THE SOVIET IMPACT

ON

INTERNATIONAL LAW

THE SOVIET IMPACT
ON
INTERNATIONAL LAW

HANS W. BAADE
Editor

OCEANA PUBLICATIONS, INC.
Dobbs Ferry, New York
1965

Originally published in Autumn 1964

by

LAW AND CONTEMPORARY PROBLEMS

DUKE UNIVERSITY SCHOOL OF LAW

Titles Published in
The Library of Law and Contemporary Problems

POPULATION CONTROL, The Imminent World Crisis
MELVIN G. SHIMM, *Editor*, (and others)

EUROPEAN REGIONAL COMMUNITIES,
A New Era on the Old Continent
MELVIN G. SHIMM, *Editor*, (and others)

AFRICAN LAW, New Law for New Nations
HANS W. BAADE, *Editor*, (and others)

ACADEMIC FREEDOM, The Scholar's Place
in Modern Society
HANS W. BAADE, *Editor*, (and others)

THE SOVIET IMPACT ON INTERNATIONAL LAW
HANS W. BAADE, *Editor*, (and others)

URBAN PROBLEMS AND PROSPECTS
ROBINSON O. EVERETT, RICHARD H. LEACH, *Editors*, (and others)

TABLE OF CONTENTS

FOREWORD

On February 28 and 29, 1964, the American Society of International Law and the Association of Student International Law Societies held a joint conference on the subject of this symposium at Duke University. This conference, which was attended by a large number of scholars and public officials, was ably arranged and managed by the Duke International Law Society.[1] All of the contributions appearing below have been originally presented by their authors at that time; they are reproduced here with a minimum of editorial revision. The Editor gladly takes this opportunity to express his gratitude to the Duke International Law Society and its officers and members for the opportunity to publish the papers presented at the conference, and for their competent and untiring work in this connection.

In the immediate wake of the momentous changes brought about on the international scene by the emergence of the Soviet Union and its bloc as one of the two principal actors in a bipolar world (bipolar, that is, because of this emergence), and on the eve of possibly equally momentous changes that could result from a détente or the re-emergence of a polycentric world power pattern, it seems somewhat presumptuous to undertake the assessment suggested by the title of this symposium. And indeed, such an assessment has not been attempted here. The aim, even if two-fold, has been much more modest. The first and foremost concern is the analysis and critique of Soviet legal doctrine and policy in specific areas of international concern, especially peaceful coexistence, international organizations (both regional and world-wide), treaties, nuclear weapons, outer space, and the colonial question. The second focus is on the economic and political consequences of Soviet foreign trade and aid, and on the legal regulation of East-West trade in the United States.

With one conspicuous exception,[2] the contributors on the various topical facets of Soviet international law teaching and practice arrive at negative, and to a varying degree hostile, conclusions as to the Soviet impact on their chosen subjects. The cumulative result would appear to be that while there has, of course, been a Soviet impact on international relations and economics, and some international response to Soviet foreign and economic policy, there has been no specific Soviet impact on international law in the sense of a positive contribution to the shaping of now generally accepted doctrines or rules.

[1] For a brief report of this conference, see Warren, *Southeastern Regional Conference and the Association of Student International Law Societies, Annual Conference, Duke University School of Law, February 28-29, 1964*, 58 AM. J. INT'L L. 744 (1964).

[2] Karpov, *The Soviet Concept of Peaceful Coexistence and Its Implications for International Law, infra*, at 14

Is such a conclusion really justified? Although not new,[3] it is still seemingly based on fragmented and occasional research, suggesting at once the dangers of specialization, language and source limitations, and, to an extent that can hardly be overlooked, individual and environmental predisposition. This is, of course, not the place for an attempt to redress the balance (if, indeed, it needs redressing); and in any event, the task would have to be undertaken by those who, like the contributors to this symposium, have more specialized knowledge and ability than does the Editor. Still, on the basis of some reflection, it is suggested that at least two areas would appear to need additional attention. The first and probably most important is the impact of specific international legal doctrines and policies which, while not Soviet in origin, were championed by the Soviet Union in such a manner that their initial and/or particularly emphatic endorsement by *this* world power accelerated their general acceptance, no matter what the discrepancies between Soviet theory and practice. Subjects that immediately come to mind in this connection are world peace, open treaties, self-determination, collective security, and peaceful coexistence.

A second subject for fruitful research might lie in the more philosophical field: To what extent has historical materialism generally, and Marxism-Leninism in particular, contributed to the theoretical foundations of modern international law? Again, it apparently has to be pointed out to international lawyers as well that "one must never make the fatal mistake in the history of ideas of requiring of a notion that it be 'true,' "[4] and that a pedantic search for self-reversals or contradictions or yawning gaps between professed ideals and actual practice is hardly more fruitful here than a preoccupation with witch-burnings would be for historians of theological dogmata.

It might well be that the essentially negative assessment of the Soviet impact on international law now prevailing among Sovietologists will not ultimately be in need of substantial revision. After all, even historical materialism appears to have been a more effective stimulant outside of the Soviet sphere than within it; Soviet social science has neither assimilated Freud, nor produced an impressive number of convincing historical studies that could serve as the foundation of a radical and reasonably well-founded re-evaluation of the past. Then, Soviet international lawyers should have added incentive to ponder the causes of a monumental lack of rapport. Is the rejection of coexistence in ideology and the insistence on partisanship in science really worth the price that has apparently been paid in the past, and that is seemingly still exacted today? And is it ultimately worthy of a great power to make its marks primarily by way of a response of others to its own challenge, not as a partner who stimulates emulation: by impact, not by cooperation?

HANS W. BAADE.

[3] For a typical recent reaction, see Schwebel, *The United Nations and the Challenge of a Changing International Law*, 1963 AM. SOC'Y INT'L L. PROCEEDINGS 83, 87.
[4] Samuelson, *Economists and the History of Ideas*, 52 AM. ECON. REV. 1, 14 (1962). This remark is specifically addressed to Marxism.

THE SOVIET UNION AND THE UNITED NATIONS*

RICHARD N. GARDNER†

After a recent speech by a State Department official on U.S. policy toward the United Nations, someone got up in the question period and declared: "You have argued that the United Nations serves the national interest of the United States and other countries of the free world. But how, according to your own analysis, can it also be said to serve the interest of the Soviet Union?"

This perceptive and difficult question is asked in one form or another in all serious discussions of the United Nations. To help find an answer, it may be useful to take a brief look at the record of Soviet participation in the United Nations, and at the prospects for the future suggested by recent developments in Soviet foreign policy.

I

THE RECORD

When we look at the record of the Soviet Union in the United Nations, we see a striking contrast between word and deed, between Communist ideology and Charter principle. In word, the Soviet Union has often found it expedient to support the United Nations. In 1947, for example, André Vyshinsky, then Deputy Minister for Foreign Affairs, had this to say:

The policy of the U.S.S.R. with regard to the United Nations calls for strengthening that body, extending and reinforcing international cooperation, unfaltering and consistent observance of the charter and the implementation of its principles.

The Soviets have hardly lived up to these fine words. Why not? Putting it bluntly, the ideological "baggage" that the Soviet Union brought with it into the United Nations has made it difficult, if not impossible, to accept the full obligations of membership. Indeed, it is hard to escape the conclusion that there is a fundamental incompatibility at almost every point between traditional Communist doctrine and the principles of the U.N. Charter:

—Communist doctrine looks forward to a monolithic world of Communist states. The United Nations Charter looks forward to a world of diversity, where each country can develop differently in accordance with the different characteristics and aspirations of its people.

* This article is based on a chapter in the author's book, IN PURSUIT OF WORLD ORDER: U.S. FOREIGN POLICY AND INTERNATIONAL ORGANIZATIONS, published by Frederick A. Praeger, Inc.

† B.A. 1948, Harvard University; LL.B. 1951, Yale Law School; Ph.D. 1954, Oxford University. Deputy Assistant Secretary of State for International Organization Affairs. Former Professor of Law, Columbia University. Author, STERLING-DOLLAR DIPLOMACY: ANGLO-AMERICAN COLLABORATION IN THE RECONSTRUCTION OF MULTILATERAL TRADE (1956); NEW DIRECTIONS IN U.S. FOREIGN ECONOMIC POLICY (1959).

1

—Communist doctrine seeks to build a Communist world through coercion. The United Nations Charter seeks to assure a world of free choice.

—Communist doctrine sees a world divided into hostile camps—Communist and Capitalist. Even the slogan "peaceful coexistence" was defined by Khrushchev as "a form of intensive economic, political, and ideological struggle" whose only outcome can be the triumph of Communism and the burial of Capitalism. The Charter sees one world in which the interests that unite nations are stronger than the interests which divide them. As Alexander Dallin has put it, the Soviet Union is "a state with a 'two-camp' world view trying to operate in a 'one-world' organization."[1]

—Communist doctrine—like all totalitarian doctrine—distrusts international organizations that the Communist leadership cannot control. The U.N. Charter establishes an international organization beyond the control of any state or party.

—Communist doctrine denies the possibility of impartial men rendering disinterested judgment in the service of international institutions. The United Nations was founded on this very assumption.

—Communist doctrine and the narrow interests of the Communist elite demand a closed society in which the population is sealed off from exposure to alien ideas. The United Nations looks to an open world in which the free play of ideas can build a community of values and attitudes.

But we do not need further illustrations of the clash between Communism and the Charter on the level of principle. What is more relevant is the collision between the Soviet Union and the United Nations in actual practice. In two decades of U.N. history, this collision has occurred in eight principal areas:

1. *Communist Coercion.* The most obvious area in which Soviet policy has collided with the Charter has been the systematic attempt of the Soviet Union to promote its political and ideological objectives by use of force. This collision was not unprecedented. In 1939, the Soviet Union had been expelled from the League of Nations only a few years after its admission for its unprovoked invasion of Finland. Those who hoped that the creation of the United Nations would bring fundamental changes in Soviet foreign policy were quickly disappointed. Indeed, many of the major crises that have beset the United Nations since its inception—in Iran, Greece, Korea, Hungary—have resulted from the attempt of the Soviet Union to impose its system by force in violation of the U.N. Charter. The fact that the Soviet Union has found it necessary to cast more than 100 vetoes in the Security Council gives one measure of the extent of the problem.

The U.N. operation in the Congo provides a recent example of how the United Nations stood in the way of the historic Soviet thrust for world domination. The Soviet Union counted on filling the power vacuum created by the withdrawal of colonial rule in Africa and elsewhere. The Congo offered a particularly good opportunity: here was the strategic key to sub-Saharan Africa, possessed of great

[1] ALEXANDER DALLIN, THE SOVIET UNION AT THE UNITED NATIONS 6 (1962).

wealth, in a chaotic condition after independence. The Soviet Union voted for the initial Security Council resolutions on the Congo—perhaps in the mistaken belief that the United Nations would confine itself to preventing the re-entry of Belgian troops. It soon began to oppose the operation when it became clear that the United Nations would act to protect the new Congolese nation against the intervention of outside forces—including those of the Soviet Union—and to preserve a unified state. By controlling the key airfields and other points of entry into the Congo, the United Nations was able to prevent the extensive intrusion of Soviet personnel against the wishes of the Central Government and thus helped to avert the transformation of that country into a cold war battleground. It was inevitable that the United Nations' attempt to implement its mandate to protect the Congo's territorial integrity and political independence would provoke the violent opposition of the principal member that was working in the other direction.

2. *Constitutional Development.* The Soviet Union has always seen the U.N. Charter essentially as a contract between rival states rather than as a constitution capable of organic growth in the service of a world community. The collision between the pursuit of Communist goals by coercion and the United Nations' defense of national independence based on free choice has with growing frequency been manifested in constitutional arguments about the interpretation of the U.N. Charter.

The central element in the controversy has been the authority of the United Nations to carry on peacekeeping activities that could frustrate the pursuit of Communist aims. The Soviet Union has insisted on the so-called "principle of unanimity" —the doctrine that no peacekeeping action can be undertaken except through agreement at every step of the way of all five Permanent Members of the Securty Council.

The overwhelming majority of U.N. members have refused to accept so restrictive an interpretation of U.N. power. Through the Uniting for Peace Resolution, they established procedures by which the General Assembly could exercise its residual authority contained in the Charter to deal with threats to international peace and security in the event that the Security Council was unable to carry out its primary responsibility in this field. And in instances such as the Congo crisis, when the Security Council initially voted a peacekeeping operation, they supported the broad exercise of authority by the Secretary-General to assemble peacekeeping forces through voluntary arrangements with individual members. The refusal of the Soviet Union to accept the legality of these procedures and of the operations they made possible thrust the United Nations into its most serious constitutional crisis.

3. *Financing.* Directly related to the conflict between the Soviet Union and the United Nations over constitutional interpretation has been the conflict over U.N. financing. In the face of the veto power of Security Council members, the United Nations had no legal right to require that the Soviet Union supply troops or logistic support for operations it opposed, but it did have the legal right to assess the Soviet Union for its fair share of the cost of peacekeeping forces voluntarily supplied by others. The exercise of this right in the Middle East and Congo operations led to

the clash over Article 19 of the Charter, which provides for the loss of vote in the General Assembly of any country more than two years behind in its total assessments. The Soviet position in this matter has been very clear: It will not pay for U.N. activities it does not like—at least in so far as the expenditures support functions it regards as beyond the normal administrative activities of the organization. As a result, the Soviet Union has even gone so far as to declare its intention not to pay that portion of its regular budget assessment which goes for the U.N. field service, the Korean cemetery, and the repayment of interest and principal on the U.N. bonds. Obviously, the collision between the Soviet Union and the United Nations on financial matters is but another manifestation of the Soviet Union's restrictive view of the U.N. Charter, and of its determination to pursue its foreign policy goals free of any possible interference from the independent activity of international organizations.

4. *International Civil Service.* Still another manifestation of the Soviet attempt to hamstring the independent operation of the United Nations has been the conflict between Soviet and Charter concepts of the international civil service. This conflict came to a head in 1961, when the Soviet Union mounted a frontal assault on the independence of the U.N. executive. Having failed to paralyze the United Nations through the exercise of its veto in the Security Council and its refusal to pay its peace-keeping assessments, the Soviet Union unveiled its Troika demand. This proposal to replace the Secretary-General by three Secretaries-General (representing the Communist states, the so-called Western states, and the so-called uncommitted states) would have given the Soviet Union the very veto over U.N. operations that it had failed to achieve by others means. This fact was very clearly perceived by the other U.N. members, and they rejected the Troika overwhelmingly.

Article 100 of the United Nations Charter represents the most modern expression yet given to the concept of the international civil service:

1. In the performance of their duties the Secretary-General and the staff shall not seek or receive instructions from any government or from any other authority external to the Organization. They shall refrain from any action which might reflect on their position as international officials responsible only to the Organization.

2. Each Member of the United Nations undertakes to respect the exclusively international character of the responsibilities of the Secretary-General and the staff and not to seek to influence them in the discharge of their responsibilities.

The Soviet Union has accepted this article neither in principle nor in practice. At the time of the Troika controversy, Walter Lippmann wrote that Khrushchev told him he "would never accept a single neutral administrator. Why? Because, he said, while there are neutral countries, there are not neutral men. You would not accept a Communist administrator and I cannot accept a non-Communist administrator."[2]

In expressing these views, Khrushchev was not developing any new Soviet policy.

[2] "Khrushchev to Lippmann—Face to Face, No. 1," N.Y. Herald Tribune, April 17, 1961, p. 1, col. 1; p. 2, col. 4.

His remarks are consistent with the Soviet Union's traditional philosophy toward the international civil service going back to League of Nations days. The concept that an individual from any country can serve an international institution in a disinterested manner rather than carry out the policies of his nation, party, or class is alien to traditional Communist doctrine. Indeed, the attitude that the Fascist countries took on the same issue in the League of Nations days indicates that the concept is equally incompatible with any totalitarian philosophy.

Soviet practice reflects precisely this traditional philosophy. The Soviet Union normally hand-picks its senior nominees for the U.N. Secretariat from the Soviet Foreign Ministry and does not permit direct recruitment of U.N. staff within the Soviet Union. It does not permit its citizens to undertake long-term careers with the United Nations but rather rotates them in and out of the Secretariat every two or three years. Most important of all, it does not permit its citizens to serve as truly independent members of the Secretariat. Newspaper accounts of the senior Soviet official in the Secretariat passing notes to the Soviet representative on the Security Council and of the espionage activities conducted in the United States by Soviet citizens in the Secretariat have dramatized the problem for all who are willing to face the facts. It is only in technical and relatively non-political assignments with the United Nations and the specialized agencies that Soviet citizens have seemed to live up fully to their responsibilities under the Charter.

The Troika demand was defeated. But the battle still goes on. Continued vigilance is necessary to protect the international civil service from these Soviet practices. Moreover, U.N. agencies continue to be threatened by "creeping Troika"—the simplistic concept not confined to the Communist bloc that the world is divided into three groups and that every individual must be regarded as the servant of one of these groups.

5. *International Adjudication.* The Soviet Union has consistently resisted the settlement of disputes by international courts or arbitral tribunals. It was obliged to accept the statute of the International Court of Justice as the price for membership in the United Nations. But it never accepted the compulsory jurisdiction of the Court—*i.e.,* the obligation to submit to the jurisdiction of the Court in an international legal dispute at the behest of another country accepting the same obligation. By itself, of course, this fact would not be conclusive: A large number of non-Communist countries have also declined to accept the Court's compulsory jurisdiction, and some of the countries that have accepted it in principle—such as the United States—have attached important qualifications. What is more significant is that the Soviet Union has steadfastly refused to submit individual cases to the Court. And it has usually declined to accept provisions in bilateral or multilateral agreements calling for compulsory jurisdiction of the Court in disputes over their interpretation.

The Soviet Union has also consistently opposed requests by U.N. organs for advisory opinions from the International Court. In the assessments case, however, the Soviet Union did participate for the first time in oral argument before the Court

5

in the person of Gregory I. Tunkin, the Legal Adviser of the Soviet Foreign Ministry. Having participated, the Soviet Union nevertheless did not consider itself estopped from continuing to challenge the validity of the advisory opinion as accepted by the General Assembly.

6. *Economic and Social Cooperation.* The Soviet Union has taken a highly restrictive view of the economic and social as well as the political activities of international organizations. At the outset of the United Nations, indeed, the Soviet attitude was even more negative on the economic than on the political side. In his opening speech at the San Francisco Conference in 1945, Foreign Minister Molotov emphasized the need for an "international security organization" and failed entirely to mention any economic and social functions.

Soviet policy in the early years of the United Nations reflected this negative attitude toward the development of international organization in the economic and social field. The Soviet Union turned up at the Bretton Woods Conference at the last moment but failed to join either the International Bank or the International Monetary Fund. It declined to participate in the drafting of the Charter for the International Trade Organization despite the elaborate state-trading provisions which were included to facilitate its membership. It never adhered to the General Agreement on Tariffs and Trade.

The pattern was the same with other international organizations in functional and technical fields. Of the Big Five nonfinancial Specialized Agencies, the Soviet Union never joined the Food and Agriculture Organization or the International Civil Aviation Organization, and for some years it refrained from membership in UNESCO, the International Labor Organization, and the World Health Organization. While it has not failed to exploit meetings of these institutions for propaganda purposes, its participation in their field operations has been marginal, and the Soviet Union has consistently opposed substantial increases in their budgets and programs.

The pattern has been the same in the case of voluntary programs of the United Nations. The Soviet Union at first declined to participate in the Expanded Program of Technical Assistance when it was created in 1949; although it joined the program in 1953 and also joined the U.N. Special Fund when it was created in 1959, its participation in both institutions has been unenthusiastic. In 1964, the Soviet contribution to the two programs amounted to $4 million out of nearly $150 million— something under three per cent of the total—as compared to its seventeen per cent share of the regular budget. Even this modest contribution is paid in rubles, the employment of which is subject to so many restrictions that the United Nations has difficulty in making full use of them. Soviet experts participating in these programs in 1963 totaled only 90 out of 2,634.

The niggardly Soviet financial contribution to the United Nations' economic and social work scarcely bears out Soviet claims of superior economic performance. Observers at the U.N. General Assembly are always amused to hear Soviet delegates boast in the Economic Committee that the Soviet Union will soon overtake the

United States in gross national product and living standards, while pleading in the Budgetary Committee that its stringent economic circumstances and balance of payments difficulties require modest contributions to the United Nations.

It is not difficult to explain why executive action by international agencies should be anathema to the Soviet Union in economic as well as political affairs. Traditional Soviet policy has sought to maintain the maximum freedom of action in both areas. Only in recent years has the Soviet Union begun to emerge from a policy based on economic autarky to play an increasingly active role in international economic relations. It is clearly determined to play that role for high political stakes—to use trade and aid as political and ideological instruments. So far, there has been little room in such a strategy for large-scale cooperative programs through international organizations in trade and aid.

The negative attitude toward economic cooperation has been reflected in another area of U.N. activity—the promotion of human rights. The Soviet bloc joined the Union of South Africa in 1948 in abstaining in the vote on the Universal Declaration of Human Rights. In the early years of the United Nations, it took a wholly negative and defensive posture in the discussion of human rights questions. While later it began gradually to exploit the propaganda opportunities in this field—as it did in economic relations—its objection to the development of any executive functions for the United Nations continued unabated. The Soviet Union has consistently opposed any proposals for the international implementation of human rights standards, even comparatively modest measures involving fellowships, research, and the reporting of national human rights practices. It has resisted the implementation provisions in the draft Human Rights Covenants for bringing disputed situations to a Human Rights Committee or to the International Court. As might be expected, it has also opposed any role for nongovernmental organizations in the submission of information in the field of human rights.

7. *Information Activities.* It is implicit in the Charter of the United Nations that the informed citizenry in member states, knowledgeable about the purposes and activities of the United Nations, will encourage the responsible behavior of their governments in conformity with Charter standards. This assumption has considerable validity in many countries of the free world. In the United States, for example, public opinion is highly sensitized to activities of the United Nations. Thanks in part to the work of the United Nations Association of the United States of America,[3] information about the United Nations and other international organizations in universities, high schools, and adult organizations is extensive and well presented. Most important, the work of this organization and widespread coverage of events in New York by the press, radio, and television insure that those who determine U.S. policy on issues before the United Nations are conscious at every step of the way of the pressures of American opinion. While there is a powerful

---

[3] The new private organization resulting from the merger of the American Association for the United Nations and the U.S. Committee for the United Nations.

anti-U.N. lobby, there is also an important constituency pressing for affirmative U.S. policies in the political and economic work of the organization. No such influence affects Soviet policy in the United Nations. Few U.N. activities take place in the Soviet Union. The Soviet equivalent of the United Nations Association is largely ornamental and does not act independently of the government to influence public attitudes. United Nations documents are not readily available to Soviet citizens. The U.N. Information Center in Moscow is located in three rooms of an apartment house in a modest residential section, and foreign visitors describe it as one of the loneliest places to be found in the city.[4] There is only perfunctory mention of the United Nations in the schools and only limited and self-serving coverage of U.N. activities in the Soviet press.

8. *Peacekeeping and Disarmament.* A central element in the disarmament plans advanced by the United States and other Western countries has been the building up of the United Nations as a peacekeeping agency—specifically, the creation of a U.N. peace force and more effective procedure for pacific settlement of disputes. The reason for this is obvious: Nations will never be willing to eliminate or even radically reduce their arms until they have some other way to maintain their security and protect their vital interests.

Here again, hopes for building up the United Nations as an executive agency have run squarely into Soviet opposition. While the Soviet Union has sometimes paid lip service to the concept of a U.N. peacekeeping role, its proposals on this subject have been devoid of substance. Moreover, Soviet bloc representatives at the Geneva disarmament conference have depreciated the peacekeeping issue as an undesirable distraction from the subject of disarmament.

II

RECENT TRENDS

One cannot fail to be impressed with the consistency of Soviet behavior on fundamental constitutional issues during two decades of participation in the United Nations. Yet Soviet tactics have not been static. They have changed with the general change in tactics of Soviet foreign policy that became evident in the early 1950s and are generally associated with the death of Stalin.

During the last decade, Soviet diplomacy in the United Nations has become more sophisticated. The Soviets recognized that the old hard line was not working and that a softer approach might yield political dividends. And they were encouraged to believe that the influx of newly independent countries from Africa and Asia would change the balance of forces in the United Nations in their favor. In recent years, Soviet publications have ceased to speak of "automatic majorities" of Western nations in the United Nations and have suggested instead that on key issues, the United States and its allies will eventually be reduced to a minority position.

---

[4] DALLIN, *op. cit. supra* note 1, at 92-93.

The fundamental element in the change of Soviet U.N. tactics was the recognition that the new nations arriving in the United Nations offered a tempting and available opportunity to influence important and, hopefully, susceptible political figures. Anticolonialism, disarmament, and trade became the central themes in the Soviet Union's new approach which culminated in Premier Khrushchev's dramatic visit to the 15th General Assembly in 1960. The more sophisticated Soviet policy was also evident in some of the Specialized Agencies and in economic forums such as the Economic and Social Council. Perhaps the most dramatic example of the shift in the Soviet line came in the field of trade. The same nation that had ignored international economic problems entirely at San Francisco and had boycotted the negotiations on the ITO and GATT suddenly turned around in the mid-1950s and started calling for an International Trade Organization with a broad mandate to promote and regulate international commerce, particularly between countries with different economic systems.

Yet the shifts on all these issues were essentially tactical ones. The Soviet Union had come to appreciate the possibilities of the United Nations as a propaganda vehicle, but it continued its negative approach to U.N. operations. During his famous visit to the 15th General Assembly, Khrushchev declared:

Experience of the work of the United Nations has shown that this body is useful and necessary, because in it are represented all the States which are called upon to solve, through negotiation and discussion, the pressing issues of international relations so as to prevent them from reaching a point where conflict and wars might break out. That is the positive aspect of the work of the United Nations. That, indeed, constitutes the main purpose of the creation of the United Nations.

Notably missing from this Soviet benediction of the United Nations was any reference to its function as an operating agency—as an instrument for building free nations and keeping the peace. This is not surprising. The Communists have been concerned by the prospect that the United Nations might achieve a greater operational capability to carry out a Charter full of dangerous thoughts about freedom of choice for all men—a capability that could bury the Communist version of history without the necessity of a major war.

III
THE OUTLOOK

This record of Soviet participation in the United Nations is not encouraging. But it is no occasion for hopelessness or despair. We must not fall into the habit of thinking that nothing can be done to strengthen the United Nations as a force for peace and welfare without the cooperation of the Soviet Union. The whole history of the United Nations—in Korea, the Congo, and the Middle East, in technical cooperation and aid to less developed countries—proves that the contrary is the case. This will continue to be so as long as the United States and other free nations work together to maintain and strengthen the United Nations' capacity to act on the basis of the common interest recognized by the large majority of its members.

Moreover, the position of the Soviet Union may not be frozen for all time. Recently, we have seen some hopeful stirrings in Soviet foreign policy. For various reasons—the confrontation over Cuba, the increase of Western military strength, its split with Communist China, and domestic economic difficulties—the Soviet Union has come to acknowledge and in certain cases to act upon the fact that, despite national and ideological conflicts, nations may share common interests in survival and welfare.

With this modification in Soviet attitudes, there has developed what some have described as a "limited adversary relationship" between ourselves and the Soviet Union—a relationship in which fundamental differences remain but do not preclude limited forms of cooperation based on mutual restraints and reciprocal undertakings that serve the national interests of both sides. Among the more significant manifestations of this new relationship have been the agreements that have helped somewhat to slow down the arms race—the partial ban on nuclear testing, the communications link between Washington and Moscow to help prevent accidental war, and the General Assembly resolution against the placing of weapons of mass destruction in outer space. Other examples have been the agreements on international cooperation in the peaceful uses of outer space and the policy of mutual example in which both countries have announced cutbacks in the production of nuclear materials.

There have also been some straws in the wind on Soviet policy toward the United Nations—the fact that the Soviet Union invited U Thant to Moscow for the signing of the test ban treaty, that it concurred in the application to large nuclear reactors of the safeguards system of the International Atomic Energy Agency, that it has made special efforts at some recent U.N. meetings to avoid polemics and facilitate the orderly disposition of major issues, and that it voted affirmatively in the Security Council on the resolution establishing the U.N. peacekeeping force in Cyprus. We have been disappointed too often in the past to assume that these are more than tactical shifts. Whether they really herald fundamental changes in attitude, only time will tell.

Certainly, there was much in what Khrushchev was saying in 1964 that sounded unusually congenial to American ears. The most celebrated example was his advice to Hungarian comrades that goulash and ballet were more important than revolution. Less widely quoted, but no less interesting, were some of the observations in his message to foreign heads of state at the beginning of the year. Among other things, Khrushchev noted that in our interdependent world, "a collision which may occur in any place and would, seemingly, have a purely local character, can quickly involve many other countries." To avoid the danger of such "collisions," Chairman Khrushchev proposed the conclusion of a treaty for the peaceful settlement of territorial disputes. In explaining this proposal, the Soviet leader appeared to modify somewhat the line that Soviet delegates had been taking in the disarmament negotiations—

that the problem of peace could be solved automatically by general and complete disarmament without the concomitant improvement of peacekeeping machinery. He asserted that measures of peaceful settlement would make it "far easier" to make progress in disarmament:[5]

In conditions in which states will no longer have to worry about their frontiers and in which any plans for changing these frontiers by force are banned by international law, many of the motives by which the states were guided in increasing their armed forces must disappear.

Chairman Khrushchev's New Year's Message also had some sympathetic and moderate things to say about the United Nations:[6]

A peaceful settlement of territorial disputes is also favored by the fact that in the practice of international relations there already exists a store of improved methods of peaceful settlement of outstanding issues—direct negotiations between the states concerned, use of good offices, request of assistance from international organizations, and so on. Although in my opinion the United Nations in its present form is far from being an ideal instrument of peaceful cooperation of states, even this organization, granted an impartial approach, can make a positive contribution to the cause of peaceful settlement of territorial and border issues.

This theme was developed further by the Soviet Union in a note sent in July 1964 to the United States and other U.N. members. The note went beyond the specific reference to territorial disputes in the New Year's Message and urged "wider use . . . of the peaceful means of settling international disputes provided for in the Charter." It said an "understanding" among U.N. members on "the strengthening of the organization's effectiveness in safeguarding international peace and security" would "help in further easing international tension, in strengthening mutual trust in relations between States and in normalizing the international situation." In stressing the potential contribution of the United Nations to world peace it warned of "certain circles that have no interest in preserving peace" and of "some countries" which are "still endeavoring by force to maintain their dominion over peoples waging the just struggle for freedom and independence." Some observers felt that these last references may have been intended to apply to a certain large Asian power as well as to Soviet adversaries in the West.

For all its interesting preambular language, however, the July note represented no progress from the traditional Soviet line when it came to details. The note re-stated the old Soviet position that all U.N. peacekeeping must be subject to the exclusive jurisdiction of the Security Council and therefore to great power veto. It also proposed to introduce the Troika into U.N. peacekeeping operations by requiring the participating of contingents from "socialist" as well as Western and uncommitted countries. The note was particularly disappointing since it came as

[5] Chairman Khrushchev's letter to President Johnson, of Dec. 31, 1963, 50 DEP'T STATE BULL. 158, 163 (1964)
[6] Id. at 162.

11

a response to new peacekeeping proposals handed to the Soviet Union in March by the United States and United Kingdom. It was poorly received by the large majority of U.N. members who are not prepared to surrender the General Assembly's residual powers to initiate peacekeeping operations.

In the face of these developments diplomatic observers could only regard Soviet professions of interest in a stronger U.N. peacekeeping role with continued skepticism. Obviously Soviet expressions of support for the United Nations can only be meaningful if the Soviet Union embraces not merely the *principle* of peaceful settlement but the *machinery* for peaceful settlement embodied in the United Nations—and does so in deeds as well as words in application to specific disputes.

In the months ahead, there will be at least two critical tests of Soviet policy in the United Nations—in addition to the outstanding difficulties between us on Cuba, Berlin, and Southeast Asia. The first test will come in the constitutional crisis that has been precipitated by the refusal of the Soviet Union to pay its dues for U.N. peacekeeping operations. The United Nations cannot work to full advantage as an instrument for peaceful settlement of international disputes until its financial crisis is resolved. If the Soviet Union is really concerned about the contribution that peaceful settlement can make to disarmament and the avoidance of war, it will pay its peacekeeping assessments. Equally important, the Soviet financial boycott of the United Nations has become a serious roadblock on the highway to peace. If the new Soviet leadership seriously wishes to consolidate recent progress toward the relaxation of tensions, it will get off the collision course in the United Nations and avoid a bitter dispute over its voting rights in the Assembly which could set back not only cooperation in the United Nations but the whole climate of international relations.

The second major test of Soviet policy will come in the current re-examination by U.N. members of procedures for initiating and financing future peacekeeping operations. The improvement of present procedures could serve the interests of all members of the United Nations. The members of the United Nations will never accept the Soviet Union's traditional position that no peacekeeping operation can ever take place without its consent, but they might accept adaptations in General Assembly procedures to give large and middle powers a greater voice than they have under present arrangements. Here again, if the Soviet Union is genuinely concerned to improve the international climate and strengthen the machinery of peaceful settlement, it will join with other members in developing rational decision-making procedures for future U.N. peacekeeping operations.

How will the Soviet Union respond to these and other tests of its U.N. policy? Seasoned diplomats and Kremlinologists, recalling past shifts in Soviet policy and innumerable disappointments of previous expectations, will be properly skeptical of the possibilities. We shall have to wait and see.

Yet there is one factor that gives us the right to be hopeful for the long run.

Soviet foreign policy ultimately reflects Soviet national interest—and the real long-term interest of the Soviet Union, as well as of other countries, would be served by a stronger U.N. that could help the great powers disengage from dangerous confrontations and prevent brush-fire conflicts between small states from triggering a nuclear war. By "real long-term interest," of course, we mean the interest of the Soviet state and people and not the interest of an elite in promoting world Communism by force. The Soviet Union will play a more constructive role in the United Nations only as the former interest takes precedence over the latter.

As Secretary of State Dean Rusk pointed out in his Hammarskjöld Lecture at Columbia University:[7]

As long as a member possessing great power was intent on promoting conflict and up-heaval—the better to coerce the world into its own image—that member might well regard the United Nations as a threat to its own ambitions.

But suppose it is agreed that all members, despite their deep differences, share a common interest in survival—and therefore a common interest in preventing resort to force anywhere in the world. Then the peacekeeping capacity of the United Nations can be seen realistically for what it is: an indispensable service potentially in the national interest of all members—in the common interest of even rival states.

[7] Dag Hammarskjöld Memorial Lecture, prepared for delivery by Secretary of State Dean Rusk, and read by Harlan Cleveland, Assistant Secretary for International Affairs, at Columbia University, New York, N.Y., on Jan. 10, 1964. 50 DEP'T STATE. BULL. 112, 116 (1964).

THE SOVIET CONCEPT OF PEACEFUL COEXISTENCE AND ITS IMPLICATIONS FOR INTERNATIONAL LAW

VICTOR P. KARPOV*

I

PEACEFUL COEXISTENCE AND SOVIET FOREIGN POLICY

The concept of peaceful coexistence has always been the general line of Soviet foreign policy. Of course, this concept has been liable to some development and improvement but its very emergence was a result of the Great October Revolution which gave birth to the socialist system.

From its very inception the Soviet state proclaimed peaceful coexistence as the basic principle of its foreign policy. The fact that the very first political act of the Soviet Russia was the Decree on Peace, the decree on stopping the bloody war, is not to be considered an accident.

The peaceful coexistence policy is not a tactical move on the part of the Soviet Union. Our desire for peace and peaceful coexistence springs from the very nature of our socialist society in which there are no social groups interested in profiting by means of war or by the arms race.

Moreover, the principle of peaceful coexistence is the only realistic policy to pursue nowadays when the world consists of nations belonging to different social systems—capitalism and socialism. In view of the present alignment of forces in the world and of the progress of military technique, it is impossible to find any other sound basis for relations between countries except that of peaceful coexistence. We cannot even discuss this principle in terms whether we should "accept" or "reject" it. The point is that today peaceful coexistence is *an indisputable fact* of international life and not someone's request or suggestion. Peaceful coexistence is an objective necessity stemming from the contemporary stage of the development of human society.

If we face facts squarely, we should admit that the essence of world politics now is the character of relations between the two main socioeconomic systems—capitalism and socialism. And capitalist and socialist countries exist side by side on our planet. The rise of socialism was an inevitable objective historical development. However, the capitalist world refused to recognize this fact and has repeatedly resorted to war to destroy its unwelcome neighbor. It is common knowledge that all these attempts have turned out to be futile.

The attempts to solve differences between the two systems by means of war have always been costly for the common people. They resulted in millions of killed and

* First Secretary, Embassy of the Union of Soviet Socialist Republics, Washington, D.C.

14

wounded, in thousands of destroyed towns and villages, and in senseless losses of human energy and ingenuity.

And now the very character of modern nuclear warfare makes planning for war as a means of settling differences between the two systems obvious insanity. None of these systems can rely upon war to secure its victory over the other. The Soviet Union does not need any war to secure victory over capitalism, although the Soviet people believe in such a victory.

It is not war that should settle the controversy between the two systems. In the final analysis, it will not be the system which produces the greatest quantity of means of destruction that will triumph, but the system which produces the most of material and spiritual values, which provides man with a better life. We are absolutely sure that one cannot drive people to paradise with a club, or drive them to communism by means of war.

Communists do not conceal from anyone their desire to attract all people of the world to the side of socialism. This is regarded by them as their prime international task. But the question is: by what means is that cause to be advanced? We are not going to attain it by unleashing wars, nor by forcing our way of life on other nations. It is through creative labor, through the great constructive force of the liberated peoples, through the revolutionary energy of the working people, that we are going to raise the prestige of socialism and to win it more and more support on the part of various nations.

Some people say that communism promotes the cause of peaceful coexistence because this favors communism and brings it certain advantage. These people are right. Peaceful coexistence, we feel, really favors our cause, the cause of socialism. And we do not conceal our belief that, in the long run, peaceful competition between socialism and capitalism will result in an overall victory for socialism.

But that would be a fair competition—a competition in the best possible satisfaction of all man's needs. Why should nations be afraid of that kind of competition? If they are sure that their cause is right, they should wholeheartedly accept this competition and do their best to win it. And if there are countries reluctant to be engaged in peaceful economic competition with the socialist countries one can but suggest that they rely more on their arms and armies in competition with socialism than on their productive capacities.

Coexistence is a continuation of the struggle between the two social systems, but struggle by peaceful means, without resort to war, without interference by one state in the internal affairs of another. It is a competition in peaceful endeavors. It implies reciprocal concessions and compromises—I would say mutual adaptation—in the sphere of interstate relations as regards the settlement of urgent practical issues in order to preserve and strengthen peace.

The point at issue now is not whether or not there should be peaceful coexistence. In fact, since socialism and capitalism are not at war they are in practice coexisting. And if we want to avoid the lunacy of world nuclear war we

15

should coexist. The only alternative we have nowadays is between peaceful coexistence and nuclear holocaust. There are no other choices.

But the point is that we should coexist on a reasonable basis.

There are some people in the West who willy-nilly accept the necessity to coexist with the Soviet Union because, although it belongs to another social system, it is a powerful nation and possesses mighty weapons. But as soon as a question arises of peaceful coexistence between a big Western power and a smaller country, these people prefer methods of coercion—economic, political and even military threats. That, of course, is a wrong attitude; and it can bring about very grave consequences.

The principle of peaceful coexistence should be universal. It should be based on the assumption that every country, big or small, chooses for itself or borrows from its neighbors what it thinks fit, without any outside imposition. This is a precondition, the only one that can make coexistence genuinely peaceful and good-neighborly.

In short, coexistence on a reasonable basis presupposes the recognition of the existence of different social systems, the recognition of the right of every people to deal independently with all political and social problems of its own country, respect for the sovereignty of other nations, adherence to the principle of non-inteference in internal affairs of other countries, and the settlement of all international issues by negotiation.

Thus, the Soviet view of peaceful coexistence of countries with different social and political systems does not simply imply an absence of war or a state of temporary and unstable armistice. It provides for the maintenance of friendly economic and political relations and envisages the establishment and development of a variety of forms of peaceful international cooperation.

And we believe that the realization of the Soviet proposals for general and complete disarmament under strict international control, the immediate and final abolition of the disgraceful colonial system, the conclusion of a German peace treaty, and the normalization on its basis of the situation in West Berlin would remove the chief causes of existing international tensions, destroy the very machinery of war, and enable all peoples to go calmly about their peaceful and creative labor.

II

PEACEFUL COEXISTENCE AND INTERNATIONAL LAW

The principle of peaceful coexistence is more and more widely adhered to by states in their international relations. It has won not only the widest moral support on the part of the peoples, but also international legal recognition. The countries of the socialist camp are guided precisely by this principle in their relations with other countries.

The principle of peaceful coexistence is reflected in the decisions of the Bandung Conference of Asian and African countries. Many countries of Europe, Asia, and Africa have solemnly proclaimed it as the basis of their foreign policy. And this idea was more than once unanimously supported in the resolutions of the United Nations General Assembly (for instance, decisions of 12th, 13th and subsequent sessions). It is very significant that the 17th session of the General Assembly unanimously resolved on December 18, 1962, to undertake further studies to promote and codify international legal principles of friendly relations and cooperation between states.

If we have a look at the United Nations Charter itself we can find out that it is based on the principle of peaceful coexistence although it does not use this very word. In its Preamble, the United Nations Charter, for example, states that the member countries undertake "to practice tolerance and live together in peace with one another as good neighbors," and to unite their "strength to maintain international peace and security." By that, the U.N. Charter in fact provides for the practice of what we call peaceful coexistence. Some other articles of the U.N. Charter are also based on a tacit recognition of this principle, and also on the recognition of such principles as the sovereign equality of states (Article 2(1)), non-intervention (Article 2(7)), the equality and self-determination of peoples (Article 1(2)), territorial integrity (Article 2(4)), and so on.

The well-known clause providing for unanimity of the permanent members of the Security Council when major decisions are to be taken is also a reflection of the principle of coexistence. In fact, if this clause had not been included into the U.N. Charter, we might have witnessed situations when a group of nations representing one social system would have tried to impose its will on another nation or other nations representing a different social system. Such a hypothetical situation would have led inevitably to complete disregard of principle of peaceful coexistence of states with different social systems and cannot but lead to the violation of the goals of the United Nations and to a dangerous aggravation of international tension.

The majority rule cannot be applied to the relations between different social systems. Such relations are inevitably to be based on mutual respect for the sovereign equality of nations, peaceful negotiation, and reasonable compromise.

That is why we consider very dangerous all attempts to change the U.N. Charter so that the unanimity rule in the Security Council is abolished. This could lead only to the collapse of the United Nations. In this connection I would like to mention the case of so-called Soviet "failure" to pay for the U.N. operations in the Middle East and in the Congo: to mention it because some governments try to resolve the financial crisis of the United Nations at the expense of the Soviet Union by using methods which run absolutely counter to the principles of international law if this law is understood properly.

This is the essence of the case: Attempts are being made to apply Article 19 of the U.N. Charter to the question of reimbursement of the expenditures incurred by U.N. operations in the Middle East and the Congo. But Article 19 has nothing

17

to do with these cases; it can be applied only to the arrears in members' payments to the regular budget. Decisions on reimbursement for the expenditures for the Middle East and Congo operations were adopted by the General Assembly, bypassing the Security Council and usurping the rights of the Security Council against the clear provisions of the Charter. (According to the Charter, the General Assembly makes *recommendations* that are not obligatory for those countries which did not vote for them.)

The same goes for the decisions of the International Court of Justice which is being used to prove the alleged legality of this illegal attempt.[1] Incidentally, the United States does not recognize that decisions of the International Court of Justice are obligatory in all cases, and has made a reservation to this effect while ratifying the Statute of the Court.[2]

The Soviet Union's position in this case is clear. We feel that the responsibility for the consequences of aggression, including financial implications, should be borne by those who have committed the acts of aggression. Any other approach would only encourage aggressors. It is primarily and precisely for this reason that the Soviet Union is not sharing, and will not share, the expenditures for the U.N. operations in the Middle East and the Congo.

We are not going to change our position under any pressure. Our position is just, and we are not inclined to compromise it. On March 21 of this year, the Soviet government issued a warning that in case of any attempt to act along the mentioned unlawful lines, the Soviet Union may be obliged to reconsider its attitude toward the U.N. activities in general.

A theoretical basis, so to say, of the attempts to make the U.S.S.R. pay for those U.N. emergency operations can be easily found in the concepts which claim that international law should prevail over the national or municipal law. This attitude is completely alien to the principle of peaceful coexistence, as it entails an encroachment upon the sovereign rights of nations and opens avenues for interference into their domestic affairs.

The same goes for the proposal to grant obligatory jurisdiction to the International Court of Justice, which some American lawyers view as one of the ways to improve the "rule of law" in international relations. This is not only contrary to the spirit of peaceful coexistence but at the same time is not adequate in present circumstances. The most burning international issues, such as the liquidation of colonial system or the solution of the West Berlin question, are *political* problems first of all, and cannot be solved by a court or an arbitration alone.

These are, broadly speaking, the main prerequisites that should ensure the application of the principle of peaceful coexistence to international law.

---

[1] Certain Expenses of the United Nations (Art. 17, para. 2, of the Charter), [1962] I.C.J. Rep. 151.
[2] Declaration of August 26, 1946, 61 Stat. 1218.

III

THE BASIC PRINCIPLES OF PEACEFUL COEXISTENCE

Speaking more specifically, we can trace the following, more detailed provisions which constitute the essence of the peaceful coexistence and which, in our understanding, should be reflected in the international law.

1. *Renunciation of war as means of settling international disputes, and their solution by negotiation.*

Compliance with this principle should lead to adoption of specific measures that would exclude war from the life of human society both by way of solemn obligations of states and by measures of physical disarmament that would liquidate all means of waging war. To achieve this goal, the Soviet government proposes the general and complete disarmament program, various measures of partial disarmament, and a non-aggression pact between the NATO and Warsaw Pact countries. Recently the Soviet government advanced a new program to this effect, which provides for an international agreement to renounce the use or threat of force in territorial and border disputes between nations. This agreement should include the following provisions:

(a) a solemn undertaking not to resort to force to alter existing borders;

(b) the acknowledgment that the territories of states should not, even temporarily, be the object of any invasion, attack, military occupation, or any other forcible measure directly or indirectly undertaken by other states for whatever political, economic, strategic, border or any other considerations;

(c) a firm statement that neither differences in social and state systems, nor refusal to grant recognition or absence of diplomatic relations, nor any other pretext may serve as a basis for the violation by one state of the territorial integrity of another;

(d) a commitment to solve all territorial disputes by peaceful means in conformity with the United Nations Charter.

2. *Equality, mutual understanding and trust between countries.*

3. *Consideration for each other's interests.*

4. *Non-interference in internal affairs of other countries.*

5. *Recognition of the right of all peoples to solve all the problems of their countries by themselves.* This should provide for all countries to refrain from "exporting" revolution or counter-revolution. Communists do believe that the idea of communism will ultimately triumph throughout the world, just as it triumphed already in the Soviet Union and in some other countries. But when we say that in competition with capitalism the socialist system will win, this does not signify by any means that we shall achieve that victory by interfering in the internal affairs of non-socialist countries. Our confidence in the victory of communism is based on a knowledge of the laws governing the development of human society. Just as in its time capitalism, as the more progressive system, took the place of

19

feudalism, so will capitalism be inevitably replaced by the more progressive and just social system—communism.

6. *Strict respect for the sovereignty and territorial integrity of all countries.* This principle should be strictly observed; and its observance is, of course, incompatible with some resolutions that have from time to time been adopted by the American Congress, as those calling for "liberation" of some integral parts of Soviet Union—of the Ukraine, Byelorussia, Lithuania, Latvia, Estonia, Armenia, Azerbaijan, Georgia, Kazakhstan, Turkmenistan and even some "Ural Area." I would say that this is roughly the same as if the parliament of Mexico, for example, would have passed a resolution demanding that Texas, Arizona, and California be "liberated from American slavery." Such an attitude, of course, is incompatible with the principle of peaceful coexistence and with international law in general.

7. *Promotion of economic and cultural cooperation on the basis of complete equality and mutual benefit.* This should lead to abolition of all forms of economic blockade, of economic sanctions, or trade discrimination.

CONCLUSION

The Soviet Union has consistently pursued, and will pursue, the policy of peaceful coexistence of states with different social systems.

We are convinced that the principle of peaceful coexistence should be the basis of the whole structure of contemporary international law. Only if it is based on the principle of peaceful coexistence can the international law best promote the cause of peace and mutual understanding between nations.

THE HISTORICAL ORIGINS OF THE SOVIET DOCTRINE OF PEACEFUL COEXISTENCE

WARREN LERNER*

The history of the doctrine of "peaceful coexistence" in Soviet foreign policy is inseparable from the history of the doctrine of "world revolution." Throughout its history, the Soviet regime has acknowledged fealty to both doctrines but varied the public support for one or the other doctrine according to the objective conditions of the time. Both doctrines lend themselves to sweeping and varied definitions and defy standard descripton. However, for the purposes of this discussion, I have taken the liberty of assigning the following broad definitions to each doctrine: "Peaceful coexistence," within the Soviet experience, is the policy which acknowledges the existence of societies antagonistic to the Soviet regime without regarding the destruction of these societies as the immediate goal of the Soviet state. By the same token, "world revolution" may be defined as a policy based on the premise that since Communist society cannot be secure in a "capitalist encirclement," the primary goal of the Soviet state becomes the destruction of the "capitalist encirclement" and the governments which compose it.

There has generally been a historical interaction between these two doctrines in Soviet foreign policy, with the result usually that the practice of one of these doctrines has been downgraded in order to facilitate the practice of the other at any given time. Since 1956, "peaceful coexistence" has enjoyed a rather intensified promotion in Soviet pronouncements on foreign affairs and has officially been proclaimed as the cornerstone of Soviet foreign policy. At the same time, the very term "world revolution" has been eschewed, and except for avowals of faith in the determinist view of the march of history such as Khrushchev's celebrated remark, "Your grandchildren will live under socialism," the concept has not been directly promoted. In line with this new emphasis on "peaceful coexistence," in 1959, Nikita S. Khrushchev offered American readers a reasonably detailed exposition of the Soviet viewpoint in the prominent American journal, *Foreign Affairs*. In his article, Mr. Khrushchev maintained that the Soviet Union's professsed policy of "peaceful coexistence" was nothing new, that it had always been the policy of the Soviet régime, and that with more than forty years of experience in practicing this policy, Soviet professions of peaceful coexistence should be better received in the West. Going on to prove his case for the historical permanence of "peaceful coexistence" in Soviet doctrine, Khrushchev stated:

From its very inception [in 1917] the Soviet state proclaimed peaceful coexistence as the basic principle of its foreign policy. It was no accident that the very first state act of the

* B.S. 1952, Boston University; M.A. 1954, Certificate of the Russian Institute 1954, Ph.D. 1961, Columbia University. Assistant Professor of History, Duke University, since 1961.

21

Soviet power was the decree on peace, the decree on the cessation of the bloody [world] war.[1]

The validity of Mr. Khrushchev's historical claim must, to a certain extent, be reaffirmed. As he points out, immediately after seizing power in Russia, in November 1917, the Bolsheviks issued a Decree on Peace which *inter alia* called for all of the participants in World War I to open immediate negotiations for the conclusion of peace. Indeed, Mr. Khrushchev could have added that Leon Trotsky, then the People's Commissar of Foreign Affairs, followed this decree by proclaiming an official doctrine of peaceful coexistence with all peoples.[2] However, to argue the case of Soviet fidelity to "peaceful coexistence" on the basis of such theoretical pronouncements is to pervert the historical record. What Mr. Khrushchev failed to mention in his article is the fact that in the early years of the Soviet state the doctrine of "world revolution" was also loudly proclaimed; in fact, it was "world revolution" and not "peaceful coexistence" which took precedence in the early formation of Soviet foreign policy. In the years 1917 to 1920, specifically, the belief in the imminence of "world revolution," and the obligation of the Soviet regime to aid and abet this revolution, reduced peaceful coexistence to an occasional slogan, a condition from which it emerged only when the immediate survival of the Soviet regime was at stake or other pragmatic considerations made its espousal desirable.

In 1918, Lenin and Trotsky were both convinced that the survival of the Soviet regime was absolutely contingent upon the outbreak of proletarian revolution in West Europe and not on "peaceful coexistence." Even in his Decree on Peace, Lenin implied that the workers of the West were expected to join the Russian workers in establishing proletarian regimes. Further statements throughout 1918 and 1919 spoke alternately of hopes and disappointments in the quest for world revolution. No thought at all was given, at least openly, to the apparent contradiction in this policy: can you preach and practice coexistence with countries and at the same time actively support—and with support by no means limited to sympathy—the overthrow of the governments of these countries? There is, of course, a marked difference in applauding a revolution and fostering or directing it.

Soviet relations with Imperial Germany in 1918 were an apt demonstration of this contradiction in Soviet foreign policy. Lenin, in a "peace at any price" policy, had been forced in March 1918, to accept the Draconian terms of the Treaty of Brest-Litovsk. Technically speaking, this treaty created a state of "peaceful coexistence" between Germany and Soviet Russia. Actually the treaty had not been accepted by Lenin out of ideological beliefs but out of sheer necessity. Nevertheless, it represented the first manifestation of "peaceful coexistence"—albeit on terms very unfavorable to the Soviet regime—in practice by the new Bolshevik government. However, on October 1, 1918, sensing a possible chance for a proletarian revolution in a Germany whose armies were on the verge of collapse, Lenin wrote

---

[1] Khrushchev, *On Peaceful Coexistence*, 38 FOREIGN AFFAIRS 3 (1959).
[2] 3 LEON TROTSKY, SOCHINENIIA [WORKS] pt. 2, at 165 (Moscow, 1926).

to Trotsky that the Soviet regime ought to supply revolutionary-minded German workers with "brotherly union, bread, and *military assistance*."[3] The fact that Soviet Russia was technically at peace with Germany and allegedly practicing "peaceful coexistence" with it apparently did not inhibit Lenin from proposing military assistance to those who might want to overthrow the German government. The simple answer was to be found in the conflicting interests of world revolution and peaceful coexistence; in this period, the priority of the former over the latter was unquestioned.

During the next several months, the Soviet régime was not able to participate directly in the progress of the German revolution, but this lack of participation was dictated by geography and the lack of a contiguous border—thanks to the resurrection of Poland in 1918—rather than by any qualms about violating peaceful coexistence.

The high point of the crusade for world revolution, regardless of the consequences, came in March 1919, when the Communist International was founded at Lenin's insistence. Though many of the organization's calls to world revolution can be dismissed as revolutionary rhetoric, the founding of a group whose raison d'être was the overthrow of the established governments of the world tarnished the image of a Soviet regime seeking "peaceful coexistence."

The following year, 1920, put Soviet intentions vis-à-vis "peaceful coexistence" to their sternest test. Hitherto, Soviet estimates that the West might accept "peaceful coexistence" had been substantially clouded by Western intervention in Russia's civil war on the anti-Bolshevik side. By 1920, most of this intervention was over and perhaps the Soviet régime was in a better position to consider the realities of "peaceful coexistence" now that the direct military threat was limited to one anti-Bolshevik army in the Ukraine. Furthermore, the failure of Soviet ventures in the West had cooled revolutionary ardor and had made the climate for "peaceful coexistence" a little more relaxed. However, before any serious consideration of a vigorous policy of "peaceful coexistence" could take place, Polish legions invaded the Ukraine and the Russo-Polish War of 1920 was launched.

The Russo-Polish War of 1920 was actually the result of a long-smoldering situation which the Russians had not been anxious to press so long as they were involved in their own civil war. The Polish invasion, however, gave the Soviet régime some second thoughts on relations with non-Communist neighbors. Hitherto, the official policy toward Poland had been one of peaceful coexistence, even if relations had been difficult. After the outbreak of open hostilities in April 1920, the Soviet leadership re-evaluated its official position and came to the conclusion that under the circumstances "world revolution" was a better policy to apply in this situation. Hence the Soviet goal in this war became not merely to defeat Poland but to install a Soviet government in Poland. Thus, after the Poles had been driven back, Red Army units crossed into Poland and immediately installed a

[3] Reprinted in 21 LENINSKII SBORNIK [LENIN's MISCELLANY] 252-53 (1933). (Emphasis added.)

Revolutionary Committee in the Polish city of Bialystok, openly recognizing this committee as the future Soviet government of Poland. The various pronouncements by leading Bolsheviks, especially by Marshal Tukhachevsky,[4] avowed that the goal of the Red Army was to create a Soviet Poland and beyond that spread the world revolution as far as possible. For a while it appeared that Soviet efforts might be successful, since by August 1920, the Red Army was in sight of Warsaw. Only a sensational and daring defense of the city by the Polish general, Josef Pilsudski, frustrated the attempt to convert Poland into the second Soviet state in the world. Failing to take Warsaw, the Red Army offensive lost its momentum and the Poles now drove the Russians back to White Russia. Both sides agreed to an armistice in September, followed by the Treaty of Riga of 1921. The first attempt to spread the world revolution by military force had failed.

The failure of the Russian drive on Warsaw was perhaps the greatest impetus toward the adoption of a policy of "peaceful coexistence" by the Soviet regime. What impressed Lenin was not the military aspect of the defeat but the fact that the proletariat of Poland fought not on the side of the Bolsheviks but on the side of its own "bourgeois" Polish government. It was this failure of the Red Army to impose a Soviet regime on Poland in 1920 and not, as Khrushchev maintains, the Decree on Peace of 1917, that gave birth to the serious pursuit of "peaceful coexistence."

That Lenin himself had finally recognized that "world revolution" was not imminent is implicit in his assessment of the Russo-Polish War, contained in a speech on foreign policy which he delivered in Moscow on October 2, 1920:

If Poland had become Soviet . . . the entire international system built by the victors [of World War I] would have been destroyed. . . . However, it turned out that although events are moving inexorably toward the workers' revolution, they are still moving too slowly as compared to the rapidity of events in Russia.[5]

While Lenin had previously conceded difficulties with various revolutionary situations, hitherto he had consistently expressed confidence in the immediate potential for world revolution. With the failure of the Polish campaign, the period of the *militant* quest for world revolution had come to an end; and it now became expedient to put into practice the doctrine of "peaceful coexistence."

The chief practitioner of the newly revived doctrine of "peaceful coexistence" was the polished and skillful Georgi Chicherin, since mid-1918 People's Commissar of Foreign Affairs. So successful was Chicherin in marketing the image of "peaceful coexistence" that by 1925 every major country in the world, with the notable exception of the United States, had extended diplomatic recognition to the Soviet régime. With some countries, notably Weimar Germany, Chicherin not only established peaceful relations but extensive trade contacts as well. Yet at the same time, the Communist International, an organization of Communist Parties of the world, continued to pursue an active policy of world revolution, promoting revolutionary

---

[4] See, for example, M. N. Tukhachevsky, VOINA KLASSOV [Class War] 138-40 (1929).
[5] Reprinted in 41 V.I. LENIN, POLNOE SOBRANIE SOCHINENII [COMPLETE COLLECTED WORKS] 324-25 (5th ed. 1963).

putsches in Germany, Bulgaria, and China—albeit with rather ludicrous results. Although the Communist International was supposedly devoid of any control by the Soviet régime, it was based in Moscow, led and controlled by Bolsheviks, and its major strategy determined by Lenin and his Politburo. If the Communist International, with rather open Bolshevik control, actively sought the overthrow of foreign governments, could the Soviet Union be said to be pursuing a policy of peaceful coexistence? The question became somewhat academic in the latter half of the 1920s when, after Lenin's death and the ascendancy of Stalin over Trotsky, the Communist International became a far less active organization whose meetings became rarer and rarer and whose members' major preoccupation became purging dissidents rather than capitalists.

If the first major step in making "peaceful coexistence" a Soviet policy came with the end of the Russo-Polish War, the second major step came with Stalin's introduction of the doctrine of "socialism in one country." This doctrine, first introduced by Stalin in 1924, and adopted by the Soviet Communist Party in the wake of Stalin's triumph, substantially downgraded the importance of world revolution. "Socialism in one country" involved such a total commitment of Soviet resources in the home country that "peaceful coexistence" not only became feasible but highly necessary. During the period of the first two Five Year Plans, that is, 1928-1938, the Soviet Union did all it could do to enhance the impression that it had no ambitions beyond its borders and was distressed lest anyone else have such ambitions. With the emergence of a Nazi régime in Germany in 1933, the Soviet Union, with its Foreign Office now under the direction of Maxim Litvinov, sought international respectability in the West as ardently as they had sought world revolution in the early years of the régime. The Soviet Union joined the League of Nations (a deliberate manifestation of support for "peaceful coexistence"), signed defense pacts with Western nations, and unlike the 1920s refrained from foreign adventures— although it could not resist meddling in the Spanish Civil War. This policy was all well and good for the cause of "peaceful coexistence," but what of "world revolution?" Had Stalin in more or less pursuing peaceful coexistence more or less abandoned world revolution? From his exile in the West, Trotsky indicted Stalin for moving the goals of Soviet foreign policy "from world revolution to the status quo."

An explanation of the new Soviet policy was offered to the outside world by one of Stalin's chief publicists, Karl Radek. In an article in *Foreign Affairs*,[6] offered as official interpretation of Soviet doctrine, Radek emphasized the willingness of the Soviet Union to seek peaceful relations with all powers and downplayed as much as he could the theme of world revolution. As for the latter doctrine, Radek offered the rather apocalyptic view that once workers in other lands had seen the triumph of "socialism in one country," they would seek to emulate the Soviet example. Considering Radek's earlier background as a rather militant—and sometimes irresponsible—advocate of revolutionary action, the dim and far-off—and maybe

[6] Radek, *The Bases of Soviet Foreign Policy*, 12 FOREIGN AFFAIRS 193 (1934).

never—view of world revolution went far to establish the official priority of "peaceful coexistence" over "world revolution."

Actually, for some purposes, Stalin had done too good a job of selling "peaceful coexistence" and in some respects had seemed to confirm Trotsky's charge that Stalin had betrayed "world revolution." In 1938, through the medium of his public letter to one Comrade Ivanov, Stalin reaffirmed his faith in eventual "world revolution":

Hence the support of our revolution by the workers of all countries, and still more, the victory of the workers in at least several countries, is a necessary condition for fully guaranteeing the first victorious country [U.S.S.R.] against any attempts at intervention and restoration, a necessary condition for the final victory of socialism.[7]

The outbreak of World War II in 1939 forced a complete re-evaluation of Soviet foreign policy. Stalin, after protecting himself with a non-aggression pact with Hitler, still had the opportunity to follow a path of "peaceful coexistence" had he so desired. Quite to the contrary, however, 1939 effectively marked a. major interruption in the Soviet practice of "peaceful coexistence." The Soviet record from 1939 to 1941—a period when the Soviet Union was officially neutral in World War II—was marked by military aggression against Poland, Romania, the Baltic States, and Finland; and resulted in the militant spread of Bolshevism to all of the Baltic States and portions of other states. This policy was interrupted by the German invasion of the Soviet Union in 1941 and the dire military plight of Russia for the next few years. Once the German military threat was repulsed, however, Soviet foreign policy renewed its militancy of the 1939-1941 period and again converted the Red Army into an instrument of world revolution. As the Red Army marched westward, it brought in its wake Soviet governments, exported from Moscow to take over the countries of East Europe. "Peaceful coexistence" was on the Soviet agenda only after the Moscow-exported governments were installed in power. From the end of World War II until Stalin's death in 1953, it was difficult to take Soviet professions of "peaceful coexistence" seriously; the record in East Europe seemed to indicate a policy much more concerned with "world revolution."

With Stalin's death, Soviet relations with the West became more stable than they had been since 1939. Once again, the prospects for further military expansion dimmed. The 1950s appeared to be a more suitable time for consolidating gains than for new conquests. As in the past, the doctrine of "peaceful coexistence" was now trotted out and loudly proclaimed. Khrushchev may have claimed that he was only continuing the eternal policy of the Soviet state, but more serious reflection will indicate that be it under Khrushchev, Stalin, or Lenin, "peaceful coexistence" has been adopted by the Soviet Union as a pragmatic measure and not as an inherent belief. "World revolution," on the other hand, is inherent in Communist doctrine; and should the international situation offer new opportunities, it might again supplant "peaceful coexistence" as it has in the past.

[7] First published in 4 Bol'shevik, p. 14 (Feb. 15, 1938).

PEACEFUL COEXISTENCE*

LEON LIPSON†

INTRODUCTION

"Peaceful coexistence" deserves provisionally to be examined as a principle or a set of principles of international law: not simply as a description of contemporary international relations, not as an index to a mood or as an expression for something desired, but as something proclaimed to be the basis for contemporary international law and indeed the most important principle within it. Is this a straw man?

A Polish Ambassador to India has written (in 1961) that coexistence is the norm applicable to present-day international relations, that coexistence besides being a concept of international relations becomes also a concept of the law of nations, that the principles of international law applied to contemporary relations are the principles of the conduct of coexistence, and that international law is the law of coexistence. The man who is perhaps the most eminent currently active Soviet scholar of international law, Professor Gregory Tunkin, said in 1958, "A new page in the development of international law constitutes the principle of peaceful coexistence," and, in 1963, "There is every ground to call present-day international law the law of peaceful coexistence."

The Committee on Peaceful Coexistence of the Soviet Association of International Law declared in 1962, "The principle of peaceful coexistence is a universally recognized principle of modern international law; ... whereas international law of the past was a law of war and peace, it has today become a law of peace and peaceful coexistence." The draft declaration of principles of peaceful coexistence submitted by the Association proposed that the United Nations proclaim that the principle of peaceful coexistence is a fundamental principle of modern international law.

More of the same is at hand; but enough has been cited to show that if there is a man of straw it is not I who set him up. Nor am I undertaking to knock him down. Though Soviet international law remains in large measure a fighting international law rather than a thinking international law, it does not therefore deserve a belligerent response.

At the same time, it should be possible to object to some of the proposals being made for a code or declaration of the principles of peaceful coexistence without falling under suspicion of opposing peaceful coexistence in the factual sense of the term. Just as it is not sufficient for genuine adherence to peaceful coexistence to make loud noises in its favor, it ought not to be necessary to make loud noises in

* The substance of this article was delivered as an address at the School of Law of Duke University in February, 1964. Recent events have not materially altered the situation.

† A.B. 1941, M.A. 1943, LL.B. 1950, Harvard University. Professor of Law, Yale University. Member of the District of Columbia and New York bars.

its favor in order to avoid the charge that one is not committed to peaceful coexistence. On the other hand the claim for peaceful coexistence as a principle of international law is not to be dismissed on the ground that it is made and pushed by the Soviet Union. It is right to "consider the source," but it is not enough. Besides, as scholars, the leaders of today's international jurists in the Soviet Union have put forward a claim to be taken seriously, and that claim in turn deserves to be taken seriously, though upon examination we may decide that the claim is unfounded.

I

THE FIGHT FOR THE SLOGAN

The term "peaceful coexistence" as such has been found in Soviet literature, bearing as early a date as 1920. Contemporary Soviet writing ascribes the idea to Lenin; he does not seem to have used the term. The Soviet scholars who inveigh against the sin of quotationism have not been able to commit it in this instance. Western scholars have recalled that it was Chicherin, the People's Commissar for Foreign Affairs, who referred to the peace treaty with Estonia in 1920 as the first experiment in peaceful coexistence with bourgeois states. Twenty years later, the bourgeois state of Estonia having been rescued by Soviet forces, it became unnecessary to coexist with her except in the sense that the robin in Don Marquis' poem coexisted with the worm it had swallowed. The first experiment in peaceful coexistence had been unilaterally successful.

It is true the slogan has become central only since about 1956. At that time it took off from the Pancha Shila, the five principles which had been proclaimed in the Sino-Indian Pact of 1954 and expanded in the Bandung Declaration of 1955. As a proclaimed principle of international law, peaceful coexistence has been treated in numerous Soviet monographs and articles since 1956 and has been pressed with vigor by Soviet representatives at national meetings of governmental and nongovernmental organizations. The thrust of the massive effort now being exerted in many forums is to place that which is called principles of peaceful coexistence in the center of contemporary international law.

To this end, the purity of the slogan as such is defended against objection from without or within. Thus, in the summer of 1962 when an attempt was made in the International Law Association to change the title of the relevant committee by dropping the term "coexistence" so as to bring the title in line with that which was used in the United Nations, the Soviet delegation quit work in the committee until the change of name was blocked. In 1963 at a meeting of the Soviet Association of International Law one Soviet jurist made the error of depreciating the slogan in a similar way. He is reported as having contended that the principles of cooperation and friendly relations between states (a term used in the United Nations) were identical with the principles of peaceful coexistence. On this he was opposed, according to published report, by eight speakers who were named and others who were not; no one is reported to have risen to his defense. I shall suggest, below, some reasons for the criticism. Here it suffices to note that the phrase "principles of peaceful coexistence" is sacred. Chairman Khrushchev has made merry over those who have trouble pronouncing the phrase; for Soviet jurists, it seems, it is not easy to stop pronouncing the phrase. We and they might save time by abbreviating it to PCX, which would also help to distinguish the slogan from the very important fact of peaceful coexistence.

II

THE CONTENT OF PCX

When PCX is offered as a legal principle and an envelope for subordinate legal principles, it is natural to seek a list, representative or exhaustive, and a principle of organization that gives unity to the list. It will not do to say that PCX in international law means that men ought to live in peace. That would be little more than to describe the commonplaces in international relations, as Professor Jennings of Cambridge has said. Nor is it enough to say that PCX means that men should live in peace and collaboration. That would be a desirable outcome, and it may be a good thing to express the aspiration, but we should not have gone far along the road to proving that something new had arrived in international law.

It is not hard to find a list; the hard thing is to find which list to use. In view of the friendly Soviet references to the Pancha Shila, we might begin there. We find that the five principles are mutual respect for territorial integrity and sovereignty, mutual non-aggression, non-interference in each other's internal affairs, equality and mutual benefit, and peaceful coexistence itself. These are noble if not quite clear; if they were more clear they might not sound quite so noble. Some aid to interpretation may be found in the course taken by Sino-Indian relations since the signing of the agreement in 1954.

We note that PCX is number five on the list. Does it embrace all or any of the others? Does any of the others embrace No. 5 as well as others on the list? In the mid-1950s several Soviet authors took up the five principles and gave to all of them the term "The Principles of Peaceful Coexistence." That was the period in which the Leninist origin of the idea was discovered.

In the Bandung Conference of 1955 the list had swollen to ten. The first four principles of the Sino-Indian Pact survive in altered or lengthened form. Several new ones included (among others) respect for fundamental human rights and for the purposes and principles of the Charter of the United Nations, respect for the right of each nation to defend itself singly or collectively in conformity with the Charter of the United Nations, abstention from the use of arrangements of collective defense to serve the particular interests of any of the big powers, abstention by any country from exerting pressure on other countries, and respect for justice and international obligations. Coexistence was lifted from the list of enumerated principles to the caption of the list.

By 1961 a politically authoritative list had appeared in Part One of the Program of the Communist Party of the Soviet Union. There PCX was defined as implying renunciation of war as a means of settling international disputes and their solution by negotiation; equality, mutual understanding and trust between countries; consideration for each other's interests; non-interference in internal affairs; recognition of the right of every people to solve all the problems of their country by themselves; strict respect for the sovereignty and territorial integrity of all countries; promotion of economic and cultural cooperation on the basis of equality and mutual benefit.

One may note certain features of these and other lists besides the fluidity of their contents. Most of the items stressed and most of the reasons advanced in their support have been conspicuous for failure to specify a concrete secondary content; that is, a content that is sufficiently arguable to have meaning. Where the content is arguable, it is tendentious. For example, the proclamation of the inalienable right of peoples to their natural resources is silent upon the form or extent of compensation or other redress in the event of expropriation. For another example, in the Soviet draft declaration submitted to the International Law Association in 1962 the proclamation of the equality of states was accompanied by the sentence, "States shall be represented in international organizations with consideration for the fact of the existence at present of three large political groupings." It is easy to see that that rider was mounted on a *troika*.

On the whole, Soviet publicists have not shown themselves jealous of the purity of the list. The slogan is one thing; the content of the principles is something else. Soviet jurists have included some principles designed to have general appeal and some that were designed for particular advantage. They have been hospitable to lists advanced by others if only the others were willing to go along with the idea that an agreed list of PCX should be worked out. Even their opposition to certain principles in competing lists, principles that likewise were designed for particular advantage, has been relatively mild. We shall presently consider an explanation for the generality and fluidity of these enumerations.

One of the ways of testing the content of PCX is to ask whether the suggested extension of the term points to all of the particulars that normally would be considered. For instance, arbitral or judicial determination of legal issues between states is not a principle of peaceful coexistence in Soviet formulation. Now, one of the Bandung principles of 1955 was settlement of all international disputes by peaceful means such as negotiation, conciliation, arbitration, or judicial settlement, as well as other peaceful means of the parties' own choice in conformity with the Charter of the United Nations. It is true that the residual phrase, "other peaceful means of the parties' own choice," can be read so as to require consent of the parties in each case before resort to arbitration or judicial settlement, or indeed any of the other specified peaceful means. Still, the reference to arbitration and judicial settlement is there.

30

In the Soviet lists arbitration and judicial settlement are smothered. Some time ago Professor Jennings asked whether this refusal to submit legal disputes to legal determination was a part of the concept of peaceful coexistence. If it was, he said, Professor Tunkin might be thought not progressive but somewhat reactionary. Chairman Khrushchev, in his New Year's message in 1964 to heads of state of other governments on the settlement of territorial disputes, proposed four points for an international agreement on the settlement of territorial disputes. The fourth point was an undertaking to settle all territorial disputes exclusively by peaceful means such as negotiation, mediation, conciliatory procedure, and also other peaceful means at the choice of the parties concerned in conformity with the Charter of the United Nations. The accordance with the Bandung Declaration is almost exact. The only exceptions are the limitation of the subject matter to territorial disputes, which after all was the general subject of the New Year's message; the insertion of a reference to mediation; and the consistent absence of a reference to arbitration or judicial settlement.

Also conspicuously absent from Soviet lists of principles of PCX is condemnation of war as such. Wars that serve the ends of Soviet foreign policy have never been termed illegal. They are given the label of wars of national liberation or revolutionary civil war or wars against the counterrevolution and are accepted as just. Sometimes the implicit *eirenicon* is that the wars being outlawed are wars between states. The abjuration of war as a means of settlement of disputes between states ought to be read with the emphasis on "between states"; disputes that are not between states may well be subject to settlement by war. Soviet doctrine has consistently preserved the negative pregnant.

So PCX is not the same as pacifism. Soviet doctrine has never accepted pacifism; but at times when the movements of pacifist interest groups or pressure groups or groups of principle in the Open World have happened to serve the ends of Soviet foreign policy, pacifism has been acclaimed exoterically. Soviet international lawyers tell us that the *jus ad bellum* is now obsolete, but they still distinguish between rightful wars and wrongful wars. A book entitled *Peace, Freedom and You*, published in Prague in 1963, is quoted in a recent Western study as containing the statement: "Peaceful coexistence creates the most favorable conditions for the fight of the oppressed nations against their imperialist oppressors. Peaceful coexistence means the maximum support to the oppressed nations, including arms."

A third absent item is a principle that would uphold free international interchange of ideas. Peaceful coexistence in the sphere of ideology has been repudiated by Soviet leaders and writers in many statements directed principally at the Soviet population but used also in the context of the Sino-Soviet dispute. As recently as 1961 Chairman Khrushchev referred to the policy of peaceful coexistence as representing in its social content a "form of intensive, economic, political, and ideological struggle of the proletariat against the aggressive forces of imperialism in the international arena"; the current Program of the Communist Party uses similar language. When it was suggested in a Soviet forum that an enumeration of principles of friendly relations between states, suggested by a Czechoslovak delegation, was transferable to PCX, the orthodox critics pointed out that such an identification ignored the character of the relationship between socialist and capitalist states as a form of the class struggle.

For the present we need not scruple to take the terms of Marxist-Leninist polemics at face value. It is not now within my scope to ask whether the states called "socialist" and "capitalist" deserve those names or whether the class struggle in the form derived by Marx in the mid-nineteenth century in Western Europe has much bearing, except for purposes of religion and myth on both sides, upon the confrontation across the Iron Curtain today. Similarly, when reporting Khrushchev's statement, I do not stop to ask whether the proletariat is in fact represented by those who most often invoke its name, whether aggression is a monopoly of one state or party, or whether imperialism is any less imperialistic when it is exercised over contiguous colonies than when it is exercised from a distance.

Another way of testing the content of PCX in international law is to reduce the general ideas to manageable proportions by imagining cases. Here the imagination ought not to be confined to illustration from Soviet practice, for the idea that it is worth working out PCX in international law has won support in other quarters. If, for example, the United States' support of the Bay of Pigs invasion of Cuba is to be justified under international law, then we have a better idea of what the justifying speaker means by the principle of non-intervention. If the Indian embrace of Goa or the Israeli advance in Sinai is praised as the righting of historic wrongs or as preventive counteraction, then we have a better idea of what the speaker means by the principle of settlement of territorial disputes by peaceful means. If the Soviet suppression of the Hungarian revolution of 1956 is supported as justifiable in international law, we have a clearer notion of the supposed content of the principle of non-interference in the internal affairs of other states. If the events that have taken place in the last three or four years along the Sino-Indian border are an explication of the inner meaning of Pancha Shila, then some of the mystery of the mysterious Orient is dispelled. If the annexation of the Baltic states during the period of the Soviet-Nazi pact is defended on the ground of the plebiscites carefully arranged there, then we can understand better the meaning being attached by the speaker to the principle of self-determination.

III

THE STRATEGY OF THE CAMPAIGN

Is the idea of PCX taken seriously by its Soviet proponents as a guide for Soviet foreign policy, or is it put forward to advance that policy, or both? A full answer would lead us into a general discussion of international relations in the cold war, of the Soviet system, of the détente and the Sino-Soviet split, of the multiple audiences for Soviet statement on peaceful coexistence and their reciprocal eavesdropping. Here a few pertinent episodes must suffice.

When the leaders of the Soviet regime were somewhat more candid than they have since become, it was reasonably clear that the idea of PCX was to serve as a tactic in the conduct of foreign policy. In 1922 Lenin wrote to Chicherin when Chicherin represented Russia at the Genoa Conference:

We Communists have our own Communist program, the Third International. Nevertheless, we consider it our duty as merchants to support (even if there is only one chance in ten thousand) the pacifists in the other [bourgeois] camp. It will be both biting and amicable and will help to demoralize the enemy. With such tactics we will win even if Genoa fails.

Though expressed in universal terms, in practice the principles of PCX have seemed to be used to indicate duties of states outside the Soviet bloc but rights of states inside the Soviet bloc. One small example is worth our attention because the evidence, noticed by some close readers of the Soviet press, was so striking. Early in 1962, Mr. Suslov, a chief Soviet Marxist theoretician, made a speech at a conference of Soviet university teachers in the social sciences. His speech was published in *Pravda* on February 4th. The *Pravda* report had him saying: "Peaceful coexistence means . . . the rejection of war, the settlement of disputes between states through negotiations. It means the refusal to export revolution and to export counterrevolution." The symmetry of the last sentence is the thing to notice. Thirteen days later the same speech was published again in the chief Soviet magazine of general political theory, *Kommunist*. In that version, peaceful coexistence means ". . . the refusal to violate the territorial integrity of states, the inadmissibility of the export of counterrevolution." The reference to the refusal to export what the Soviet leaders call revolution was omitted; and the action seems not merely an omission but a deletion, made at a late stage of the printing in *Kommunist*, perhaps from galley proof or page proof, for the key sentence in *Kommunist* is now very widely spaced.

The strategic uses of "principles of PCX" vary with the audience. Afro-Asian audiences are assured that the Soviet Union sides with them in their campaigns for the Pancha Shila and, more fundamentally, that the Soviet Union as an important European power takes seriously a form of words that the Afro-Asians take seriously. With certain other audiences the aim is to influence non-Soviet disarmament, to attract East-West trade, to enlist support for various other current objectives of Soviet foreign policy. With Communist audiences the declaration of adherence to PCX is a taking of sides on one of the main issues between the Chinese and Soviet Communist leaders, which may be defined as the question whether the expansion of the Communist system can be rapidly achieved without actions that increase the risk of world-wide nuclear war.

Recently, before a Soviet audience, some Soviet international lawyers took pains to distinguish the concept of peaceful coexistence "as the fundamental principle of international law which is also the basis of the foreign policy of peace-loving states" from "the concept of coexistence of the two systems as an indication of the stage of history referred to by V. I. Lenin, a stage which is inevitable by virtue of the fact that the socialist revolution does not triumph simultaneously in all countries." All of the audiences eavesdrop on one another with differing success. That complicates the task of Soviet publicists, but they are assisted by the durable propensity of us all to hear what we wish to hear and to close our ears to what we would rather not hear.

PCX obtains only between states of different social systems, to use Soviet language. In the last analysis that comes down to states with diverse attitudes toward the Soviet Union. Relationships between states in the open world are not characterized in Soviet terminology as PCX; neither are relationships between states in what Soviet writers call the socialist camp. Between socialist countries the governing principles are those of proletarian internationalism, a term now being replaced (since the proclamation of the end of the period of dictatorship of the proletariat) by the term socialist internationalism. Principles of PCX are no part of the law of socialist internationalism, because there can be no class struggle between comradely, freely collaborating, brotherly states, and principles of PCX are meant to guide the class struggle.

In the higher phase of interstate relations that has been attained within the socialist camp, as we are told, genuine equality prevails. The principle of non-aggression becomes superfluous between socialist countries, for under those conditions aggression is too unthinkable to be worth warding off. The rights of national minorities are so well protected in socialist countries that there is no point in recognizing the principle of the protection of national minorities as being a principle of international law for those states. The provisions of the declaration on the rights of man with regard to the protection of democratic rights and freedoms of the representatives of various nations are likewise read out of the field of play for this part of the world. So are the provisions of the Convention on Genocide, and so it goes with slightly varying language for the principle of the equality of states, for the principle of non-intervention in the internal affairs of other states, and others.

What ought we to make of the idea that emerges: that legal principles are not applicable to him who propounds them if he states that he never violates them? The Soviet writers at this point would appear to be distinguishing their polity from lesser breeds within the Law. From the standpoint of international relations, what underlies this limitation of the principles of PCX to relationships between the Soviet bloc and the open world is the implication that that is the only important confrontation in the world today. The Soviet concept of PCX, in short, presupposes bipolarity and the cold war, rather than offering a way out of the cold war. Indeed, when combined with the repudiation of peaceful coexistence in the realm of ideology, it furnishes a Soviet equivalent of the cold war. The emphasis upon confrontation between socialism so-called and imperialism so-called lines up states on two sides of the Iron Curtain, ignores *pro tem* other bases of division and alliance, purports to set out rules for the conduct of states across the Curtain, and scores points in the Sino-Soviet debate.

IV

PCX AND CUSTOMARY INTERNATIONAL LAW

We can now arrive at some conjectures as to the utility of PCX in Soviet plans for the development of international law, after rehearsing briefly the position of the Soviet Union in the international legal community and recalling some of the other techniques the Soviet Union has applied in order to improve that position. The Soviet Union began its statehood under conditions of Soviet theory that implicitly denied the validity of traditional international law as the regulating idea of the system of nation-states. Upon coming into the international community the Soviet Union was very much in a minority. Even today, though it is stronger with satellites and friends in power and out of power throughout the world, the Soviet Union finds it useful for morale and ideology to emphasize at times that it is beleaguered by a hostile majority. Not only were many of the doctrines of international law disagreeable or hampering to Soviet leaders but the process by which international law was made and applied seemed under Soviet analysis to be necessarily exclusive and anti-Soviet. The facts indeed lent some support to this opinion despite the elements of humbug and hypocrisy that disfigured its expression.

In such a situation Soviet theory in international law, whatever its twists in regard to the course of Soviet foreign relations, made use of a variety of techniques to depreciate existing processes of the development of international law and to enlarge the role to be reserved for the Soviet Union in those processes. There was the time when international law was generally repudiated. Later, international law was to be accepted during a period of transition, admitted to be necessary before the time when international law could be discarded along with the general system of separate nation-states. There was the assertion that a state whose polity was based upon a new and just social theory had the right and duty to repudiate those particular doctrines of international law that offended that theory. There was the continued insistence upon the primacy of treaties as sources of international law, the belittling of the role of custom, the stress upon the necessity of the consent of a state before that state could be bound by a rule. When the United Nations Charter was adopted, with institutional arrangements allowing a very important role to the Soviet Union and its text corresponding in many ways to demands upon which Soviet representatives had insisted, Soviet publicists extolled what was called the international law of the Charter over what was called traditional or, indeed, obsolete international law. I have listed these various techniques roughly in the chronological order of their appearance, but there was no neat sequence of invention-use-abandonment-replacement. Many of them are alive today though not all of them flourish. They all have been overshadowed, even if not quite superseded, by the emphasis upon the principles of PCX. The picture I am drawing may have foreshortened the mental processes of Soviet lawyers, who perhaps did not plan it that way all at once; and the engine that I believe they have tried to build may not march along the intended route, and even the route may change. But as of today the course seems clear.

What counts for this purpose is not that PCX shall have one content instead of another, or indeed that it shall have any content at all. The content will become important at the second stage of the campaign. At the first stage, which is the stage of the present, what counts is that something under the name of PCX, preferably without definition, should win recognition as lying at the heart of international law; that it should be acknowledged the world over that to define PCX is the most urgent task of contemporary international law; that it should be acknowledged that the process of defining PCX requires participation and consent of the Soviet Union; and, by implication, that any existing principle or norm of prior international law that has not been accepted by the Soviet Union as part of or consistent with PCX in general statement or in particular application has to be rejected as being for that reason invalid.

It is there, in my opinion, that we have the chief significance of the campaign for PCX in contemporary Soviet work on international law. It is there, too, that we have an explanation for the hospitality of the Soviet publicists toward so many of the items furnished on provisional lists of principles of PCX by Americans, Yugoslavs, Indians, and others. They are hospitable because at the present stage the content of the term does not matter. Arguments about the content can and expediently should be postponed until the stage that would follow after the centrality of the as yet undefined principles had been conceded by the rest of the world. To that end, which is nothing less ambitious than a veto power over the formation and application of customary international law, many particular questions of content can be sacrificed for the time being.

CONCLUSION

If we now find PCX as principles of international law to be either truisms or religious dogmas (like the reference, in the Soviet draft declaration of principles of PCX, to "mankind's advance toward the most just social system which is Communism") or tactics in particular Soviet moves in foreign policy, or an effort to secure the veto in the formation and application of customary international law, does it follow that we ought to oppose any further effort to codify and declare the principles of PCX?

There is respectable argument to the negative. We are urged that we ought to consider the difficulties that even the best modern Soviet international lawyers must face in coping with the heritage of the past, in the policy of the Chinese Communists, in the views of some of their own Soviet colleagues, in their personal inner debate. We are urged to allow for the technical underdevelopment of Soviet international law: underdevelopment due not to any lack of intellectual quality but to years of isolation and difficulties of training, political interference, the constrictions of Soviet dogma. We are urged to be grateful for the relatively mild expression, the relatively friendly approach. We are urged not to set our faces against the de-Stalinization of the cold war. The détente, we are told, is genuine but it is fragile, it requires concessions. If Soviet international lawyers find one form of words so agreeable to them or so binding upon them by virtue of politically authoritative pronouncement, then the concession here is in an area that will not do much harm.

These arguments are not without substance; but the substance is more diplomatic than scholarly. As an amateur diplomat or even as a professional diplomat one might be well advised to take those arguments into account. But if one were acting in that capacity many other factors ought also to be considered and the balance might tilt in another direction. As scholars, we ought not to say that that has sense which seems to us to lack sense or that that is full which seems to us to be empty.

And yet the very process of examining the campaign for PCX ought to lead us to consider the beam in our own eye and to ask ourselves whether we have devised adequate procedures for the development of international law, whether we are proceeding as fast as we ought in the re-evaluation of the international situation, whether we are doing our duty in the effort to make law more just and peace more worthy. The attempt to answer those questions will not leave us complacent.

Chairman Khrushchev once let fall from his lips the famous and now often regretted boast, "We will bury you." He has insisted many times that the statement was only meant figuratively, that it was not meant to refer to particular individuals, that it was compatible with peaceful coexistence, that it has been misunderstood. But the best answer on Khrushchev's behalf was, as I have observed elsewhere, made for him more than twenty years before he made his statement. In 1936, at the exercises celebrating the tercentenary of the founding of Harvard College, President Conant moved that the meeting be adjourned to the same day of the same month of the year 2036. Ex-President Abbott Lawrence Lowell intervened: "Before putting that motion [of adjournment] I want to say a word in its favor. If I read history aright human institutions have rarely been killed while they retain vitality. They commit suicide or die from lack of vigor, and then the adversary comes and buries them. . . ."

INTERNATIONAL ORGANIZATIONS FROM THE SOVIET POINT OF VIEW

KAZIMIERZ GRZYBOWSKI*

I

THE HISTORICAL BACKGROUND

Soviet current policies in the United Nations Organization and in relations with the free world at large have their roots in the early days of the revolutionary régime, when the October Revolution gave power to the Bolshevik Party. At that time Russia, one of the great European powers, was on the brink of military disaster due to her involvement in war and her alignment with the Entente in conflict with the Central Powers. The defeat of the imperial army sowed the seeds of the revolution. At the same time, the new régime was painfully aware that in order to survive and to save the country from foreign conquest and political disintegration it must drastically change the situation. It was imperative that Russia be extricated from the war.

The idea of political and military disengagement was by no means the monopoly of the Bolshevik Party. It had its partisans in the imperial government, in certain political circles in Russia, and even among the members of the imperial family. The strength of the Bolsheviks lay in the fact that only they had a political theory and a philosophy of neutrality in that period of history and in that particular situation. Lenin's views, formulated in his major work, *State and Revolution,* served to make virtue of Russia's inability to fulfill the terms of the Alliance, and furnished a plan for action. According to Lenin the war was an imperialist war, fought not for the ideals of liberation, but for control of markets and world supply of raw materials. The real aim of the warring parties was to increase their dominions by the enslavement of the weaker nations. The decree on Peace, which was one of the first acts of the new régime, declared that: "To continue this war for the sole purpose of determining how to shape out control of the subjugated nations by the rich and powerful countries was a major crime against humanity."[1]

In order to stop the war, the Bolshevik régime proposed an immediate conclusion of peace, and sued for peace itself.

The decree repudiated the alliance with Western powers. In order to justify it, the Bolsheviks published secret treaties and agreements between Russia and other members of the Entente regarding post-war territorial settlements which indeed anticipated vast acquisitions for Russia, France, and Britain. Furthermore, the new

* M.L.L. 1931, Dr. iur. 1932, University of Lwow, Poland; S.J.D. 1934, Harvard University. Lecturer in International and Comparative Law, University of Lwow, 1936-39. Senior Research Associate, Rule of Law Research Center, Duke University. Author, SOVIET LEGAL INSTITUTIONS: DOCTRINES AND SOCIAL FUNCTIONS (1962); THE SOCIALIST COMMONWEALTH OF NATIONS (1964).
[1] S.U. RSFSR (Soviet Laws), 1917-18, no. 1.

régime looked with suspicion at various plans of the Western Powers to help Russia in her war effort. According to Potemkin's *History of Diplomacy*, which was to establish the official record of those times for the instruction of posterity, in the Fall of 1917 Britain, the United States, and France had reached an agreement to cooperate in "assistance" to Russia. The United States assumed responsibility for the reorganization of Russian railways, and Britain, for the development and equipment of the sea transport, while France undertook to give assistance to the army. However, the terms of the agreement were changed in a manner which in Russian eyes was proof of the far from friendly intentions of the Western Allies. Assistance to the Murmansk railway was assigned to Britain, while Western and South Western railways were to come under the French control. The Russians feared that the new agreement was not only a case of gross intervention in the internal affairs of Russia, but a first step towards her partition into foreign spheres of influence.[2] ¡Thus, as the new masters saw it, Russia's war sacrifices earned her nothing but defeat and humiliation, and held a prospect of enslavement at the hands of her imperialistic friends. To serve the nation and the interests of humanity the Bolshevik régime felt entitled to seek a separate peace with the Central Powers.

The decree on Peace, which declared void all secret treaties which were to benefit Russian landowners and the capitalist class, the ruling class in the Empire, was followed by another measure, this time aiming at the economic disengagement of Russia. The decree of People's Commissars of January 28, 1918 annulled "finally and without exception" all foreign loans to the previous régime as contrary to the new political reality.[3]

Stated in those terms, the policy disengagement remained for a long time the guiding line of Soviet foreign policy. Its main idea was that the socialist state is, by its very nature, free from those entanglements which result from the struggle and ambitions of the imperialist powers: Soviet policy is such that it cannot be affected by the conflicts and internal contradictions of the world economic and political order.

The fullest exposé of the position of the socialist Russia in world affairs was made by the Russian delegation to the Genoa Conference (April-May 1922), which sought to re-establish the economic and political unity of Europe. One of the key problems vis-à-vis Russia was the reconstruction and revival of her industrial and economic assets, to make her again a partner in foreign trade. This was impossible without foreign capital, and the members of the Conference sought to convince the new Russian régime that its repudiation of foreign loans and nationalization of foreign enterprises were obstacles to effective economic cooperation. Before new capital was made available, the Russian government had to mend its ways and make some concession to foreign interests. However, this plea fell on deaf ears. The Russian delegation refused to discuss the matter in terms of practical steps and came out

[2] 2 Istoria Diplomatii (History of Diplomacy) 302 (1945).
[3] S. U. RSFSR (Soviet Laws), 1917-18, nos. 353, 386.

with a broad statement of principle, which justified its past policy, and asserted that the Russian régime was entitled to discuss terms of economic cooperation on the basis of new agreements and commitments. In its memorandum of May 11, 1922, the Russian delegation stated that:

. . . revolutions, which are a violent rupture with the past, carry with them new juridical relations in the foreign and domestic affairs of states. Governments and systems that spring from the revolution are not bound to respect the obligations of fallen governments.[4]

However, principle or no principle, as time went on, the Russian government was forced to modify somewhat its position as regards the binding force of the acts of the previous Russian government. In an exchange of notes with the British government and later on various different occasions, the Soviet government either confirmed the validity of a number of earlier agreements, or withdrew its basic opposition to being bound by the tsarist treaties. Either by governmental proclamation, by reference in new laws, or official accessions, and even indirectly by publishing the texts of treaties in force, a number of international agreements pre-dating the revolution was recognized as remaining in force.[5] In particular, the Soviet régime found it useful to continue its cooperation with other countries within the framework of various technical and specialized organizations.

In the course of the twenties, the Soviet Union slowly built up its membership and participation in already established international organizations, including various technical arrangements. The Soviet Union became a party to the International Metric Union, International Telegraph Union, International Convention Concerning Protection of Underwater Telegraph Cables, Convention Concerning Establishment of an International Union for the Publication of Customs Tariffs, Convention Concerning Establishment of a Permanent International Agricultural Institute, International Office for Public Health, International Agreement for the Creation of an International Office Dealing with Contagious Diseases of Animals, Universal Postal Convention, Convention for the Creation in Paris of an International Office of Chemistry, Convention for the Unification of Certain Rules of International Air Traffic, and so on.

However, while the Soviet Union sought to cooperate in technical organizations, it refused to be involved in political schemes for the preservation of peace. It remained a partisan of the doctrine of political disengagement, which, as its leaders believed, saved the revolution. Not invited to become a member of the League of Nations, the Soviet government maintained an attitude of criticism and disapproval of the régime for the preservation of peace established under its auspices.

A subtle change in the Soviet line occurred in the late twenties, when the Soviet Union decided to join the General Treaty for the Renunciation of War as an Instrument of National Policy (Kellogg-Briand Pact—Treaty of Paris) of August 27, 1928.

[4] CMD. No. 1667, at 42-43 (1922).
[5] Cf. note 7 infra.

This was a first demonstration of Soviet active interest in some forms of collective security. The 1928 Treaty was followed by three regional agreements connected with its provisions. On February 9, 1929 the Soviet Union signed a Protocol concerning the entry into force of the Paris Treaty for the Renunciation of War (Litvinov Protocol) with Danzig, Poland, Estonia, Latvia, Lithuania, Persia, and Romania. On July 3, 1933, the Soviet Union concluded a convention on the definition of aggression with Afghanistan, Estonia, Finland, Latvia, Persia, Poland, Romania, and Turkey, and the next day a similar convention with Czechoslovakia, Turkey, and Yugoslavia.

The new line of policy which slowly took shape in the late twenties and early thirties was largely due to the growing change in the political climate in Europe. While initially the Soviet Union could maintain a posture of neutrality in a world which faced no real chance of major conflagration, the emergence of the dictatorial régimes in Italy and Germany, and the growing might of the Japanese Empire and its conquests on the Asian mainland made the Soviet Union vitally interested in the preservation of the status quo and in preventing wars. Soviet leaders saw themselves slowly becoming the main targets of political propaganda campaigns and even attacked by military force in Soviet territorial possessions. In those circumstances the Soviet Union was forced to abandon its policy of isolation, and to seek contact and cooperation with the forces of stability and political status quo.

In 1933, in a move to strengthen its position, Soviet intransigence as regards non-compensation for the nationalization of foreign property was abandoned. The actual concession was not important and involved no financial outlay on the part of the Soviet Union. In November 15, 1933, the Soviet government concluded a Gentlemen's Agreement (Litvinov Assignment), with the United States concerning the settlement of the pre-Soviet Russian government debts to the United States. The following day the Soviet Union and the United States exchanged notes establishing diplomatic relations between the two countires. In 1934 the Soviet Union joined the League of Nations and the International Labor Organization (ILO).

Soviet policy of active participation in various collective security schemes was closely associated with the person of Maxim Litvinov, who after long years in the Soviet foreign service finally reached the position of the foreign commissar of the Soviet Union. There seems to be no doubt that Litvinov himself was earnestly convinced that Soviet security could not be assured except by adhering to the policy of collective security. However, his position in the government and in the Party was not strong enough to commit the Soviet Union to this policy. Soviet entry into the League was understood as an act of political demonstration and a new line in the Soviet political tactics rather than a genuine change of heart. There was little evidence that the Soviet Union rendered more than lip service to the aims and goals of the League of Nations. At any rate its contribution to the prestige and power of the League could not but only delay (if at all) the process of disillusionment with the effectiveness of the great organization, which barely a dozen years earlier was a source of hope for the world.

Similarly, Soviet representatives in the ILO have done little to promote the work and the aims of the Organization. In spite of the fact that Soviet delegates participated in five of its annual sessions (19-23), the Soviet government did not accede at that time to a single of its conventions or agreements seeking to establish international standards of employment and improve world labor conditions. Some of the conventions prepared at that time and approved, also by the Soviet delegation at the ILO meetings, were ratified by the Soviet Union only after the death of Stalin (1953). A Soviet manual describing Soviet participation in the work of the ILO suggested that Soviet delegates to the ILO used its sessions mainly to "expose willful lies concerning the position of Soviet labor and to inform the public of the great achievement of the socialist country."[6]

As time went on, Soviet leadership became convinced that the policy of collective security was not a realistic policy, committing an error of judgment similar to that made by the governments of the other great powers of Europe. (Munich Agreement of 1938.) In March 1939 Litvinov was replaced by Molotov, who until that time was the chairman of the Council of the People's Commissars, and Stalin assumed direct responsibility for the government of Russia, taking in turn Molotov's position. The new leadership came to terms with Germany and became a party to the Ribbentrop-Molotov Pact (August 24, 1939). More than twenty years after Soviet leaders had successfully experimented with the disengagement maneuver the Soviet government again resorted to the same policy.

II

SOVIET PARTICIPATION IN UNIVERSAL INTERNATIONAL ORGANIZATIONS SINCE 1945

In the perspective of historical experience, the question which must be asked today is, what is the nature of the Soviet government participation in international programs involving technical cooperation with other countries, or in organizations seeking to guarantee peace and collective security in the world?

In the post-World War II period, the Soviet Union built up its membership in international organizations to the imposing number of some two hundred forty associations concerned with activities of interest to more than one country. In all probability in the entire world there is no other country with a government involved in so many international activities. This high figure is primarily due to the unique approach of the socialist countries to international relations. In more traditional societies a good deal of international contact is left to private individuals and private associations. In the Soviet Union and other socialist states, activities of business and professional association, of scholars, artists, labor leaders, humanitarians,

[6] MEZHDUNARODNOE EKONOMICHESKIE ORGANIZATSII (INTERNATIONAL ECONOMIC ORGANIZATIONS) 138 (1962 ed.).

if they extend beyond national boundaries, are a matter of foreign relations and a government monopoly. Thus the Soviet government in its official capacity is represented in all type of international associations which, so far as other countries are concerned, are not inter-governmental organizations. These include those established for the promotion and advancement of international research and exchange of information in the field of natural sciences, of humanities (history, Slavic studies), social studies (International Penal Law Association), cancer, rheumatism, shipbuilding and construction of roads and bridges, which although international in scope are "private" in nature. In addition the Soviet Union takes part in various organizations active in the field of trade and economic cooperation, international trade union activities, the International Red Cross Organization, and so on. Not all international organizations of which the Soviet Union is a member are international in the traditional sense. Yet, even with those corrections, Soviet membership in international organizations is quite impressive.

Soviet membership in inter-governmental organizations falls in three categories:

By far the largest is that group of international associations which were set up to deal with concrete, mostly technical problems of international cooperation. They include railway transport, electric power and its transit, communications including wireless, protection of natural resources (North Pacific Fur Seal Commission, International Whaling Commission, North Pacific Fisheries Commission, and so on). However, the Soviet Union remains uncommitted to international programs for the protection of copyright and of industrial property, as such rights are differently conceived and protected by the socialist states for reasons determined by national policy rather than out of respect for individual initiative and personal creation.

The second category of Soviet international involvement represents those forms of collective activity which, broadly speaking, form the United Nations system of international organizations.

In addition to the U.N., of which the Soviet Union is one of the original members, the Soviet Union is a member of the International Labor Organization (since 1954 also Ukraine and Byelorussia have joined ILO); the Economic and Social Council, Trusteeship Council, Bureau of Technical Assistance of the United Nations (the Soviet Union contributes financially to that organization since 1953); the Universal Postal Union, World Meteorological Organization, World Health Organization, UNESCO (since 1954), and the International Atomic Energy Agency.

The Soviet Union is not a member of the following technical organizations which are a part of the U.N. system: International Bank for Reconstruction and Development; International Monetary Fund; International Finance Corporation; Food and Agricultural Organization; International Civil Aviation Organization; Inter-Governmental Maritime Consultative Organization.

Soviet lack of interest in these organizations, especially those that are designed to render financial and economic assistance to underdeveloped countries, seems to be indicative of a fundamental opposition to international control of this type of activity, and may be dictated by a number of reasons. It cannot be excluded that the Soviet Union, a country with one of the largest national budgets in the world is unable to contribute to those activities in proportion to its position and influence in world affairs, a matter of prestige which is an important consideration in Soviet international policies. In addition the Soviet Union has its own program of economic assistance to other countries, which it administers according to policies dictated by its national interest, and which obviously is in conflict with the policy of international bodies. The same reason may inspire Soviet non-participation in the Inter-Governmental Maritime Consultative Organization, which is to bring agreement and cooperation in this aspect of international economic activity, and where the Soviet Union has aspirations exceeding its present possibilities.

Soviet participation in various United Nations activities underwent a subtle change since the death of Stalin and subsequent removal of Molotov from the control of foreign policies of the Soviet Union. Soviet foreign policy became more active and more inclined to compromise (*e.g.*, Austria and Laos). The Soviet Union joined UNESCO; and its participation in the International Labor Organization ceased to be a purely nominal affair. Since 1954 the Soviet government began to take active part in ILO's efforts to establish uniform labor conditions in the world by ratifying some of the numerous international conventions prepared and voted at ILO sessions.[7]

It must be said at once that by no means the Soviet Union became more amenable to identify its policies fully with those of the United Nations. The change, however, signified a more rational attitude to the work of the U.N., and to cooperation with its programs, when this was in the Soviet Union's interest.

[7] Convention concerning decrease of work hours to forty hours per week (ILO no. 47) of June 22, 1935, ratified by the Soviet Union on June 4, 1956.

Convention concerning annual holidays with pay (ILO no. 52) of June 24, 1936, ratified by the Soviet Union on July 6, 1956.

Convention fixing the minimum age for the admission of children to employment at sea (ILO no. 58) of October 24, 1936, ratified by the Soviet government on July 6, 1956.

Convention fixing the minimum age for admission of children to industrial employment (ILO no. 57) of June 22, 1937, ratified by the Soviet Union on July 6, 1956.

Convention concerning the age for admission of children to non-industrial employment (ILO no. 60), ratified by the Soviet Union on July 6, 1956.

Convention concerning medical examination for fitness for employment in industry of children and young persons (ILO no. 77) of October 9, 1946, ratified by the Soviet government on July 6, 1956.

Convention concerning the restriction of night work of children and young persons in non-industrial occupations (ILO no. 78) of October 9, 1936, ratified by the Soviet Union on July 6, 1956.

Convention concerning freedom of association and protection of the right to organize (ILO no. 87) of July 9, 1948, ratified by the Soviet Union on July 6, 1956.

Convention concerning the night work of young persons employed in industry (ILO no. 90) of July 10, 1949, ratified by the Soviet Union on July 6, 1956.

Convention concerning the application of the principles concerning the right to organize and to bargain collectively (ILO no. 98) of July 10, 1949, ratified on July 6, 1956.

Convention concerning equal remuneration for men and women workers for work of equal value (ILO no. 100) of June 29, 1951, ratified by the Soviet government on April 4, 1956.

Convention concerning maternity protection (ILO no. 103) of June 28, 1952, ratified by the Soviet government on July 6, 1956.

Soviet attitude towards some of the work done at the U.N. seems to indicate that a common policy uniting capitalist and socialist countries in certain fields of international activity is affected by the ideological difficulties stemming from different conceptions as to the historical sense of our times.

III

REGIONAL ORGANIZATIONS WITHIN THE SOVIET BLOC

In contrast, in relations between the socialist countries, the Soviet Union has demonstrated vigor and initiative in developing programs to realize a concrete vision of a future world order, of which the present political and economic alignment of the socialist nations is only a beginning.

To achieve this purpose the Soviet Union and the associated socialist countries of Europe and Asia have set up a system of international organizations and cooperation programs, strictly confined to the community (or Commonwealth) of socialist nations.

In the military field this cooperation began with a network of bilateral alliances and resulted in 1955 in establishing a Warsaw Treaty Organization which is a military alliance comparable to NATO. Economic cooperation of the socialist countries is directed by the Council for Mutual Economic Aid (COMECON). Established in 1949 to regulate and render technical assistance in trade relations. COMECON grew into an important center dealing with all forms of economic relations, with the ultimate purpose of intergrating the socialist countries into one system based upon a regional plan for the distribution of various economic responsibilities and functions. The Council for Mutual Economic Aid is in charge of planning, technical and scientific assistance, and research to bring about this ultimate goal.

Started as a fairly modest organization, COMECON consists now of a great number of technical organizations, including permament commissions for individual industrial branches or specific fields of economic activities, located in the capitals of the COMECON countries, and an international bank established in 1962 to finance various phases of economic cooperation. The principle of integration is that the industrial system of the Soviet Union and its vast natural ˜esources, including all types of fuels, raw materials, rare metals, and its enormous market potentialities are to serve as a base for the economic systems of other socialist countries.

COMECON assists the economic activity of the member countries by unification of international trade regulations; by planning various phases of the integration program, stressing the development plans conceived in the perspective of common needs of the entire bloc; and assisting in the realization of the cooperative projects designed to serve the economy of a number of COMECON countries. The latter include various transport facilities (pipelines and power grids), railway communications, development of air and sea fleets, developments of extractive industries, and market research to place commodity surpluses available in the member countries.

COMECON activities are supported by a number of technical organizations in charge of special fields of international cooperation between the socialist countries. These include railway and river transport organizations, conferences of government departments dealing with communications and custom formalities, the Joint Institute for Nuclear Research, the Danubian Commission, and various organizations for the protection of the maritime and fresh water fisheries.

Taken as a whole, the scope of economic and political cooperation of the Commonwealth of the Socialist Countries, centered upon the idea of their economic integration, is without precedent in international relations. Its purpose is to organize a vast area stretching from Central Europe to the Pacific Ocean washing the shores of Asia into a single economic system. In terms of historical experience it is comparable to the growth of the American economy. In terms of plans of social and economic integration it is comparable to the Common Market. Yet it is fair to mention that the simile is valid in a limited sense only. American economy filled the great void, and was the achievement of individual initiative. The Common Market programs bring about the economic integration of Europe by releasing economic initiative from the restrictions of national boundaries with as little interference of governmental authority as possible. Unification action is concerned with the equalization of social and opportunity conditions, and with prevention of discrimination by the governmental authorities of the participating countries. In addition, Common Market programs are only a return to the economic unity of Europe, which was already once a historical reality.

In contrast the program of the socialist integration envisions a totally novel experience. It relies primarily upon the cooperation of governments and of specialized governmental agencies. It is centrally planned and calls for detailed agreements between the governments concerned. It is therefore not surprising that in terms of governmental organization, it surpasses anything hitherto experienced in the history of human government. It is also not surprising that in terms of actual performance the results fall far short of achievements in the art of administrative buildup.

IV

CooPERATION IN UNIVERSAL INTERNATIONAL ORGANIZATIONS: EQUALITY AND VETO

In summarizing the history of the East-West cooperation within the framework of the United Nations it would not be unfair to state that absence of accord in practical cases is due to differences in some basic concepts between the socialist and free economy countries. They have to do with the aims and goals of the international cooperation, the role of the United Nations in our times, and the meaning of some basic concepts of international law. The end result of those differences is that the Soviet Union and its allies among the socialist countries are unable to agree to common approach with the Western powers in situations in which ideological differences are involved. They are opposed to efforts which are aimed at the stabilization of social and economic conditions. They see the purpose of economic assistance not in the strengthening of the free institutions, but in the development of planned economy systems. In the Soviet view, economic cooperation and movement of capital should not be the business of individual initiative, but the instrument of national control of economic resources. National independence has a meaning in the socialist political dictionary that will not be found in more traditional systems of political thinking.

These differences, which frequently give occasion to Soviet use of veto power, are the ultimate reason why a vast majority of U.N. members seek new ways and techniques to fulfill the basic aims and purposes of the United Nations Organization, which again is a source of irritation and conflict between the socialist and free economy countries. The growing membership of the United Nations is a source of pressure upon its institutions to effect change and to increase the influence of the smaller countries. The growing needs of the modern world and the presence of great forces of destruction call for a reform of the United Nations Organization to make it more effective, and a better tool in meeting some of the basic problems of our times.

It would not be true to state that the Soviet Union is insensitive to the trends in the public opinion of the world, and if it sees no possibility to make concession to that point of view it is so because of important reasons fundamental to its position.

A good deal of Soviet attitude to international cooperation with the states of different social order is due to the feeling of isolation, of the Soviet Union specifically, and of the socialist states as a whole in a world in which the free economy countries still vastly outnumber the members of the Soviet bloc.

This sense of isolation was born at the moment when the Soviet régime realized that the October revolution would not be followed by communist revolutions in other countries of Europe. As a result, any plan of political or economic cooperation with the outside world had to resolve the question of how to neutralize the capitalist majority in any situation in which it would have a bearing on conditions and circumstances of cooperation. Lenin's notes made on Chicherin's memorandum in connection with the departure of the Russian delegation to the Conference of Genoa (April-May 1922), which came with full documentation ready to justify a total rejection of all plans for reconciliation, were almost exclusively concerned with this problem. In order that the Russian delegation might have some chance of success at the conference table which would draft plans of cooperation, Lenin insisted that the Conference should include participation on equal footing of colonial and dependent nations. The Conference should also admit workers' organizations, and accept a general principle of nonintervention of international organizations in the internal affairs of the member countries. Similarly, Lenin insisted on full equality and numerical parity of representation in all procedures concerned with the settlement of disputes between the socialist and capitalist nations. As regards international arbitration, Lenin thought that only such court of international arbitration which would consist of an "even number of members, delegated by both parties, so that half of the members would be imperialists and half communists,"[8] would be acceptable to the new Russian government.

The same concern with numbers manifested itself when it became obvious towards the end of the last World War that the Soviet Union would not be able to retain the position of isolation and would have to participate in the activities of the United Nations Organization. The formula for political action in the new world was the unanimity and concerted action of all big powers so conceived that the opposition of one would block all effective action. In his report to the Supreme Soviet on November 6, 1944, Stalin warned that the actions of the future international organization in safeguarding peace shall only be effective if the great powers "shall act in the spirit of unanimity and agreement. They will not be effective if this basic premise is violated."[9]

The immediate post-war experiences in the conference room, where Soviet leaders were forced to sit and debate various political and legal problems, have strengthened even further their dislike of voting procedures. Diplomacy and negotiations had little to do with deciding questions by putting them to vote. Molotov, who was the chief Soviet delegate to the Paris Peace Conference of 1946, on several occasions complained bitterly against the voting technique. During the closing session of the Peace Conference, he denounced the "voting machine" which forced him to abandon many of his "just" claims. He indicated that the Soviet delegation favored the unanimity principle, which makes it impossible to settle international questions at the expense of the weaker party. He spoke darkly of the dangers associated with the technique of decision by the majority vote:

> Veto prevents an agreement of three or four of the big powers to conspire against one of them. Veto promoted cooperation between the major powers, which is in the interest of all United Nations and of the entire world.[10]

He was convinced that the unanimity principle is superior to the majority vote.

> The principle of veto requires that great powers must pay attention to their common interests . . . preventing the emergence of groupings or of blocs of states directed against other states, and making it difficult to intrigue with aggressors behind the backs and contrary to the interests of the peace loving nations.[11]

As the number of the socialist countries grew into a system of socialist states, the principle of veto became a basic condition to the cooperation between two state

---

[8] *Zajavlenie sovetskoi delegatsii na pervom plenarnom zasedanii Genuezkoi konferentsii (Declaration of the Soviet Delegation on the First Plenary Meeting of the Genoa Conference),* in 5 DOKUMENTI VNESHNEI POLITIKI SSSR (DOCUMENTS ON FOREIGN POLICY OF THE USSR) 191-94 (1961).

[9] Pravda, Nov. 7, 1944.

[10] MOLOTOV, RECHY NA PARYZSKOI KONFERENTSII (SPEECHES AT THE PARIS CONFERENCE) 116 (1946).

[11] *Id.* at 118.

systems. The Soviet right to veto any political decision made by the Security Council guarantees the equality and sovereign rights of the socialist states. It became thus a principle of peaceful co-existence within the United Nations Organization. Chairman Khrushchev stressed the wisdom of the Founding Fathers of the U.N. who "accorded equal rights to each of the great powers, members of the Security Council, including the Soviet Union, although at that time socialist countries were in an absolute minority. At that time only the Soviet Union and the Mongolian People's Republic were socialist states. Nevertheless, the Soviet Union was given the same rights as all other members of the Security Council." In his opinion the socialist states were given the same rights to influence the course of public affairs in the world as all other capitalist states.[12]

Furthermore, the right of veto was a political necessity. As a Soviet jurist wrote:

> The Soviet Union could not but take into account that in the course of the pre-war years the policy of Western powers towards the Soviet Union was reactionary and high-handed. It had to remember that anti-Soviet policy was the backbone of the foreign policy of the Western Powers. . . .[13]

In support of the Soviet government position Soviet jurists came out with a number of legal doctrines, which have promoted the principle of unanimity of great powers in the Security Council, and of the institution of veto to the central principle of the decision mechanism in the United Nations.

The highly authoritative 1957 edition of the Soviet treatise on international law prepared with the participation of the leading Soviet jurists expressed the view that:

> The negative vote of a permanent member (of the Security Council) means that the decision was rejected. If the permament member decided to refrain from voting, indicating that this should not be considered as a negative vote . . . the Council has the right to adopt the decision. Absence of a permanent member of the Council, announced before hand, makes it impossible for the Council to adopt any decision, except in matters of procedure, as in this case there is no agreement between all the members of the Security Council.

It is necesary to state in this connection, the absolute illegality of decisions made by

[12] N. S. KHRUSHCHEV, ZA MIR, ZA RAZORUZHENIE, ZA SVOBODU NARODOV (FOR PEACE, DISARMAMENT AND FREEDOM OF PEOPLES), 288. *Cf.* also Bobrov, *Printsip ravnopravia dvukh system v sovremennom mezhdunarodnom prave (The Principle of Equality of the Two Systems in Contemporary International Law)*, [1960] SOVETSKOE GOSUDARSTVO I PRAVO, No. 11; N. A. USHAKOV, PRINTSIP JEDINOGLASSIA VELIKIKH DERZHAV V ORGANIZATSII OBJEDINONNIKH NATSII (THE PRINCIPLE OF UNANIMITY OF THE GREAT POWERS IN THE UNITED NATIONS) 39-40 (1956).

[13] USHAKOV, *op. cit. supra* note 12, at 39.

"The Security Council differs from all other organs of the United Nations also in this respect, that it alone has the authority to make decisions, which are obligatory for all members of the Organization, while the Charter contains no obligation to fulfil the recommendations passed by the General Assembly, or other main organs of the United Nations. Only the Security Council has the power to adopt measures, to uphold international peace and security, while the General Assembly, which was authorized to examine "all problems connected with maintaining international peace and security" must all such problems, requiring such a measure, submit to the Security Council prior or after its examination." *Id.* at 51.

the Security Council in 1950 in the matter of Korea in the absence of repersentatives from the Soviet Union and the People's Republic of China.[14]

Soviet jurists also found that the veto principle is strengthened by the fact that in contrast with the League of Nations, which had set up the principle of equality of the Council and the League Assembly, the United Nations Charter made a distinction between the respective positions of the General Assembly and of the Security Council assigning, them different responsibilities. In this setup, the position of the General Assembly is definitely inferior:

. . . permanent members of the Security Council bear singular responsibility for the preservation and strengthening the world peace and security . . . which is expressed . . . in this, that according to the Charter, the Council is this organ, which is exclusively competent to institute international sanctions to support international peace and security. The United Nations Organization differs in this particular point from the League of Nations, that the Security Council is the only UNO body, which can institute measures of this type.[15]

As the unanimity principle in its United Nations version is the only platform on which socialist and free economy countries can establish working relations, it assures the universal character of the U.N. As it is absolutely necessary to preserve this universal character, the unanimity principle is the cornerstone of the present public order of the world. It must be adhered to, come what may. As Judge Winiarski from Poland, one of the important representatives of this trend of thought in the International Court of Justice, stated in his separate opinion in the case of *Certain Expenses of the United Nations*:

. . . it has been asserted that the purposes and in particular the maintenance of international peace and security may provide legal justification for certain decisions, even if these are not in conformity with the Charter, and that in any event a consideration of the purposes must furnish guidance as to the interpretation of the Charter. In the case before the Court, however, this argument certainly has not the importance, which there is temptation to attribute to it; . . . The Charter has set forth the purposes of the United Nations in very wide, and for that reason too indefinite terms. . . . It does not follow, far from it, that the Organization is entitled to seek to achieve those purposes by no matter what means. The fact that an organ of the United Nations is seeking to achieve one of those purposes does not suffice to render its action lawful. . . .
The intention of those who drafted it, was clearly to abandon the possibility of useful action, rather than sacrifice the balance of carefully established fields of competence. . . . It may be that the United Nations is sometimes not in a position to undertake action which would be useful for the maintenance of international peace and security, or for another of the purposes indicated in Article 1 of the Charter, but that is the way the Organization was conceived and brought into being.[16]

Professor Krylov developed this line of thought somewhat further:

[14] MEZHDUNARODNOE PRAVO (INTERNATIONAL LAW) 330 (1957).
[15] USHAKOV, *op. cit. supra* note 12, at 65; see also, F. I. KOZHEVNIKOV (ED.), MEZHDUNARODNOE PRAVO (INTERNATIONAL LAW) 321, 325 (1957).
[16] [1962] I.C.J. REP. 230.

The sovereign equality of the UN members finds expression in the fact, that each country has only one voice. The fact that some decisions of the United Nations organs are made by the majority vote does not affect that sovereignty, in particular as the U.N. General Assembly makes only recommendations, which do not create obligations upon individual states unless expressly accepted by such states. Furthermore, General Assembly decisions imposed upon the dissenting minority by the mechanical majority vote, if the minority's interests are in accordance with the aims and principles of the Charter of the United Nations, must be regarded as deprived of legal force. The minority has the right to reject those decisions.[17]

Summary

To summarize, Soviet attitude to the role of international organizations in our time seems to reflect a set of conflicting principles. The Soviet government on the whole has no reservation against participation in the work of technical and specialized organizations, provided they do not have a general purpose of economic assistance. Soviet leaders are fully aware that some of the technical problems of our civilization call for international cooperation.

The Soviet government sees the importance of collective effort and the full identification of national interests with those of the larger group of nations within the framework of the socialist system of states.

International cooperation within the U.N. framework is conditioned by the practical, case-to-case coordination of the interests of the socialist states with those of states belonging to the different social and economic order. Soviet participation in the United Nations represents a limited engagement and partial identification of its national interests with those of the world at large. In this connection, the concept of national sovereignty and of the legal equality of all members of the international community becomes rather a concept of the legal equality and of political independence of the two state systems, which must not, either directly or indirectly by means of an international organization, interfere in each other's domestic affairs.

[17] Krylov, Istoria sozdania Organizatsii Objedinonnikh Natsii (The History of the Creation of the United Nations Organization) 258 (1952). Cf. Morozov, Organizatsia Objedinonnikh Natsii (United Nations Organizaton) 168 (1962).

SOVIET TREATY LAW: A QUANTITATIVE ANALYSIS

Jan F. Triska*

Introduction

The purpose of this paper is to discover and define, by way of quantitative analysis of Soviet treaties and Soviet treaty-making data, the more recent trends, tendencies, developments, conditions and propensities characteristic of the Soviet law of treaties.[1]

It is true that an analysis based on quantitative or "hard" data does not necessarily possess greater evidential weight than an analysis based on qualitative or "soft" data. This depends upon the problem under investigation. A rigorous content analysis[2] of Plato's writings, for example, would tell us little about Plato's philosophy and ideology, try as we may, though it may yield less exalted information not obtainable otherwise. On the other hand, there are legitimate questions which can be answered through quantitative inquiry better than any other way. For example, the question whether relations among states depend upon and are conditioned by the volume, scope, frequency, type, and speed of the inter-state transactions, can best be answered quantitatively by any analysis of the transactional data correlated with an empirical scale of relationships between states.

The questions raised in this paper from the evidence and data gathered, explored, cross-examined and compared are entirely modest. They are directed to what may be called the "hard core" of Soviet foreign policy—*i.e.*, that component of policy which expresses articulation and normalization of relationships, commitments, stability, conservation of forces but assimilation to change and concession to progress, resolution of conflicts, and attempt for creation of more favorable situations—namely treaties, agreements, and conventions. These questions are based on comparison of Soviet treaties— (1) their numbers, (2) contracting parties, and (3) types— in the 1958-1961 period with that of (a) the 1917-1957 period and, in some instances, with (b) the last four years of the 1917-1957 period, namely 1953-1957. The units of analysis are Soviet agreements and treaties, the time span is forty-five years, and the technique is comparative. The overriding interest here is the relation of data to hypotheses construction: The multiform interaction data upon which the research rests are used either to formulate or to test hypotheses.

---

* J.U.D. 1948, Charles University (Prague); LL.M. 1950, J.S.D. 1952, Yale University; Ph.D. 1957, Harvard University. Associate Professor and Associate Executive Head, Political Science Department, and Director, Studies of the Communist System, Stanford University.

[1] I am indebted to Professor Richard R. Brody of the Institute of Political Studies, Stanford University, for comments on and criticism of this paper; and to Messrs. Stephen R. Fox and William L. Tuohy of the Department of Political Science, Stanford University, for their research assistance.

[2] By content analysis is meant a systematic attempt to codify the matter contained in a defined set of communications with a view of obtaining measures of the substantive material contained in it.

The quantification of Soviet agreements is, of course, only a prelude to the subsequent analysis—an essential prelude to the main theme. It is the analytical portion of the paper which contains the major effort, namely (1) finding the amount of change in the new data, (2) ascertaining the strength of relationship among the new data, (3) defining, on the basis of different particular ranges of data within the three groups, the degree of change' over the whole range of data, and (4) discovering the degree of correlation between the data and the social reality in which the agreements were made. To this end, a set of hypotheses either emerging from or based upon the quantification of the data is offered in the last portion of the paper.

I

NUMBERS

In the four-year period between January 1, 1958, and December 31, 1961, the U.S.S.R. allegedly concluded 870 international engagements—793 bilateral and 77 pluri- or multilateral.[3] Compared with the 2,586 international arrangements Soviet Russia was purported to have concluded in the first 41-year period of its existence (2,086 bilateral and 500 pluri- or multilateral),[4] as well as with the total of 702 agreements it concluded in the 1953-1957 period, the record of the four most recent years makes it abundantly clear that the U.S.S.R. increases its contractual engagements over time, and substantially so. In fact the tendency noted in our book in 1962[5] has been amply validated by the more recent data.

The average annual number of Soviet contractual engagements for the 1917-1957 period (leaving out the brief and relatively unproductive year of 1917) was 62.9; in the 1953-1957 period, the annual average was almost tripled to 175.5 agreements (in this four-year period the Soviet government concluded twenty-eight per cent of all its contractual engagements for the 41-year period); and in the 1958-1961 period, the average jumped to 217.5 agreements per year—a 23.9 per cent increase over the previous four-year period but a truly spectacular increase of 246 per cent over the previous 41 year period. This dramatic increase in frequency and volume of Soviet treaties took place, however, in the bilateral sector: While the 1917-1957 yearly plurilateral and multilateral average was 17.5 agreements and conventions, the 1958-1961 yearly average increased only by ten per cent to 19.3 conventions and agreements. The Soviet government thus continued to favor bilateral over both plurilateral as well as multilateral arrangements, and increasingly so: While the 1917-1957 ratio of the former to the two latter combined was over four to one, the

[3] Slusser & Ginsburgs, A Calendar of Soviet Treaties, January-December 1958, 7 Ost Europa Recht 100-31 (1961). Ginsburgs & Slusser, A Calendar of Soviet Treaties, January-December 1959, 8 Ost Europa Recht 132-64 (1962); and Ginsburgs, A Calendar of Soviet Treaties, January-December 1960, 9 Ost Europa Recht 120-59 (1963), and A Calendar of Soviet Treaties, January-December 1961, 10 Ost Europa Recht 116-48 (1964).

[4] Robert M. Slusser & Jan F. Triska, A Calendar of Soviet Treaties, 1917-1957 (1959).

[5] Jan F. Triska & Robert M. Slusser, The Theory, Law, and Policy of Soviet Treaties 4 (1962).

1958-1961 ratio of bilateral to pluri- and multilateral treaties was over ten to one, or more than double that of the 41-year average.

Tested against new empirical evidence, then, our original hypothesis has been amply validated: The U.S.S.R. indeed tends to increase the number of its contractual commitments over time, strikingly so in the bilateral sector but only moderately in the pluri- and multilateral sector, *i.e.*, on the regional as well as on the international levels.

II

CONTRACTING PARTIES

In the 1958-1961 period, the U.S.S.R. entered into bilateral contractual engagements with 65 states. However, it concluded 706 or about ninety per cent of all of its agreements with only 36 of these states. Of these, 55.3 per cent were with the other 13 communist party-states[6] (sixty-five per cent of these with the East European communistic party-states), 29.0 per cent with the developing countries, 9.0 per cent with the leading Western states and 6.5 per cent with Finland (24 agreements), Austria, and Japan (11 agreements each).[7]

The comparison of the more recent data with data gathered previously indicates that alterations and changes here took place along the functional-ideological continuum and away from geographical orientation. In the 1917-1957 period, the fifteen leading Soviet treaty partners were (1) Finland, (2) Poland, (3) Germany (and West Germany), (4) Romania, (5) Communist China, (6) and (7) Czechoslovakia and Bulgaria, (8) Hungary, (9) Yugoslavia, (10) East Germany, (11) France, (12) the United Kingdom, (13) Italy, (14) Norway, and (15) Albania. They were thus primarily Soviet neighbors (and their neighbors' neighbors) and secondarily leading West European countries. The reshuffling which took place in the 1958-1961 period— to (1) Poland, (2) Bulgaria, (3) Mongolia, (4) Czechoslovakia, (5) Hungary, (6) East Germany, (7) and (8) North Korea and Romania, (9) India, (10)-(12) China, North Vietnam and Indonesia, (13) and (14) Afghanistan and Finland, (15) Cuba, (16) and (17) Albania and Ghana, (18) UAR, (19) Yugoslavia, (20)-(22) United Kingdom, United States and Guinea, (23) France, (24) West Germany, (25) and (26) Cambodia and Iraq—affected both categories: (A) As to the neighbors' group, the switch was (a) towards the communist party-states of Eastern Europe, the economically accelerated part of the socialist camp, namely (1) Poland, (2) Bulgaria, (4) Czechoslovakia, (5) Hungary, and (6) East Germany, all members of the Council of Mutual Economic Assistance and of the Warsaw Pact, and in the case of

---

[6] By communist party-states I mean those 14 states which are ruled by communist parties, namely, the U.S.S.R., the Chinese People's Republic, People's Republic of Albania, People's Republic of Bulgaria, Hungarian People's Republic, Democratic Republic of Vietnam, German Democratic Republic, Korean People's Democratic Republic, "Heroic People of Cuba," Mongolian People's Republic, Polish People's Republic, Romanian People's Republic, Czechoslovak Socialist Republic, and Socialist Federal Republic of Yugoslavia. Cf. Pravda, April 14, 1964, p. 1.

[7] The Soviet-Austrian agreements fall into the diplomatic formalities and trade agreements categories while Soviet-Japanese engagements deal chiefly with fisheries and trade.

TABLE I

Soviet Bilateral Contracting Parties

	1917–1957			1958–1961	
Rank	Contracting Party	Treaties & Agreements	Rank	Contracting Party	Agreements
1	Finland	134	1	Poland	58
2	Poland	127	2	Bulgaria	39
3	Germany (& West Germany)	107	3	MPR (Mongolia)	35
4	Rumania	81	4	Czechoslovakia	33
5	Communist China	73	5	Hungary	32
6-7	Czechoslovakia & Bulgaria	70	6	GDR (East Germany)	30
8	Hungary		7-8	KPDR (North Korea); Rumania	28
9	Yugoslavia		9	India	27
10	East Germany		10-12	CPR (China); DRV (North Vietnam); Indonesia	25
11	France		13-14	Afghanistan; Finland	24
12	United Kingdom		15	Cuba	22
13	Italy		(16-17	Albania; Ghana	19
14	Norway		18	UAR (Egypt)	18
15	Albania		19	Yugoslavia	17
			20-22	U.K.; U.S.; Guinea	16
			23	France	
			24	FGR (West Germany)	13
			25-26	Cambodia; Iraq	12
			27-29	Austria; Italy; Japan	11
			30-33	Iran; Ethiopia; Norway; Morocco	8
			34-37	Nepal; Sudan; Brazil; Ceylon	7
			38-40	Iceland; Tunisia; Somalia)	6

Bulgaria, Czechoslovakia and Hungary also members of the Danube Commission, and (b) away from the economically decelerated Asian portion of the camp, chiefly Communist China (from 5th to 10-12th place), but also North Korea (from 4-5th in 1957 to 7-8th place) and North Vietnam (13th in 1957, 10 to 12th in 1958-1961).[8] Predictably, Mongolia moved contractually much closer to the U.S.S.R., while Albania came to be grouped with the Far Eastern party-states. Just as predictably, the now "neutralist" Yugoslavia moved from 9th to 19th place on the Soviet contractual scale.[9] On the other hand and significantly, Romania slipped from 4th place

[8] With Communist China, North Korea and North Vietnam the U.S.S.R. concluded two, six, and six agreements respectively for industrial aid in this time period, while it concluded fifteen and twelve agreements with Bulgaria and Poland. Trade, scientific-technical aid, and economic agreements bear out the same or similar frequency-volume patterns.

[9] The Soviet Union concluded seventeen agreements with Yugoslavia—two in 1958, four in 1959, five in 1960, and six in 1961. Of these seventeen agreements, four were constituted by the protocol and plan of cultural and scientific collaboration between the Soviet Union and Yugoslavia (for the years 1958, 1959, 1960, and 1961). This agreement covered the fields of art, science, cinema, higher education, publishing, radio and television. Similar plans were agreed upon by the Soviet Union and each of the other twelve communist party-states; they seem to be designed for the maintenance of and increase in ideological unity and understanding.

Four more of the eleven Soviet-Yugoslav agreements dealt with the work of the Soviet-Yugoslav

to the 7-8th place, thus suggesting already at this time the cooling off of Soviet-Romanian economic relations, which became obvious to us only last year. Cuba moved from nowhere [except for the establishment (in 1942) and suspension (in 1952) of diplomatic relations, no Soviet-Cuban agreements existed prior to 1960] to 15th place in 1961 with a spurt of 22 agreements,[10] thus within two years approaching the four year records of Communist China and North Vietnam with 25 agreements each. (This Soviet-Cuban rapprochement is somewhat reminiscent of the 1955 Soviet-Yugoslav renewal of relations, with its 18 Soviet-Yugoslav agreements.) Finland moved from first to 13-14th place on the Soviet contractual scale, an indication of growing functional disaffinity between the U.S.S.R. and Finland,[11] and

commission on scientific-technical cooperation. There are similar Soviet commissions with the other communist party-states, apparently another measure for cohesion within the party-states system.

Of the three other agreements between the Soviet Union and Yugoslavia, one is a consular convention and the other two trade agreements—perhaps the only two agreements of the eleven of any actual consequence. Entered into on January 28, 1959, and January 30, 1960, respectively, the 1959 plan called first for the exchange of Yugoslav steel pipes, rolled ferrous metals, lead, copper sheets, leather wear, mercury, cables, cement and woolens for Soviet wheat, coal, oil and oil products, rolled ferrous metals, tin sheets, wire, ferrous alloys, asbestos, manganese ore, machinery and equipment, medicines and chemicals, and so on; the 1960 plan was similar, but included a call for $108 million worth of trade both ways. The six agreements concluded in 1961 concerned cultural matters (3 agreements), trade (2 agreements) and technical-scientific matters (1 agreement).

[10] On February 13, 1960, three agreements were concluded between the Soviet Union and Cuba: A joint communique concerning a visit by Anastas Mikoyan to Cuba; a trade and payments agreement (a) in which the Soviet Union promised to purchase one million tons of sugar annually for the next four years, and (b) creating a Soviet-Cuban mixed trade commission; and a credit agreement providing Soviet credit to Cuba of up to $100 million at 2.5% per annum. One week later an exchange of notes took place between the U.S.S.R. and Cuba concerning a provisional Soviet trade mission in Cuba. After these agreements were concluded, diplomatic relations were finally re-established between the two contracting parties on May 8, 1960.

The Soviet-Cuban relationship became even closer on June 18, 1960, when the two partners issued a joint communique on trade and economic questions and another on cultural relations; they also signed an agreement on delivery of Soviet oil and oil products; and an agreement (between the State Bank of the U.S.S.R. and the National Bank of Cuba) on procedure for payments for goods delivered in accordance with the agreement on trade and payments and the agreement granting a Soviet loan to Cuba. All this, together with the final joint communique issued by the U.S.S.R. and Cuba on talks concerning trade, economic, and cultural relations of June 20, 1960, made Cuba a Soviet contracting partner high on the Soviet treaty scale. A month later, Raul Castro visited the U.S.S.R. and expressed Cuban gratitude for Soviet political and moral support and economic aid. He said he appreciated the Soviet readiness to use any means to prevent an armed attack on Cuba by the United States.

Later in 1960, Cuba and the U.S.S.R. agreed to employ Soviet technical aid in Cuban industry and geological survey work, and to send Cuban specialists and technicians to the U.S.S.R. for training. Other contractual engagements concluded before the year's end included an agreement on cultural cooperation; a trade protocol for 1961 based on the agreement on February 13, 1960, and foreseeing an increase in trade turnover; an agreement for Soviet technical aid in geological prospecting for oil and other minerals; an agreement providing for Soviet aid in the training and education of Cuban specialists in various fields of the national economy; and a joint communique issued after Guevara's visits to the U.S.S.R.—concerning international questions, trade, and scientific and cultural cooperation.

In 1961, Cuba concluded four more agreements with the U.S.S.R.—on technical-scientific, technical-industrial, cultural and economic cooperation.

[11] Against the Soviet-communist party-states' agreements, the twenty-four Soviet-Finnish agreements of 1957-1961 appear quite non-committal. There are some settlements of claims, agreements on border and customs regulations, agreements concerning fishing and navigation, and renewals of trade protocols. There is only one agreement providing for Soviet-Finnish industrial-technical cooperation, and only three agreements which deal with broader economic problems.

Norway was displaced, from 14th to 29-32nd place, by more responsive Soviet contractors from Asia and Africa.

(B) The leading West European states all disappeared from their relatively high positions on the scale of Soviet contracting parties (Germany was 3rd, France 11th, the United Kingdom 13th, and Italy 14th) and reappeared outside of the fifteen leading Soviet treaty partners, namely in the 20th-23rd and 26-28th places. Also, a certain amount of switching around took place: A non-European power, the United States, moved into the lead and became now with the United Kingdom the ranking Soviet treaty partner from the West (20-22nd on the scale both with 16 agreements), followed by France (23rd with 15 'agreements), West Germany (24th with 13 agreements), and Austria and Italy (27-29th with 11 agreements).

(C) The leading West European states were displaced on the Soviet contractual scale by the developing states 'of Asia and Africa—India (9th),[12] Indonesia (10-12th),[13] and Afghanistan (13-14th).[14] These favorable Soviet contractual respondents were followed by Ghana (16-17th place), United Arab Republic (18th), Guinea (20-22nd place), Cambodia and Iraq (25-26th), Morocco, Iran, and Ethiopia (30-33rd), Nepal, Sudan, Brazil and Ceylon (34-37th) and Iceland, Tunisia, and Somali (38-40th).

III

Content

Robert Slusser and the present author maintained in 1962 that the U.S.S.R. concluded chiefly trade and commercial agreements: about every third Soviet agree-

[12] Soviet-Indian contractual interactions fall primarily into the spheres of trade and industrial-technical aid agreements. The Soviet Union decided to aid India in the construction of a thermal power station, in construction of an oil refinery, and in geological survey work in the extraction of oil and gas. The Soviets gave assistance to the Indian Technological Institute for the training of engineers and technical aid to Indian agriculture; provided for Indian industrial specialists to come to the U.S.S.R. to study; sent Soviet specialists to India to work and train Indian specialists; and agreed to build Indian industrial complexes through mutual cooperation. Soviet officials visited India three times (including a visit by Premier Khrushchev). A five-year trade agreement between the two nations was signed on November 16, 1958, and another agreement "foreseeing a considerable increase in the variety and volume of trade" was signed in March, 1960. Finally, a Soviet-Indian credit agreement providing a Soviet credit of 1.5 billion rubles over twelve years was concluded in September, 1959.
Nevertheless, India's interaction with the West was higher, in the 1958-1961 period, than with the U.S.S.R.
[13] The U.S.S.R. granted a large amount of credit to Indonesia. On July 28, 1959, the U.S.S.R. supplemented the $100 million credit granted three years earlier to Indonesia by providing a $12.5 million credit for building a 100,000 seat stadium in Djakarta (to be ready for the Asian Games in 1962). On that same day, the Soviets granted an additional credit of $5 million for construction of a technological faculty in Ambon and for training Indonesian specialists. A Soviet-Indonesian agreement of February 28, 1960, provided for a Soviet long-term (seven years) credit of $250 million for help in the use of atomic energy for peaceful purposes, construction of works associated with this field, and training of specialists. The 1961-1963 trade agreement between the U.S.S.R. and Indonesia, signed on July 9, 1960, called for trade to increase yearly; in 1963 to be thrice the amount of 1959.
[14] The Soviet-Afghanistan pattern of agreements exhibits a remarkable similarity to that of the Soviet-East European communist party-states. The technical-scientific, technical-industrial, technical-agricultural, cultural and trade and commerce agreements are all there, and in high numbers. Afghanistan ranks on the Soviet treaty scale as high as Finland.

ment or treaty during this period concerned trade or commercial issues and problems. The second largest group of Soviet contractual engagements, or slightly less than one-fourth of the total, dealt with political problems ranging from formal issues of diplomatic relations (174 agreements) to treaties of alliance and fraternal mutual assistance (414). The remaining Soviet agreements and treaties concerned so-called functional problems, oscillating from many—legal issues, communication, transportation and cultural problems—to few—technical military questions, armistices and suspension of hostilities, and territorial questions.

In view of the somewhat changed character and content of the agreements encountered in the 1958-1961 period, it seemed preferable to let the new data form the categories rather than force the former categories on the new data. As a consequence, the classification employed here is slightly different from that used in our previous study. The 14 new categories embrace international contractual engagements dealing with (1) trade and commerce (202 agreements); (2) technical-economic aid in areas of industry and industrial production (136 agreements); (3) diplomatic affairs—recognition of states and governments, exchanges of ambassadors, establishment of relations, diplomatic visits, consular conventions, and so on (110 agreements); (4) cultural issues, including cultural and educational exchanges and assistance and collaboration in science (110); (5) scientific questions and technical aid in scientific and cultural problems (87); (6) economic aid, payments agreements, economic collaboration and credit agreements (79); (7) matters dealing with international waters, navigation, and fishing (35); (8) matters of transportation, customs, travel, citizenship, and border demarcation (29); (9) issues of communication (18); (10) technical-economic aid in areas of agricultural and/or geological development (16); (11) matters concerning peaceful uses of atomic energy and disarmament (20); (12 and 13) health problems, social-security plans, and aid in building hospitals (10), and settlements of international claims (10); and (14) military aid or other military issues (8).

The 14 categories include both bilateral as well as pluri- and multi-lateral engagements; of the latter, the highest number concerns matters dealing with international waters, navigation, and fishing (15) and diplomatic and consular affairs (15); matters of transportation, customs, and travel (11); economic aid and payments agreements (8); and issues of communications (6).[15]

[15] Included in this number are meetings of the Soviet-sponsored Danube Commission, those of the Council for Mutual Economic Aid, the Joint Institute for Nuclear Research protocol on further expression of scientific collaboration, and the meetings and declarations of the members of the Warsaw Pact. Also, agreements such as the International Convention for the Northwest Atlantic Fisheries and thirteen other multilateral agreements in the spheres of international waters, regulation of vessels, or regulation of fishing were concluded. Other agreements concern such matters as telegraph regulations, protocol on road signs and signals, convention concerning customs facilities for touring, and so forth. Also included are the several agreements which the U.S.S.R. concluded as a part of the business of the United Nations.

Agreements of an international multilateral scope which were of political interest were those in which the subjects of Berlin or nuclear disarmament arose. On September 1-14, 1958, the Soviet Union participated in the Second United Nations Conference on Peaceful Uses of Atomic Energy. On August 30,

Comparing the above cross-classification with the results contained in our previous study, the new data tell us the following: (1) The major categories concerning economic issues and questions (namely trade and commerce; economic aid, payments agreements, etc.; technical economic-industrial aid; and technical economic-agricultural aid) total 433 agreements or 49.7 per cent, a 15.4 per cent increase over the 41 year period. (2) The change is even more striking with reference to the political treaties. Even if we include, in addition to the legitimate diplomatic affairs category (100 agreements), the more questionable categories of peaceful uses of atomic energy (and disarmament) agreements (20) as well as the military aid agreements (8), the total amounts to a mere 138 agreements or 15.8 per cent of all the agreements concluded in this period. Not only does this represent a drop of eight per cent from the previous long period, but the political treaties—the solemn treaties of alliance, mutual political assistance, non-aggression, peace, and so on— are entirely missing here, a truly striking change from the past. (3) With reference to the functional group, changes have occurred as well: armistices and suspensions of hostilities, just as repatriation problems, do not appear in this time period. The former legal category tends to appear in the form of socio-cultural aid. Instead of the humanitarian questions category, the more satisfactory technical, scientific and cultural aid categories have been employed. Health questions reappear in the 1958-1961 period, and the U.S.S.R. continued to agree to help solve them. The communication and transportation categories remain as well. All in all, the functional groups, formerly 40.1 per cent strong, declined only 6.8 per cent to 33.2 per cent in the 1958-1961 period. Should the more questionable "political" agreements concerning military aid and peaceful uses of atomic energy be included at least partly here, the functional group would show increase rather than remaining much the same. In any case, the major changes here occurred in the aid and assistance agreements—cultural, scientific, technical—where the numbers of agreements have risen sharply in the 1958-1961 period.

All in all, Soviet economic agreements showed a sharp rise; Soviet political agreements dived into decline (in fact, "solemn" political treaties disappeared al-

the United States and the United Kingdom announced declassification of information on controlled thermonuclear reactions; the U.S.S.R. made a similar announcement on September 1. October 31 through December 19, 1958, was the time of the Geneva conference on the discontinuance of nuclear weapons tests. At the time, the most important result was the tacit de facto agreement on cessation of nuclear tests by the U.S.S.R., United States and Great Britain. In reply to Soviet notes proposing a summit conference of Heads of Government, of March 2, 1959, to take place at the end of April in Geneva or Vienna, the Western Powers agreed. As a result the conference in Geneva met on May 11 to discuss questions relating to Germany and Berlin. The first half of this meeting was held from May 11 to June 20, and the second half from July 13 to August 5. The final communique mentioned "frank and comprehensive discussion" of the Berlin question and stated that the discussions would be "useful for the further negotiations which are necessary in order to reach an agreement."

On September 8, 1959, a joint communique was issued by the Foreign Ministers of France, the United States, Great Britain, and the U.S.S.R., concerning creation of a committee for the study of questions of disarmament. Finally, on December 30, 1959, there was an exchange of notes concerning a Four Power Conference "to discuss the main problems affecting the attainment of peace and stability in the world." The four contracting parties agreed to meet on May 16, 1960, in Paris.

TABLE 2

CLASSIFICATIONS OF SOVIET AGREEMENTS ACCORDING TO THEIR CONTENT

Rank	Category-type	1917–1957 Total	1958–1961 Total
1.........	Economic (chiefly trade and commerce)	850 (34.3%)	433 (49.7%)
2........	Political a ⎰General political issues b ⎱Diplomatic	414 174 588 ‾‾ (23.8%)	138 (15.8%)
3........	Functional or technical treaties a ⎰Legal issues b ⎪Communications c ⎪Cultural questions d ⎪Transportation e ⎬Repatriation of citizens f ⎪Health problems g ⎪Humanitarian issues h ⎪Armistices & suspension of hostilities i ⎪Military (technical questions) j ⎱Territorial questions	293 169 162 146 90 71 55 36 10 5 1037 (40.1%)	299 (33.2%)
	Totals	2475	870

1958–1961

Rank on totals	Category-type	# Bilateral	# Pluri-& Multi-lateral	Total
1..............	Trade and commerce	198	4	202
2..............	Technical-industrial	132	4	136
3 & 4..........	⎰Cultural	110	0	110
	⎱Diplomatic	95	15	110
5..............	Technical-scientific	82	5	87
6..............	Economic	71	8	79
7..............	Fishing; int'l waters	20	15	35
8..............	Transportation, customs, travel	18	11	29
9..............	Disarmament; peaceful atomic uses	14	6	20
10..............	Communications	12	6	18
11..............	Technical-agricultural	14	2	16
12 & 13..........	⎰Settlement of claims	10	0	10
	⎱Health problems	9	1	10
14..............	Military	8	0	8
	Totals	793	77	870

together); and Soviet functional agreements, shifted into new categories, mildly gained in number.

IV

HYPOTHESES

The quantification of Soviet treaty data which produced the above findings yielded the following hypotheses:

(1) The rapidly diminishing cultural, social and economic homogeneity of the expanding international system; the constantly accelerating pace of international relations; the instant and dire need in new areas for fresh and imaginative approaches and solutions, more often than not brought about by rapid technical and technological advances; and the increasing inadequacy of international custom and customary law (sure but slow) in the new situations—clearly emerge as the reasons that favor international agreements over other interstate means and solutions. Rational, specific, adaptable, stabilizing, equitable, innovating, flexible, proportionate and rapid, international agreements appear to offer solutions in situations where no other available tools seem to work. Not unlike the other units in the international system in this respect, the U.S.S.R. finds itself constantly augmenting and amplifying its international contractual engagements.

(2) Forty-seven years after its uneasy beginning, the Soviet Union is a great world power. It has reached heights undreamed of by the revolutionary Bolsheviks. It is a powerful state, politically satiated for the time being by all standards, notwithstanding its ideological claims to the contrary. It plays a crucial role in the international system which it helped to establish—and which it respects in its own way as much as its bourgeois partners do, even if this means the recognition of neutralism and neutrals in the world or acceptance of communist neutralism in Yugoslavia. The U.S.S.R. has traveled a long way since 1917, but it has arrived. It is an established, powerful, have-state which is vesting a great deal of interest in the known present in contrast to the less certain future, and is unwilling to take excessive risks. The longer this Soviet behavioral stance endures in the world system, the more likely international agreements will continue to serve the U.S.S.R. well.

(3) As a ranking member of the communist system, a subsystem of the international system, the U.S.S.R. has additional responsibilities. The growing restlessness of some of the units here as well as their growing propensity toward stratification, segmentation, heterogeneity, diversity, and conflict, appears to call increasingly into play those means of intercourse that are in harmony with the growing emphasis of the member units on cooperation which indeed is volitional, consensual, voluntary and permissive rather than primitively assertive. The more widely the shared demand for utility and functional integration based on mutual advantage appears to be dictating, in this stage of the communist community building, the kind of tools which should be used, the more likely will international agreements, with their decentralizing but assimilating qualities, appear to be ideal for that purpose.

(4) At the same time, however, the rapidly accelerating Soviet propensity toward contractual engagements and involvement appears to be making no appreciable dent in the older Soviet pattern of participation in *bilateral* rather than any other contractual engagements. Neither multilateral or world, nor plurilateral or communist system agreements have been appreciably rising, either in proportion to accruing

Soviet responsibilities in either system or in proportion to the great spurt in its bilateral agreements.

(5) The volume and scope of the 1958-1961 Soviet contractual transactions and the compatibility, effectiveness, frequency, speed, and range of those transactions indicate changing Soviet relationships with the contracting parties. The objective contractual typology, however, appears to confirm the sentiment or commitment pattern:

(a) In terms of modernization and development, the several East European party-states are closer to each other and to the U.S.S.R. than to any other communist party-state. Given their ideological, social, historical, geographical, ecological, and system affinity, it is not unexpected that in terms of collaboration, coordination, integration, and supranational planning, the U.S.S.R. and Poland, Bulgaria, Czechoslovakia, Hungary, and East Germany would have a higher degree of contractual interaction among themselves than with other contracting parties.

The very high position of Mongolia on the Soviet scale of bilateral contracting parties is not entirely surprising. Still, Mongolia moved to the third place on the scale only in 1961 with a spurt of 13 new agreements (from 6-7th place in 1960 with 22 agreements on its record then). Perhaps one of the most sensitive indicators of the intensity of the Sino-Soviet relationship, Mongolia continues to play this characteristic role.

(b) The developing Asian countries high on the Soviet contractual scale were sustaining an overall high degree of interaction with the U.S.S.R., as tested in another recent study[16] where an interactional input-output correlation between the U.S.S.R. and those "uncommitted" nations was found to exist at better than .001 level of significance (*i.e.,* the probability was less than one in a thousand that the similarities in the orderings were due to chance).[17] The interaction pattern thus offers an additional test of the overall interactional behavior of these nations.

(c) The leading Western states, themselves highly developed, can effectively assist the U.S.S.R. to speed up its own development as well as that of the most accelerated communist party-states' economies. Hence their high places on the scale.

(6) The observable Soviet propensity, growing over time, to conclude chiefly economic and trade but also functional, cultural and technical agreements instead of political treaties may be considerd to be due to the following causes:

(A) International relations, upset by the Second World War, were being reset—by agreement, conflict, or default—in the decade after the war. The new setting had been accomplished *de facto* within five and *de iure* within 10 years. The

[16] JAN F. TRISKA WITH DAVID O. BEIM AND NORALOU ROOS, THE WORLD COMMUNIST SYSTEM (Stanford Studies of the Communist System, mimeo., 1964, 59 pp.).

[17] The only exception was India, which could be termed the classic neutral; economically dependent on the West but attempting to play the role of the "honest broker" between the two systems. Its average international input-output index (with the U.S.S.R.) had been found negative, *i.e.,* closer to the West than to the communist system. *Ibid.*

vanquished, which temporarily disappeared, had emerged again; the victors had decided who among them won the most; the liberated nations joined or were joined in new political systems; and the bulk of the former colonial but now developing nations had made their choices and cast their lot.

This was the time of decisions and actions greatly influencing subsequent developments, the international take-off period. The new systems—the socialist camp, the North Atlantic Treaty Organization, as well as the neutralist Asian-African alignment—were constructed at this time. The new political style in the world was set. The ideological commitments or impositions made at this crucial period froze into systems which permitted only limited defection, trading of partners and loyalties, deviations, or alienations. What followed after 1955 were at most amendments, not new constitutions. Politics gave way, as Engels once said, to administration.[18]

This world trend is faithfully mirrored in the pattern of the 1958-1961 Soviet agreements. The constitutive and essential gave way to the administrative and the developmental. The former basic laws were now being implemented by multiplying and proliferating ordinances and decisions. The "solemn" treaties became simple agreements. The stage of Soviet development—in international relations, in the communist system as well as in the East European regional setting—was chronicled in the kinds of Soviet international engagements. They were more numerous, though politically less significant, than ever before.

(B) Seldom have international contractual and legal relations aroused so much sustained concern throughout the world as have Soviet treaties because of the alleged propensity to violate them. The distrust and suspicion thus evoked has not been associated with Soviet economic and trade agreements, nor with their functional, cultural or technical agreements, and not even with their formal political agreements concerning diplomatic and consular affairs. It has been associated primarily with their major "solemn" political treaties, and in particular those treaties and pacts guaranteeing the territorial integrity of the Soviet treaty partners as well as non-aggression and non-interference in their domestic matters by the U.S.S.R.

And these are precisely those treaties missing in the 1958-1961 period. I submit that the lack of interest in concluding such treaties is probably mutual. It is conditioned by the past Soviet record, the lack of mutually perceived need, the hardening of the borders between the several systems throughout the world, and by the Soviet preference for "peaceful economic competition" with the West for the allegiance of the developing countries, the only soft border left in the world today.

[18] Friedrich Engels, Herrn Eugen Dührings Umwälzung der Wissenschaft ('Anti-Dühring) (3d ed. 1894), reprinted in 20 Karl Marx, Friedrich Engels, Werke 1, 262 (1962).

CONCLUSION

The Soviet policy propensity is to proliferate considerably its bilateral contractual engagements over time, chiefly in the economic, trade, and also the functional sphere, and with states which politically, economically and/or functionally are the closest to the U.S.S.R. What does this imply in terms of the more enduring tendencies, conditions, trends, and developments of Soviet treaty law and policy?

(1) With respect to the Soviet treaty law, I submit, it tends to diminish the dissimilarity to Western treaty law. The political-ideological orientation of Soviet treaty law noted in our 1962 study[19] referred primarily to problems concerning unilateral termination of treaties, a problem disappearing with the disappearance of Soviet political treaties. With the observed tendency on the part of Soviet treaty-making toward political and economic advantage chiefly via economic utility and function, the trend has been from the ideological to the pragmatic and from the hegemonial to the consensual.

(2) With reference to the Soviet treaty policy, the new Soviet de-emphasis of the political treaties bias tends to confirm further our 1962 conclusion. We said then that improvement upon, rather than a risky challenge of, the *status quo* characterizes current Soviet treaty policy, and that the dominant accent is on economic and trade treaties and agreements. I would add now only that the trend appears to be even more clearly leading from "solemn" treaties to practical agreements, from political to economic engagements, from the normative to the descriptive, and from a high-faluting stochastic model to complex reality than we had suspected in 1962.

(3) Finally, with regard to the conflictual nature of Soviet treaties, it appears that the earlier elimination of major and substantive areas of conflict leaves only minor peripheries and objectives for the contest, more significant to the contestants in alleged prestige value than in actual strategic worth. As reflected by the new agreements, the world of the U.S.S.R. is getting more complex, functional, utilitarian, pragmatic, and conservative. The contractual conflict dangers to the Soviet Union seem to be more threatening from the camp of its allies than from that of its adversaries. The Western states seem to have rejected both withdrawal from contact as unrealistic and integration of interests as unattainable. Observing the *caveat emptor* rule, they are in various degrees contractually involved with the U.S.S.R. in an attempt for mutual advantage, and benefit, and attainment of common interests. Both parties appear to agree now that agreements based on compromise make the new relationship preferable to the past non-treaty situation, and that specific compromises may be contributive to a gradual reduction of antagonism.

In fact, it is Communist China which has recently accused the U.S.S.R. of treaty violations, and on a large scale at that. According to an editorial in *Hung Chi,* the ideological journal of the Chinese Communist Party's Central Committee, and

[19] TRISKA & SLUSSER, *op. cit. supra* note 5, at 172.

reprinted by *Jen Min Yih Pao,* the Chinese Communist Party daily on February 4, 1964,

The leaders of the C.P.S.U. [Communist Party of the Soviet Union] have violated the Chinese-Soviet treaty of friendship, alliance and mutual assistance, made a unilateral decision to withdraw 1,390 Soviet experts working in China, to tear up 343 contracts and supplementary contracts on the employment of experts, and to cancel 257 projects of scientific and technical cooperation, and pursued a restrictive and discriminatory trade policy against China.[20]

Still, our hypotheses, either tested in or emerging from the quantification of our measurable variables, *i.e.,* Soviet agreements, 1958-1961, as well as our conclusions, are based on limited data. Ideally, one should have (a) a larger sample, reaching as close as possible to the the present; (b) other interactional data for the same time period and contractual parties that could be coupled with the sample for greater depth; and (c) an elaborate and extensive content analysis of the texts of the treaties by electronic computers.[21] At the present, these additional data are either unobtainable or, because of their marginal nature, too costly for the purpose.

[20] N.Y. Times, Feb. 7, 1964, p. C.
[21] Cf. Stone, Bales, Namenwirth & Ogilvia, *The General Inquirer: A Computer System for Content Analysis and Retrieval Based on the Sentence as a Unit of Information,* 7 Behavioral Science 484 (1962).

"WARS OF NATIONAL LIBERATION" AND THE MODERN LAW OF NATIONS—THE SOVIET THESIS†

GEORGE GINSBURGS*

INTRODUCTION

What exactly do Soviet spokesmen understand by "wars of national liberation?" The answer would seem simple enough and yet is not, for no authoritative definition of the concept has ever been offered by its Soviet advocates. Rather, over the years its official uses have varied, and the record shows that, in practice, three broad categories of cases can be distinguished in which the formula has been applied to situations involving armed hostilities: "Wars of liberation, waged to defend the people from foreign attack and from attempts to enslave them; or to liberate the people from capitalist slavery; or, lastly, to liberate colonies and dependent countries from the yoke of imperialism."[1] Though the conflicts so described have many features in common, to be sure, technically they stand far apart.

For the purposes of this paper, attention will be focused on the last type of contingency, namely, "wars . . . to liberate colonies and dependent countries from the yoke of imperialism," since that is the meaning normally attributed today in the U.S.S.R., as well as outside that country, to the expression which represents the object of our analysis. As for the other two kinds of "wars of liberation," they will be considered to the extent alone that they prove germane to the topic on which we propose to concentrate, and only in so far as one can extrapolate from what has been said concerning the rules of state behavior valid in the context of the subject to which we intend specially to address ourselves here.[2]

Having thus pinpointed where our principal interest lies, we can now proceed to dissect the current Soviet thesis on modern "wars of national liberation," taking

† This paper is the latest in a series of studies by the author on various aspects of the Soviet attitude, in theory and practice, toward the laws of war. For the earlier publications, see Ginsburgs, *A Case Study in the Soviet Use of International Law: Eastern Poland in 1939*, 52 AM. J. INT'L L. 69-84 (1958); *The Soviet Union as a Neutral, 1939-1941*, 10 SOVIET STUDIES 12-35 (1958); *The Soviet Union, Neutrality and Collective Security, 1945-1959*, 2 OSTEUROPA-RECHT 77-98 (1959); *Laws of War and War Crimes on the Russian Front During World War II: The Soviet View*, 11 SOVIET STUDIES 253-85 (1960); *Neutrality and Neutralism and the Tactics of Soviet Diplomacy*, 19 AMERICAN SLAVIC AND EAST EUROPEAN REVIEW 531-60 (1960); *The Soviet Union, the Neutrals and International Law in World War II*, 11 INT'L & COMP. L.Q. 171-230 (1962). All translations from the Russian into the English language, unless otherwise indicated, are the author's.

* Assistant Professor of Political Science, University of Iowa.

[1] HISTORY OF THE COMMUNIST PARTY OF THE SOVIET UNION (BOLSHEVIKS), SHORT COURSE 167-68 (1939) (edited by a Commission of the Central Committee of the C.P.S.U.(B.)).

[2] It must be remembered, however, that the classification of conflicts as one or another type of "just" war is not subject to any hard and fast rule. A conflict may well start out as one kind of "just" war and then turn into another, or the same conflict may at one and the same time fall into two categories. The Korean war, for instance, is usually described in Communist literature as a revolutionary civil war against the South Korean capitalists and a war of national-liberation from "U.S. imperialism."

66

it point by point and discussing and evaluating its constitutive elements as we go along.

I

THE LEGAL NATURE OF COLONIAL WARS

To begin with, in accordance with a long-standing tradition, conflicts generically identified as colonial wars (regardless of the variety of names associated with these incidents in popular history) have been viewed in most quarters as a species of domestic strife, and hence as standing beyond the purview of international law. Until recently, nations which were thought suitable to be brought under colonial rule and atttempted to fight against the fate in store for them or which, once reduced to thhat subject status, tried to overthrow their bondage and regain their freedom, saw themselves denied the protection of international law. The standard rationale was, of course, that the latter extended solely to the relations between so-called civilized states that formed a select club which excluded all communities that the in-group chose to classify as backward, barbarian, savage, inferior, or the like.

The Kremlin, on the other hand, has always maintained that these military campaigns to secure fresh colonial possessions or to hold on to those already acquired in the face of a native challenge to such alien exploitation must properly be treated as international wars in every sense. Rejecting any discriminatory differentiation among the world's organized political entities on the old grounds of race, religion, level of social or economic development, and so forth, Soviet legal doctrine has instead defended throughout the notion of their perfect juridical parity. By that token, it has refused all along, *ex principio,* to accept any excuse for depriving any duly functioning national community of its equal rights under world law.

And, it should be further noted, in Soviet theory this proposition obtains not only for those communities which can validly claim to form effectively self-ruling state-like organisms, no matter how rudimentary their governmental system, but also for such national movements as are still merely in the process of struggling to create their own independent polity. Interestingly enough, so as to be able to propound this thesis, the Soviets have had to broaden somewhat the scope of their basic definition of subjects of international law (otherwise very restrictively understood), in order to accommodate this particular doctrinal element.

Indeed, whereas today the trend in most of the world moves more and more in the direction of a qualified recognition that international law no longer applies to states alone, but encompasses a variety of international personalities other than states as well, including, possibly, individuals, the Soviets have to date adamantly opposed most aspects of such an expansion of international law. Their jurists, with rare exceptions, continue to cling to a very conservative conception of what can constitute a subject of international law. The single, marked concession in this respect, as already mentioned, is in the case of "peoples fighting for national liberation." Here, Soviet jurisprudence does make a certain allowance, acknowledging that in effect

there arises the question of the possibility of ascribing nations to the class of subjects of international law. Practically, such a question arises after a nation has acquired the traits of a state, having formed some organ (national committee, etc.) which in the early stages then acts in the name of the nation. Given the existence of such organs, a nation fighting for its independence and which is in the phase of inaugurating its own state, as a rule, acts as a subject of international law.[3]

The exception still represents but a minimal departure from the basic principle in that the formal emergence of the nation on the international arena remains tied to the condition that it show evidence of possessing a quota of state-like attributes, no matter how embryonic their level of development or low their standard of performance.

Another, younger school of thought, however, which has been gaining in popularity lately in Soviet juridical circles, now goes further and proposes to waive even these token requirements.[4] As its exponents look at the issue, every nation *qua* cohesive and distinct social unit is inherently seized of the quality of "national

[3] Evgeniev, in F. I. KOZHEVNIKOV (ED.), MEZHDUNARODNOE PRAVO (INTERNATIONAL LAW) 87 (1957). For others who maintain essentially the same point of view, see D. B. LEVIN, OSNOVNYE PROBLEMY SOVREMENNOGO MEZHDUNARODNOGO PRAVA (BASIC PROBLEMS OF CONTEMPORARY INTERNATIONAL LAW) 79 (1958); L. A. MODZHORYAN, SUBYEKTY MEZHDUNARODNOGO PRAVA (SUBJECTS OF INTERNATIONAL LAW) 8 (1958); *id., Osnovnye prava i obyazannosti subyektov mezhdunarodnogo prava (Basic Rights and Duties of Subjects of International Law)*, SOVETSKII EZHEGODNIK MEZHDUNARODNOGO PRAVA 1958, at 289 (1959); F. I. KOZHEVNIKOV, UCHEBNOE POSOBIE PO MEZHDUNARODNOMU PUBLICHNOMU PRAVU (OCHERKI) (PUBLIC INTERNATIONAL LAW TEXTBOOK (OUTLINE)) 51 (1947); V. I. LISOVSKII, MEZHDUNARODNOE PRAVO (INTERNATIONAL LAW) 65 (1955); *id.,* MEZHDUNARODNOE PRAVO (INTERNATIONAL LAW) 69 (2d ed. 1961); S. B. Krylov, in E. A. KOROVIN (ED.), MEZHDUNARODNOE PRAVO (INTERNATIONAL LAW) 158 (1951); G. I. TUNKIN, OSNOVY SOVREMENNOGO MEZHDUNARODNOGO PRAVA (BASIC PRINCIPLES OF CONTEMPORARY INTERNATIONAL LAW) 17 (1956).

[4] Tuzmukhamedov, *Natsionalno-osvoboditelnaya revolyutsiya i nekotorye voprosy mezhdunarodnogo prava (Revolution of National-Liberation and Some Questions of International Law)*, UCHENYE ZAPISKI (INSTITUT MEZHDUNARODNYKH OTNOSHENII), No. 10, Legal Series, at 120-29 (1962); G. B. STARUSHENKO, PRINTSIP SAMOOPREDELENIYA NARODOV I NATSII VO VNESHNEI POLITIKE SOVETSKOGO (THE PRINCIPLE OF SELF-DETERMINATION OF PEOPLES AND NATIONS IN THE FOREIGN POLICY OF THE SOVIET STATES) 143-45 (1960); Blishchenko, *Vazhnyi vopros mezhdunarodnogo prava (An Important Question of International Law)*, [1960] SOVETSKOE GOSUDARSTVO I PRAVO, No. 1, at 152 (review of Yu. G. BARSEGOV, TERRITORIYA V MEZHDUNARODNOM PRAVE (TERRITORY IN INTERNATIONAL LAW) (1958); Yu. G. BARSEGOV, TERRITORIYA V MEZHDUNARODNOM (TERRITORY IN INTERNATIONAL LAW) 68-155 (1958). Recently, Korovin, too, has started echoing this theme. See Korovin, *Suverenitet i mir (Sovereignty and Peace)*, 9 MEZHDU-NARODNAYA ZHIZN 9-18 (1960).

However, most Communist legal authors, it should be noted, continue to treat "national sovereignty" not as an independent concept but as synonymous with "the right to national self-determination." Thus, see Modzhoryan, *Borba demokraticheskogo lagerya za natsionalnuyu nezavisimost i natsionalnyi suverenitet (The Struggle of the Democratic Camp for National Independence and National Sovereignty)*, [1953] SOVETSKOE GOSUDARSTVO I PRAVO, No. 1, at 52, 56; *Ponyatie suvereniteta (The Concept of Sovereignty)*, *id.* [1955], No. 1, at 68, 70; Evgeniev, *Pravo subyektnosti, suverenitet i nevmeshatelstvo (Legal Personality, Sovereignty, and Non-Intervention)*, *id.* [1955], No. 2, at 75; C. BEREZOWSKI, NEKOTORYE PROBLEMY TERRITORIALNOGO VERKHOVENSTA (SOME PROBLEMS OF TERRITORIAL SOVEREIGNTY) 63-67 (translated from the Polish by V. L. Kon, 1961). Earlier, Korovin, too, shared this view. See, for example, his *Nekotorye osnovnye voprosy sovremennoi teorii mezhdunarodnogo prava (Some Basisc Questions in the Contemporary Theory of International Law)*, [1954] SOVETSKOE GOSUDARSTVO I PRAVO, No. 6, at 34, 43.

sovereignty." This "national sovereignty" is the quintessence of what constitutes a nation, both spiritually and materially; it corresponds to the sum total of those inalienable rights of a given human group which stamp it as a nation. This core element is the source from which flow all the secondary rights that accompany this "national identity"—*inter alia,* the right to political, economic, and cultural auto-determination. Once possessed of "national sovereignty," a nation can be deprived of it only if the community itself is totally destroyed. Otherwise, a nation always retains this attribute, regardless of its technical juridical status at a particular moment in history. Thus, a community reduced to subject stature, though not politically sovereign, on the plane of "national sovereignty" remains the equal of its independent counterparts, notwithstanding the loss of its facilities for self-government. Its faculties for self-government no nation presumably can lose forever, again short of its physical annihilation.

Every nation, then, by virtue of its natural endowment with "national sovereignty" stands as a full-fledged subject of modern international law. For, so the advocates of this viewpoint say, contemporary state practice openly recognizes the principle of "national sovereignty" as part of the general corpus of international law and, consequently, assures every national entity, in that capacity alone, all the rights and privileges of complete jural personality. Proof positive for the accuracy of the assertion that "a whole series of rights of nations, not yet formally organized as states, are nonetheless recognized by international law" and that "these rights have become international legal norms" is found in the fact that, "for instance, the principle of equality and self-determination is ratified by the Charter of the United Nations Organization (UNO), the rights of nations are protected by the convention of 1948 prohibiting genocide, the Geneva conventions of August 12, 1949, the Geneva agreements on Indochina of 1954. . . ."[5]

In either case, whether insisting that a nation display a modicum of organizational features associated with statecraft before it can attain international dimensions, or waving aside all technical prerequisites in connection with that process, Soviet jurists are agreed that "a nation struggling for self-liberation" *ipso facto* satisfies whatever criteria, if any, it must meet to achieve international stature. Hence, it forthwith qualifies as a subject of international law in every sense of the word. Indeed, it is claimed, the great merit of Soviet teaching on the topic of subjects of today's international law and its major contribution to the current doctrine in this sphere lie precisely in its elaboration and defense of this theme, a stand seen as amply vindicated by the present course of world events. In Communist quarters, the verdict on this point is unanimous and its tone uniformly jubilant, for the message it undertakes to convey is that

. . . the recognition as subjects of international law not only of States, but also of nations struggling for their independence, is an indispensable deduction of the Soviet doctrine of

⁵ Tuzmukhamedov, *supra* note 4, at 121.

international law which is confirmed by the success of the national-liberation movement of oppressed peoples, above all in Asia and Africa.[6]

While the Soviets have thus found it easy to insist in abstract terms that there now exists a principle of international law prescribing that armed hostilities in colonies and dependent territories be unreservedly classified as international wars, citing rules of positive law in support of this contention has proved more difficult. Moscow's spokesmen have, therefore, mostly rested content with vague general references to the spirit and, less frequently, isolated samples of the letter of the U.N. Charter. True, one can point to the clauses of the Geneva conventions of 1949 enjoining that the usual laws of war be observed in prosecuting civil and colonial wars too. And, as is shown above, Soviet jurists have not overlooked this aperture. Yet, this innovation, which most Soviet sources acclaim (rightly) as belatedly bearing out the U.S.S.R.'s position in this matter and the insertion of which in the agreements they attribute (with no good justification)[7] solely to Soviet exertions on its behalf at the Conference,[8] has but a strictly technical connotation. Whatever its origins—and one must give the Soviets due credit for their prolonged efforts to gain universal recognition for the proposition in question—it still represents no more than a humanitarian endeavor to alleviate the sufferings caused by all armed conflicts through maximum application of jural limitations to the exercise of public violence, irrespective of its formal nature. However, to argue from this that colonial struggles have been raised by these conventional rules to the full status of international wars would be analogous to announcing that, since the Geneva conventions of 1949 deal with conditions arising from belligerency, wars are thereby legalized and the explicit stipulations of the United Nations Charter to the contrary expressly overridden. The contention simply does not hold.

Besides the Geneva conventions of 1949, Communist legal experts claim to have found material evidence to support their thesis in the Geneva agreements of 1954 concerning Indochina. According to this line of reasoning, colonial campaigns and their organic concomitants, wars of national liberation, had always been international wars, but it took the end of the struggle for Indochina to secure formal acceptance of this fact by the "bourgeois" world. In the words of an authoritative Polish lawyer,

[6] Krylov, *K obsuzhdeniyu voprosov teorii mezhdunarodnogo prava (Concerning the Discussion of Theories of International Law)*, [1954] SOVETSKOE GOSUDARSTVO I PRAVO, No. 7, at 76.
[7] As Pictet, *The New Geneva Conventions for the Protection of War Victims*, 45 AM. J. INT'L L. 469 (1951), points out, "the new conventions [signed at Geneva] do not go as far as the Stockholm drafts [of 1948], which proposed that the conventions should make specific provision for civil war as well as for war between states." The U.S.S.R. attended the Geneva conference, but not the Stockholm session.
[8] See, *e.g.*, Sharmanazashvili, *Kolonialnaya voina—gruboe narushenie mezhdunarodnogo prava (Colonial War—A Serious Violation of International Law)*, [1957] SOVETSKOE GOSUDARSTVO I PRAVO, No. 10, at 59. See, too, Latyshev, *Zhenevskie konventsii 1949g. o zashchite zhertv voiny (The 1949 Geneva Conventions for the Protection of Victims of War)*, id. [1954] No. 7, at 121-25; Amelin, *Mezhdunarodno-pravovaya zashchita uchastnikov grazhdanskikh i natsionalno-osvoboditelnykh voin*, SOVETSKII EZHEGODNIK MEZHDUNARODNOGO PRAVA 1958, at 397-406 (1959).

. . . the Geneva agreements recognized that national-liberation wars, by which peoples realize their right to self-determination, as just wars are from the standpoint of law legitimate wars. Recognizing the international legal character of national-liberation wars, they coincidentally recognized that questions of self-determination cannot be regarded as internal legal processes of the metropolitan country or the empire, that the hands of the colonial powers are not free to pacify and suppress national-liberation movements.[9]

To get around the obvious criticism that, after all, the 1954 Geneva agreements represented no more than an *ad hoc* arrangement between a limited number of countries to resolve a purely local dilemma, the author further maintains that, in this respect, the documents adduced by him belong to the same category as the sundry Hague conventions on the laws of war, the several Geneva conventions and protocols on the same subject of pre-war and post-war vintage, the Statute of the Nuremberg tribunal, and so forth. In his opinion, all these multilateral treaties, together with the 1954 Geneva documents on Indochina, amount to no more than the end product of a long process of codification, and so merely "confirm certain principles, express customary law in treaty norms, or contain a recognition of earlier practice applied in a concrete case."[10] Citing the passage in the judgment of the Nuremberg tribunal to the effect that, "indeed, in many cases treaties do no more than express and define for more accurate reference the principles of law already existing,"[11] he concludes that "the substantive stipulations of the Geneva agreements must be understood the same way":

The basic principles of the Geneva agreements even before the adoption of these documents represented the accomplishments of progressive humanity, were legal principles which even the most reactionary forces did not deny. Their recognition, however, carries a purely theoretical, declarative character. In the Geneva agreements they acquired concrete real form and content linked to life.[12]

As such, then, he finds the latter totally analogous to the provisions of the Charter of the United Nations and to other like rules that bind even those states which

[9] M. LACHS, ZHENEVSKIE SOGLASHENIYA 1954G. OB INDO-KITAE (THE 1954 GENEVA AGREEMENTS ON INDO-CHINA 189 (tr. from the Polish by E. I. Brainin and K. A. Radvillovich, 1956). The same argument is echoed by G. B. STARUSHENKO, *op. cit. supra* note 4, at 135; Tuzmukhamedov, *Mirnoe sosushchestvovanie i natsionalno-osvoboditelnaya voina (Peaceful Coexistence and National Liberation War)*, [1963] SOVETSKOE GOSUDATSTVO I PRAVO, No. 3, at 87, 92-93.

[10] LACHS, *op. cit. supra* note 9, at 190.

[11] 22 TRIAL OF THE MAJOR WAR CRIMINALS BEFORE THE INTERNATIONAL MILITARY TRIBUNAL, *Judgment* 464 (1948); 2 NYURNBERGSKII PROTSESS, SBORNIK MATERIALOV (THE NÜRNBERG TRIAL, COLLECTION OF MATERIALS) 453 (1951).
Not all Communist lawyers, it should be noted, subscribe to this theory of "codification" in the case of the Statute of the Nüremberg Tribunal, for instance. Thus, Baumgarten, *Etatischeskii vzglyad na mezhdunarodnoe pravo (The State-Oriented View of International Law)* (tr. from the German by F. A. Kublitskii), in GOSUDARSTVO I PRAVO V SVETE VELIKOGO OKTYABRYA (STATE AND LAW IN THE LIGHT OF THE GREAT OCTOBER), 82-83 (1958), frankly admits that the Statute is a "law *ad hoc,* an international criminal law and, what is more, one with retroactive effect," but nevertheless claims that it is good law because "the validity of the criminal law contained in the Statute is based on the fact that in content as well as in form it corresponds to the demands of the overwhelming majority of the peoples of the globe justly to punish those who before and during the Second World War showed themselves to be enemies of the human race."

[12] LACHS, *op. cit. supra* note 9, at 191; *id.,* MNOGOSTORONNIE DOGOVORY (MULTILATERAL TREATIES) 191 (tr. from the Polish by G. F. Kalinkina) (1961).

never formally subscribed to them. Hence, he sees them as a general statement of contemporary international law of universal validity.

Ingenious as the argument sounds, it nevertheless fails to convince, for neither in conception, substantive scope, effect, breadth of focus, and interest did the Geneva accords of 1954 come anywhere close to the conventions with which they are thus equated. For that matter, much of what was agreed to just ten years ago is today a dead letter. This, of course, is also true of the Hague and earlier Geneva conventions, but these have been outdistanced by the progress of history and the advance of technology. In any event, no country has as yet refused outright to abide by the basic precepts of these latter treaties, even when seeking to re-interpret or set aside some particular clause, and these treaties still bear the signature, adherence, or oral acceptance of probably every country in the world. As against this, the Indochina accords never transcended the bounds of a circumscribed plurilateral transaction, which remained, as far as the overwhelming majority of the global community was concerned, purely *res inter alios acta*. Furthermore, as noted before, the solutions proposed in these documents have since for the most part broken down and been tacitly abandoned even as between the original contracting partners.

Added to that, it is hard to discern in the contents of the 1954 Geneva agreements any general principles of the order of the fundamental postulates formulated in those other conventions to which they are here pronounced kin; instead, the language of the former retains throughout the flavor of a technical blueprint with a narrowly delimited purpose and *raison d'être*. And, finally, whereas the older treaties named in this connection, though drafted by a small portion of the earth's nations, were nonetheless expected to attract wider, nowadays world-wide, endorsement, no solid evidence can be found of such practical intent behind the arrangements for bringing back peace to Indochina.

As for "national sovereignty," international law knows of no such concept. At best, it leaves the impression of a meta-juridical *Grundnorm* of sorts, an "ideal" construction which has no firm roots in the infrastructural pattern of current jurisprudential thought and finds no substantive reflection in its superstructure of positive law rules culled from state practice.

Let us assume, however, for the sake of argument, that colonial wars are international wars in the eyes of modern international law. The next step would logically be to assume that the prescriptions of international law on the proper conduct of war would then apply to these conflicts too. Well, in part they do, since all Soviet commentators insist that the colonial power waging the fight to preserve its ascendency over the dependent territory must be bound by each and every provision of international law pertaining to the modalities of civilized warfare. For that matter, the very object in pleading that colonial wars are international wars is precisely to put those who do so in a position to advance this further claim. But when it comes to drawing the inevitable companion conclusion, namely, that the movement struggling for national liberation must equally observe the established norms of international law on how to wage war, there the Soviets suddenly begin temporizing; and all at once their attitude turns thoroughly ambiguous.

Curiously enough, the avenue of escape seized upon so as to avoid ending up in such a spot is one provided by Engels who wrote in 1857 that "in a popular war the means used by the insurgent nation cannot be measured by the commonly recognized rules of regular warfare, nor by any other abstract standard, but by the degree of civilization only attained by 'that insurgent nation."[13]

On historical and sociological grounds, then, according to Engels, so-called backward and primitive peoples cannot and should not be held to the observance of the laws of war unilaterally promulgated by the more "civilized" powers and reflecting the values and level of technical development of the more advanced societies. To do so would, in his estimate, be altogether illogical, impracticable, and dishonest. At the same time, Engels asserted, the natural inability of any "insurgent nation" of this type to grasp the meaning of the laws of war in force between the European countries in no way absolved the latter from the obligation to implement the regulations devised by themselves and accurately reflecting their own outlook on what constituted proper behavior in the course of armed hostilities as among enlightened states. As he saw it, simple objective reality dictated that in a given conflict each of the contestants should follow that set of rules regarding the conduct of military operations which best corresponded to its value system and, actually, it could be expected to do no more or act otherwise, as long as it did no less. So, while primitive peoples fought as their tradition demanded of them, civilized nations, he felt, ought, in turn, to prosecute war in conformity with the standards they normally embraced, or a least pretended they embraced and sometimes enforced in their relations with neighboring communities which they tolerated as equals.

The historical and moral element in Engels' argument is irrefutable. The sight of a so-called progressive nation posing as a *sine qua non* for its own behavior that some tribe it was engaged in pacifying should abide by the modern laws of war or else forgo every claim to be dealt with in accordance with these laws does strike the impartial observer as ludicrous. On the other hand, while one can sympathize with Engels' conclusions and concede their scholarly soundness, it is nevertheless necessary to admit that in practical terms they seem sadly unreal. As an ideal and abstract construction, they stand beyond reproach. But, it is here suggested, in daily life a Gresham's law of sorts operates in the legal sphere as well as in the field of high finance. That is to say, in the confrontation between two unequal systems of legal tradition, it is believed that the inferior one will at first prevail, in the sense that the superior product will come down to the level of the other and compete with it on its own plane, instead of *vice versa*.

This, unfortunately, appears to be particularly true in warlike situations, where

[13] Engels, *Persia and China*, N.Y. Daily Tribune, June 5, 1857, reprinted in K. MARX & F. ENGELS, ON COLONIALISM III, 115 (Moscow, n.d.).

the common denominator regulating the behavior of the combatants is ordinarily the lowest standard discernible in the practice of the opponents. In general, of course, metropolitan troops everywhere do show a marked inclination to behave differently on home territory and overseas or abroad, and even more differently when in a familiar social environment as compared to when they find themselves shipped to a strange location and surrounded by people whom they are conditioned to regard as an inferior form of life. Aside from this factor, however, in the midst of any hostilities there seems to be a natural tendency to treat the enemy just as he treats you and no better. Hence, regardless of academic appeals to historical and economic determinism, it is the pattern set by the more "primitive" party which has almost always obtained, to the near exclusion of the higher standards which the other belligerent ordinarily professes to recognize.

Without being unduly cynical, one may suggest that this has ever been a part of human character and, as the record indicates, contrary opinion has so far proved thoroughly unrealistic, be it that of Engels in his time or that of Communist writers on diplomatic affairs who echo him today.[14] Sad to say, the temptation to recipro-cate with like action must just be too irresistible, all strictures notwithstanding. To demand that international law enjoin the colonial powers to wage war according to the lofty ideals set forth in the latest conventions, while the national liberation movements to all intents and purposes behave as they please because they are not sufficiently mature to grasp the essence of these alien rules, is also to tax credulity. Swinging from one extreme to the other cannot furnish and, indeed, has not fur-nished a workable answer to a problem already difficult enough as it is. Apologists for unbridled imperialism may have been altogether wrong. But then, current apologists for unbridled anti-imperialism, with the Communists in the forefront wielding pseudo-legal arguments such as the above, are no less so. Both insist on misusing and abusing international law for their own immediate ends, with sorry results every time and in a manner unacceptable to most who think of international law as a constructive, rather than a destructive, instrument in the relations between states.

II

COLONIAL WARS AND THE NOTION OF AGGRESSION

The drive to gain recognition for the principle of internationalization of colonial wars and wars of national liberation serves yet a further purpose—that of bringing such conflicts within the scope of the notion of aggression. In effect, it must be remembered that the latter concept, as defined in Soviet pronounce-ments, always applies only to actions lying within the realm of inter-state relations.[15] By this token, armed conflicts within a state and also between two halves of a

---

[14] Meleshko, in KOROVIN (ED.), *op. cit. supra* note 3, at 506.

[15] See YURIDICHESKII SLOVAR (LEGAL DICTIONARY) 12-15 (1953); P. I. KUDRYAVTSEV (ED.), 1 YURIDICHESKII SLOVAR (LEGAL DICTIONARY) 15-19 (2d ed. 1956).

divided country do not fall within the rubric of such use of force as can be qualified as an act of aggression.[16]

If today, as was common practice in the past, the proposition were successfully defended that the ties between a metropolitan power and its dependent territories were regulated by domestic law alone, then whatever conflicts disrupted the association technically could not belong to the category of incidents to which the epithet of aggressive would apply. Yet, the Soviets are and all along have been intensely interested, for reasons that will quickly become apparent, to extend this frame of reference to military hostilities in the colonies as well. By asserting that any struggle between a colonial power and a native independence movement amounts to a formal international war since it represents an armed collision between two distinct entities, each fully acknowledged as a subject of international law in its own right, the Soviets are ultimately able to claim that such a clash is automatically eligible to be judged in the light of whether an aggression has been committed. The next logical step, of course, is to determine who is the aggressor and who the victim and what remedial measures must be taken in an emergency of this sort.

In reality, the Soviets bother little with a detailed assessment of the circumstantial evidence in such instances, for, thanks to *a priori* reasoning, the answer is immediately forthcoming from them that such outbreaks of violence definitely represent every time a case of aggression, since one party to the contest must be pursuing a colonial policy which has provoked the fighting and the resulting colonial wars stand *eo ipso* condemned as acts of deliberate aggression. Let us take this one step further and consider what the Soviets postulate as constitutive elements of aggression. The prime determinant ingredient, one may gather from all their statements, is which side stooped to overt use of force first. The party so found guilty of resort to arms is thereby branded an aggressor.[17] The situation seems simple enough and, on the face of it, the criterion for passing sentence sounds not altogether unreasonable. What makes it thoroughly suspect, however, is the ideological context in which the decision as to who started the shooting is rendered, for here all at once extrinsic and totally subjective standards are seen to intrude on a process originally touted as a strictly objective kind of operation.

In order to illustrate best how this turnabout is consummated, one need but quote from the original sources. Thus, examine, for a moment, this revealing passage from one of Lenin's works, penned in 1915, in the midst of World War I, in which he wrote:

[16] *E.g.*, speech by A. Ya. Vyshinskii at a meeting of the U.N. Political Committee, Oct. 12, 1950, Pravda, Oct. 5, 1950; Tavrov, *Prestupnaya voina amerikanskikh imperialistov protiv koreiskogo naroda* (*The Criminal War of the American Imperialists Against the Korean People*), 1 TRUDY INSTITUTA PRAVA AKADEMII NAUK SSSR 100 (1951).

[17] Cf. K. A. BAGINYAN, AGRESSIYA—TYAGCHAISHEE MEZHDUNARODNOE PRESTUPLENIE, K VOPROSU OB OPREDELENII AGRESSII (1955) (AGGRESSION—A MOST SERIOUS INTERNATIONAL CRIME, ON THE QUESTION OF DEFINITION OF AGGRESSION), *passim*.

The epoch of 1789-1871 left deep traces and revolutionary memories. Before feudalism, absolutism and alien oppression were overthrown, the development of the proletarian struggle for Socialism was out of the question. When speaking of the legitimacy of "defensive" war in relation to the wars of *such* an epoch, Socialists always had in mind precisely these objects, which amounted to revolution against medievalism and serfdom. By "defensive" war Socialists always meant a *"just"* war in this sense (W. Liebknecht once expressed himself precisely in this way). Only in this sense have Socialists regarded, and now regard, wars "for the defence of the fatherland," or "defensive" wars, as legitimate, progressive and just. For example, if tomorrow, Morocco were to declare war on France, India on England, Persia or China on Russia, and so forth, those would be "just," "defensive" wars, *irrespective* of who attacked first; and every Socialist would sympathize with the victory of the oppressed, dependent, unequal states against the oppressing, slave-owning, predatory "great" powers.[18]

It is indeed significant that the Kremlin's current theses on so-called wars of national liberation should sound as but a faithful echo of this Leninist proposition enunciated almost half a century ago, so that the mere change of a few words would suffice to bring it into full conformity with the official line presently expounded by Moscow on every opportune occasion. On this count, at least, the Soviet ideological record has so far evidenced a remarkable, and rare, continuity in attitudinal patterns.

In fact, lest there remain some doubts whether these views are still held in the U.S.S.R. today, an excerpt from an article published in its leading legal journal forty two years later will put them to rest. It is worth citing at length, for not only does its formulation closely parallel Lenin's original thought, but it also brings the latter up to date to reflect current world conditions, so that, were Lenin dealing with the subject now, one ventures to suggest that he would not have phrased the idea very differently or done so much more eloquently. The relevant paragraph reads as follows:

The national-liberation war of a dependent people against the colonial power will always be a just, defensive war from the political as well as the legal standpoint, independently of who initiated the military action. The whole thing is that in the given instance the fact of initiation of a national-liberation war by a dependent colonial country has no significance for the determination of the aggressor, since the state of dependency and disenfranchisement of the colonial peoples is the result of an imperialist aggression committed earlier, expressing itself in the annexation of these territories. This means that the national-liberation war begun by a dependent, disenfranchised people will represent but a lawful act on its part in response to an act of aggression committed earlier by the imperialist state which led to the forcible enslavement of said people and the territory which it occupies. The people of a dependent or colonial country preserve the right to counter action to an imperialist aggression for the duration of the whole period of annexation of the given country or part of its territory. At any moment the oppressed people, living on the territory annexed by the imperialist state, have the right to launch a national-liberation struggle against this imperialist state. Such a struggle will be just and legitimate, since, in the first place, neither aggression nor annexation

[18] V. I. LENIN, SOCIALISM AND WAR (THE ATTITUDE OF THE R.S.D.L.P. TOWARDS THE WAR) 15-16 (Foreign Languages Publishing House ed., 1952). Originally written in July-August, 1915.

enjoy the benefits of a statute of limitations, and, in the second place, international law forbids aggression and consequent annexation puts them outside the law.[19]

The implications of this contention are crystal clear. Stripped of jargon, what it all really amounts to saying is this: colonialism is an absolute evil, fathered by aggression and tainted by original sin that has never been expiated. Hence, every state possessing colonies *ipso facto* stands convicted of having perpetrated in the past an act of flagrant aggression and, as a corollary proposition, every subject people retains forever the right to repay this old crime against the law of nations with suitable reprisals aimed at enabling it to recover its former independence. Such action by an insurgent movement can never be qualified as an aggression, regardless of the specific circumstances surrounding its genesis and evolution, since the prior lawlessness of the imperial power which reduced the area to dependent status in the first place absolves it of any guilt. By that token, wars of national liberation represent, as an axiom, licit responses to sufficient provocation, defensive measures by their very nature. Conversely, resistance on the part of the imperial power to these lawful aspirations so as to preserve a status already rooted in a violation of international law is, by the same definition, offensive and aggressive. If the colonial régime persists in clinging to its former positions and uses arms to defend it ill-gotten privileges, it merely compounds the offense and adds a second crime to its tarnished record.

The errors and distortions inherent in this line of reasoning are too numerous to treat them all in detail. Only its more fundamental inaccuracies will be pointed out here. To begin with, such a projection of the rule of international law prohibiting aggression back through the ages is totally unwarranted. The notion of aggression as a breach of positive international law is of very recent vintage. It neither applies to earlier times in which different juridical values obtained, nor can it be reasonably so transposed to judge previous events by certain criteria in vogue today but alien to the historical context in which these incidents occurred. To do so is simply to play fast and loose with all commonly recognized standards of objective inquiry and, one may interject, also to behave in a thoroughly un-Marxist fashion. Nonetheless, contemporary Soviet writers do not scruple to revise international law for the sake of ideological and political convenience. That the final results of this drastic re-write job have no scholarly merit bothers them not a whit. Nor is it probable that they will develop strong compunctions in the near future toward continuing to pursue this sort of game.

If all this were to remain on the plane of theory alone, it could simply be disregarded. Not so, however, for what at first blush may seem an academic exercise has had some disturbing practical consequences. In a series of recent test cases involving use of force or overt threat of use of force by newly emergent nations against European powers—*e.g.,* India in the Goa dispute; Indonesia in the

[19] Sharmanazashvili, *supra* note 8, at 60.

quarrel over West New Guinea—the main excuse given by the ex-colonies for resort to arms has faithfully echoed the theme struck by Moscow. Portugal in one instance, the Netherlands in the other (and there are more examples), all were now pronounced to be guilty of aggression and of having been guilty of aggression for centuries. Their very stay in the disputed territories was brought up as prima facie evidence of an aggressive past, proof of an unrepentant aggressive present, and tantamount to a promise of an equally aggressive future; to use military means against such sinners was not only permissible, but literally laudable, for not only did it serve to wipe away an ancient debt, so the thesis runs, it also upheld international law by punishing an obvious transgressor. What this has to do with the established legal order and how one can square it with known legal principles remains for some students of the current scene an incomprehensible enigma.

The next objection that comes to mind in connection with this question hinges on the fact that, historical veracity apart, the whole *plaidoyer* simply smacks of an enthusiastic espousal of the tribal rule of an eye for an eye, and a tooth for a tooth. One may counter that by pointing out that even if the original methods by which certain countries acquired colonies were very seldom simon pure, two wrongs have never yet made a right. One trouble with reprisals, as any cursory glance at the annals of diplomatic history will disclose, is that their use in a given situation merely leads to a steadily rising curve of mutual recriminations and a growing incidence of lawlessness, and that every time one party to a conflict takes liberties with the law under the pretext of avenging a wrong, the other discovers a ready reason to adopt a like course, and so on *ad infinitum*. The whole process leaves very little room for legal considerations and soon degenerates into a frantic race to see which side will bypass and circumvent the law faster and offer the more plausible rationalizations for its arbitrary conduct.

True, as mentioned before, in the midst of fighting a partial breakdown of the law, even that branch of the law specially devised for warlike conditions may very well be inevitable in any case. This has happened so often it seems almost a fixture of the international scene whenever peace gives place to armed hostilities. But this is still altogether different from coolly advocating such a dismantlement of the established jural fabric ahead of time; and there is something grossly contrived and frankly expedient about digging into the past for reasons to help excuse otherwise reprehensible plans one is harboring for the future.

The third, and last, comment on this score is that an approach of this genre again plainly puts the stamp of approval on adherence to a double standard in international law. Indeed, having thus been branded a past aggressor and virtually placed beyond the pale of the law, a colonial power is expected then meekly to submit to whatever treatment is meted out to it, without reacting, without protecting its interests, without recourse to any remedy except, as it were, to take its medicine without a whimper. It cannot even take defensive measures, for, according to the present point of view, the national-liberation movement is presumed to be acting in self-defense and there can be no self-defense against self-defense.

So, while one party to the conflict apparently may, in line with this thesis, behave literally as it pleases, the other must do nothing. No matter what policy the one pursues, it is hailed as fully justified in the eyes of the law, whereas the other stands just as surely condemned for whatever it tries to accomplish on its own behalf, virtually an outlaw bereft of all legal protection or safeguards. How practicable any scheme of international relations predicated on such notion can be is best left to the imagination.

III

WARS OF NATIONAL LIBERATION AND THE U.N. CHARTER

A. The Soviet View

Not content with denouncing colonial wars and defending wars of national liberation on the above grounds, Soviet spokesmen have also appealed to the United Nations Charter in support of their stand. Ordinarily, the argumentation here revolves around one or more of the following propositions. In almost every case, the point of departure lies in the citation of those clauses of the Charter which refer to the principle of "equal rights and self-determination of peoples," mention the obligation of member-states endowed with colonial possessions to help the latter develop self-government and of those administering trust areas to promote the "progressive development" of their wards "towards self-government or independence." The very inclusion of these provisions in the Charter is always credited to the strenuous efforts of the U.S.S.R. in sponsoring these ideas at the San Francisco Conference and successfully urging their adoption on the rest of the participants.[20]

Having taken due note of the several articles in the Charter featuring such formulas, Communist authors then unanimously interpret the language of the document so as to equate self-determination and self-government with outright political independence as a separate state. While they concede that the concept of self-determination covers more ground than just political emancipation, they insist that it is imperative that it also include the right to sovereign self-rule. A given people need not, according to them, choose such a future for itself, but it must at least have the opportunity to decide that issue on its own. Likewise, though a few Soviet commentators admit that the drafters of the Charter intentionally distinguished between "self-government" and "independence," reserving the use of the second

[20] S. B. .KRYLOV, 1 MATERIALY K ISTORII ORGANIZATSII OBYEDINENNYKH NATSII ʾ(MATERIALS ON THE HISTORY OF THE UNITED NATIONS) 158-67 (1949); id., ISTORIYA SOZDANIYA ORGANIZATSII OBYEDINENNYKH NATSII, RAZRABOTKA USTAVA ORGANIZATSII OBYEDINENNYKH NATSII (HISTORY OF THE CREATION OF THE UNITED NATIONS, DRAFTING OF THE CHARTER OF THE UNITED NATIONS 1944-1945) 156-172 (1960). See, too, Levin, Printsip samoopredeleniya natsii i likvidatsiva kolonializma (The Principle of the Self-Determination of Nations and the Liquidation of Colonialism), [1962] SOVETSKOE GOSUDARSTVO I PRAVO, No. 8, at 9a.

expression in conjunction with the régime of trust territories,[21] all nevertheless completely reject the thought of self-government meaning anything inferior to independence.[22] To them—and, one should add, not to them alone[23]—genuine self-government logically leads to, and culminates in, total independence; and the whole process must not stop short of having reached this, its natural, objective.

Such a one-sided interpretation of the Charter is open, of course, to serious criticism. On the other hand, it must be acknowledged that there has been in recent years a consistent trend in neutralist circles and among newly emergent nations admitted into the United Nations to give these passages of the Charter precisely that reading. In this endeavor, one need hardly add, they always meet with the enthusiastic backing of the Soviet Union and its allies. And, while not free of weaknesses, this introductory part of Moscow's anti-colonialist brief still represents its most solid segment. From here onward, the quality of the reasoning steadily deteriorates.

However, let us assume for the sake of discussion that the testimonials to self-determination and self-government displayed in the Charter can both be reduced to the uni-dimensional idea of full-fledged independent status for the beneficiary nations. The next Soviet move is to proclaim that "the principle of self-determination of peoples is one of the most important principles of contemporary international law."[24] That, together with the explicit endorsement conferred on it by the Charter, makes it doubly binding on the members of the Organization who thereby assume, so the thesis runs, a solemn legal obligation of first-rate magnitude to enhance its universal observance. For colonial powers this means doing everything possible to hasten the progression of their overseas holdings along the path to complete independence or, in any event, to free choice of their subsequent political destiny. The advance of the subject peoples to freedom, therefore, must unfold without interruptions, proceed at maximum speed, and have a minimum duration.

In fact, from an examination of the Soviet record in the United Nations and elsewhere, one gains the conviction that, in the last analysis, Moscow expects a state administering a colony or a trust area to set the latter at liberty at the first sign of a demand on the part of the local population that the mother-country relinquish the reins of authority. In other words, to pursue this exposition of the Charter's

---

[21] E.g., S. B. KRYLOV, I MATERIALY K ISTORII ORGANIZATII OBYEDINENNYKH NATSII (MATERIALS ON THE HISTORY OF THE UNITED NATIONS) 159 n.8 (1949).

[22] See, for example, G. I. TUNKIN, VOPROSY TEORII MEZHDUNARODNOGO PRAVA (QUESTIONS OF THE THEORY OF INTERNATIONAL LAW) 8 (1962); C. BEREZOWSKI, op. cit. supra note 4, at 47-48; Korovin, Mezhdunarodnoe pravo na sovremennom etape (International Law at the Present Stage), 7 MEZHDU-NARODNAYA ZHIZN 24 (1961); Starushenko, Protiv izvrashcheniya printsipa samoopredeleniya narodov i natsii (Against the Distortion of the Principle of Self-Determination of Peoples and Nations), [1958] SOVETSKOE GOSUDARSTVO I PRAVO, No. 1, at 63-66.

[23] Thus, A. ROSS, CONSTITUTION OF THE UNITED NATIONS 185 (1950).

[24] Baratashvili, Printsip samoopredeleniya narodov v Ustave OON (The Principle of Self-Determination of Peoples in the U.N. Charter), in G. I. TUNKIN (ED.), VOPROSY MEZHDUNARODNOGO PRAVA (QUESTIONS OF INTERNATIONAL LAW) (UCHENYE ZAPISKI, INSTITUT MEZHDUNARODNYKH OTNOSHENII), vyp. 2, at 57 (1960).

provisions, every state with non-self-governing possessions incurs a legal responsibility to prepare these for early independence and grant them this wish whenever they ask for it. This legal duty, it should be noted, is said to apply not only to the members of the United Nations, but to represent a universal rule valid for all states. The Charter, so the theory goes, only "affirmed" an already existing norm of general international law to that effect and, anyway, the Charter itself is now described as an authoritative statement of modern principles of international law for the entire world community.[25]

To this legal duty unilaterally imposed on states with dependencies corresponds the legal right of the United Nations, acting under the Charter and general international law, to demand due performance. However, this fills only half the picture, for the primary right in this sphere allegedly resides not in the Organization, but in the colonial peoples themselves. The rationale for reaching this conclusion again stems from the axiom that subject nations stand throughout as equal subjects of international law, and that their relations with the metropolitan authorities are therefore regulated by the precepts of international law, including the most important of all—the rule enunciating the right of peoples to self-determination. This last principle, then, obtains in full in the conditions of association of a subject people with the dominant country—with the result, it is claimed, that "the consummation by the colonial peoples of their right to self-determination . . . [is] not the internal business of the home state, but . . . a question of international character."[26] So, where the mother-country bears the duty to give effect to the principle of self-determination, its possessions hold the concurrent right to secure from it prompt and adequate fulfillment of its responsibilities on that score. Hence, the obligation which, according to Moscow, both the Charter and general international law recognize as vested in the imperial states to bring a quick end to colonialism within their domains does not constitute a voluntary expression of an abstract sense of duty or a unilateral donation bestowing a gift or a favor, but an enforceable reciprocal relationship in which the rights of one partner correspond to the duties of the other.

The construction is supremely important, for it means that when a colonial state fails to behave as prescribed in the matter of promoting the independence of the component parts of its empire it is deemed to have forthwith committed more

---

[25] In this case, the Soviet government chose to interpret the Charter as an agreement *erga omnes*, but on other occasions it has seen fit to defend the view that non-member states are not bound by the Charter. Presumably, it all depends on which clause is involved, on the general situation, and where Soviet interests of the moment lie.

[26] Baratashvili, *supra* note 24, at 65. The same theme is developed in G. B. Starushenko, *op. cit. supra* note 4; L. V. Speranskaya, Printsip Samoopredeleniya v Mezhdunarodnom Prave (The Principle of Self-Determination in International Law) (1961); Baratashvili, Za Svobodu i Nezavisimost Narodov (For the Freedom and Independece of Nations) (1960); Kozhokhin, *Raspad kolonialnoi sistemy imperializma i sovremennoe mezhdunarodnoe pravo (The Disintegration of the Colonial System of Imperialism and Contemporary International Law)*, Vestnik Leningradskogo Universiteta, No. 23, seriya ekonomiki, filosofii i prava, vyp. 4, at 116 n4 (1958).

than just an infraction of international law *in principio* or to have been caught in a breach of promise or an act of bad faith. Instead, it is taxed with a violation of the terms of a specific quasi-contractual undertaking toward a specific party. By the same token, the latter may now lawfully resort to appropriate reprisals to redress the wrongs thus inflicted upon it.

Soviet sources are unanimous on this last point. Any attempt to hinder a dependent area's aspiration toward political freedom *ipso facto* constitutes a flagrant infringement of the right to self-determination guaranteed under international law to all peoples, subject nations as well as communities organized as sovereign states. Accordingly, it is asserted, "any resistance to the free realization by the peoples of the right to self-determination represents a violation of the norms of international law—intervention in the domestic affairs of another nation." And, "armed intervention aimed at preventing a people from realizing the right to self-determination is aggression, that is, the gravest international crime."[27]

To sum it up, then, reluctance on the part of a metropolitan state to foster independence in its colonies or any manner of opposition on its side to a native freedom movement is *eo ipso* an offense against international law and the U.N. Charter. Should the home-country resist such a challenge to its rule by force of arms, it is again, by definition, guilty of naked aggression in the legal meaning of that term. In either case, the lesson drawn from the situation is that "the peoples of the colonies are fully entitled with arms in hand to seek liberation from the yoke of a colonial power evading a peaceful settlement of said question and be the first to start military action against it with the object of destroying its military forces stationed in these countries."[28] If these troops decide to fight back, the imperial government is guilty of yet another breach of the law of nations, for "the position of an imperialistic colonial state which by means of use of armed force attempts to keep a colony in its sphere of domination is contrary to the law."[29]

Sweeping as this may sound, the Soviet offensive against "colonialism" does not stop there, but rushes onward to even greater extremes. Up to here, the attack had followed the path of contending that any policy intended to perpetuate the disenfranchised status of the dependent territories or to impede their accession to full independence went counter to the principle of self-determination laid down by the Charter and recognized by international law. The next step takes the form of a denunciation *in toto* of colonialism *per se* as fundamentally incompatible with the spirit and the letter of today's world legal order, regardless of its

[27] Baratashvili, *supra* note 24, at 60; G. V. SHARMANAZASHVILI, PRAVO MIRA (THE LAW OF PEACE) 71-76 (1961); *id.*, PRINTSIP NENAPADENIYA V MEZHDUNARODNOM PRAVE (THE PRINCIPLE OF NON-AGGRESSION IN INTERNATIONAL LAW) 66-81 (1958); K. A. BAGINYAN, NARUSHENIE IMPERIALISTICHESKIMI GOSUDARSTVAMI PRINTSIPA NEVMESHATELSTVA (THE VIOLATION BY THE IMPERIALISTS STATES OF THE PRINCIPLE OF NON-INTERVENTION) 110-20, 132-42 (1954); Piradov & Starushenko, *Printsip nevmeshatelstva v sovremennom mezhdunarodnom prave (The Principle of Non-Intervention in Contemporary International Law)*, SOVETSKII EZHEGODNIK MEZHDUNARODNOGO PRAVA 1958, at 249 (1959).
[28] Sharmanazashvili, *supra* note 8, at 60.
[29] *Ibid.*

practical manifestations. Thus, even colonialism as a general phenomenon on the global scene, namely, in a historical conjuncture where it has not generated conflict, nevertheless now finds itself condemned as an offense against basic precepts of international law.[30] A similar argument, has already been encountered earlier, resting on the proposition that all dependencies are established through an act of aggression and that the original sin of violence underlies every instance of colonial rule. The present theme eschews this line of reasoning (impossible to uphold in international law in any event), in favor of another approach, and focuses instead on the formula featured in article 1, paragraph 2, of the U.N. Charter.

According to this clause, the purposes of the Organization include that of developing "friendly relations among nations based on respect for the principle of equal rights and self-determination of peoples, and to take other appropriate measures to strengthen universal peace." By juxtaposing the words "equal rights and self-determination of peoples" and "other appropriate measures to strengthen universal peace," Soviet jurists extrapolate from the language of the paragraph the thesis that respect for equal rights and self-determination of peoples represents a condition of universal peace. Conversely, failure to observe this rule in effect amounts to a threat to the peace or breach of the peace within the meaning of the Charter. Or, to phrase it differently, "the full and consistent implementation of the principle of equal rights and self-determination of peoples goes hand in hand with the maintenance of peace and international security."[31]

Colonialism, from Moscow's vantage-point, personifies the very negation of the idea of equal rights and self-determination. Hence, the very existence of colonies already marks that many concrete incidents of threats to peace which, in turn, can only be resolved through the total and immediate liquidation of every instance of colonial rule in conformity with the freely expressed will of the inhabitants of the interested subject areas. The prospect that any nation so consulted should elect to continue as another's subject is dismissed *ex principio* as an absolutely impossible contingency. But, in the meantime, and as long as a single case of colonialism survives anywhere on the face of the earth, universal peace remains in acute jeopardy, for, as Soviet spokesmen never tire of repeating, "violation of the principle of self-determination means violation of the principle of peaceful co-existence or the bases of the U.N. Charter itself."[32] Since the

---

[30] N. V. CHERNOGOLOVKRIN, KRUSHENIE KOLONIALIZMA I MEZHDUNARODNOE PRAVO (THE DISINTEGRATION OF COLONIALISM AND INTERNATIONAL LAW) 26 (1963): "The colonial regimen is in flagrant contradiction with the Charter of the UNO. . . ."

[31] Osnitskaya, *The Downfall of Colonialism and International Law*, 1 INTERNATIONAL AFFAIRS 39 (Moscow 1961). See, too, Bokor-Szegö, *The Colonial Clause in International Treaties*, 4 ACTA JURIDICA ACADEMIAE SCIENTIARUM HUNGARICAE 262 (1962); Lyubomudrova, *Samoopredelenie natsii—odno is osnovnykh uslovii mezhdunarodnogo sotrudnichestva i mirnogo sosushchestvovaniya (The Self-Determination of Nations—One of the Basic Conditions of International Cooperation and Peaceful Coexistence)*, in S. B. KRYLOV & V. N. DURDENEVSKII (EDS.), MEZHDUNARODNO-PRAVOVYE FORMY MIRNOGO SOSUSHCHESTVOVANIYA GOSUDARSTV I NATSII (INTERNATIONAL LEGAL FORMS FOR THE PEACEFUL COEXISTENCE OF STATES AND NATIONS) 16-58 (1957).

[32] Tuzmukhamedov, *supra* note 9, at 87.

key function of the United Nations consists precisely in maintaining and preserving world peace, colonialism is therefore seen as a blow at the very foundations
on which the Organization rests. From that it takes but one short step to voice
the companion slogan that, given the fact that it endangers peace merely by being
there, "colonialism in any form is the worst crime against humanity."[33] And
those responsible for it stand as morally convicted criminals before the bar of
world opinion by virtue of their imperial status alone.

With such a perspective on the place and role of colonialism on the international
arena, it comes as no surprise to find Soviet spokesmen and publicists alike vigor-
ously advocating use of force to eradicate this unspeakable evil and to protect
the legitimate interests of the victimized parties. Resort to violence to safeguard
a lawful right so vital as self-determination is thereby elevated to the rank of an
inherent attribute fully equal to that of individual and collective self-defense to
which, let it be noted *en passant,* it is said to be closely related. Indeed, not
only is such a course of action a legal right, it becomes tantamount to a legal
obligation, an instrument for the redemption, even if somewhat belated, of international law. Or, as one Soviet source prefers to put it,

. . . refusal to oppressed peoples of the right to make use of national-liberation war as an
extreme and temporary measure in response to the forcible attempt to hold them back
in a position of colonial dependency and imperialistic oppression runs counter to
established, universally recognized principles and norms of international law. With
fire and sword the western powers seized and kept "their" colonies. But aggression
and annexation cannot remain unpunished. . . . Refusal of the necessity of punishment
for aggression and annexation means the recognition of lawlessness in international relations.[34]

Furthermore, the right in question resides not only in the colonial nation
directly affected by its adverse experience with colonial servitude; the United
Nations is likewise vested with full authority to take appropriate action, including,
if need be, collective sanctions to uphold respect for the right to self-determination
and, coincidentally, to enhance peaceful co-existence. However, this does not
exhaust all the possibilites envisaged in certain quarters. Occasionally, one also
hears the added claim made, the most extreme of all to date, to the effect that "the
refusal of the colonists to grant independence to a people or return to a state
part of its national territory gives the Afro-Asian states the full right individually
and collectively to resort to force."[35] If taken literally, this would be equivalent
to pronouncing an anathema on any recalcitrant colonial power, proscribing it

[33] *Id.* at 89; Modzhoryan, *Raspad kolonialnoi sistemy i OON (The Disintegration of the Colonial System and the U.N.),* SOVETSKII EZHEGODNIK MEZHDUNARODNOGO PRAVA 1960, at 125 (1961).

[34] Tuzmukhamedov, *supra* note 9, at 90. He adds (p. 91): "National-liberation wars can be equated with one of the forms of international sanctions, the application of which on the basis of the UNO Charter is being demanded ever more insistently by the peoples toward colonial powers per-sisting in their illegal policy of barring the self-determination of dependent peoples."

[35] *Id.* at 88-89; V. K. SOBAKIN, KOLLEKTIVNAYA BEZOPASNOST—GARANTIYA MIRNOGO SOSUSCHEST-VOVANIYA (COLLECTIVE SECURITY—THE GUARANTEE OF PEACEFUL COEXISTENCE) 409 (1962).

and branding it an outlaw, on which is declared an open season. A state so designated becomes fair game for all—primarily, of course, for those nations which, as former victims, enjoy precedence in exacting retribution.

Still, no logical reason exists for restricting the right to mount such a crusade against the hated "colonialists" to the ex-colonies alone, though it may seem more politic at the moment to phrase the idea that way. Otherwise, in the spirit of this scheme apparently anyone can take a hand and cover himself with glory as a champion of law and order and the rights of the weak and oppressed. Just as the pirates of old, the imperial powers are thus suddenly transformed into *hostes humani generis,* objects of universal opprobrium on whose head anyone can, indeed ought to, visit the dire punishment they so richly deserve.

B. A Critique

So many objections come to mind in looking over these statements of the Soviet position concerning the purported impact of the Charter on the phenomenon of colonialism that one hardly knows quite where to begin. First, it should perhaps be reiterated that, Soviet contentions to the contrary notwithstanding, self-government and self-determination have ordinarily not been understood as synonymous with state independence, and that in its insistence on equating them Moscow high-handedly disregards altogether the technical side of the question. Even Communist sources concede that the drafters of the Charter chose their words carefully and deliberately and that, on this occasion, they purposefully picked these different terms, fully aware of their non-identity.

To say that the language of the Charter has since undergone such interpretation that now this earlier distinction has evaporated does not resolve the issue, for this is not merely part and product of the common process of tacit revision of some elements of the Charter. It would be difficult to quarrel with the latter, since all so-called "living documents" go through the same experience. However, if and when an effort is made to represent the matter as though a given viewpoint, known to be of recent vintage, has really always held sway and to picture it as an absolute and long-established truth, contrary to all sense of history and spirit of objective inquiry, this is pushing it a bit too far. Even if what the Soviets maintain the Charter means with respect to self-determination has become perfectly respectable as of late in some circles, they cannot convincingly make that claim *ab aeterno.*

Equally objectionable are many of the Soviet assertions concerning self-determination as a legal right. In taking that stand, they blithely ignore the fact that, from the moment of the concept's inception in its twentieth century Wilsonian garb, many of the world's leading jurisprudential minds have refused to recognize it as a principle of positive law at all. Even now one finds it described more often than not as "a programmatic policy statement," "a political formula," "a meta-juridical norm," in fact, anything but a legal prescript.[36] The opposite opinion, too, of course, commands its quota of adherents; and the two camps are usually locked in a doctrinal dialogue. But, what sets non-Soviet champions of self-determination as a legal right apart from their Soviet colleagues is that the latter waste no time on debate, as though the possibility of an alternative conclusion simply did not exist. The answer is by no means quite that self-evident. By failing to discount the valid criticism which their thesis invites, instead passing it *sub silentio*, Soviet jurists badly weaken their stand rather than strengthening it, as is their hope.

A further comment needs to be made in this connection. Let us again assume for the sake of argument that currently self-determination is indeed a formal legal right. That still leaves unresolved the question of its *locus*. As already mentioned, Moscow's view on this score is that the right legally rests with the colonial and dependent nations themselves, with the United Nations acting as an institutional guarantor of due performance. Such a contention fails to convince. The Charter, on which Soviet publicists rely so heavily to make this point, is not entirely clear. But it nonetheless manages to convey the impression that the right at stake here would enure to non-member, non-sovereign entities to which the text refers in this context not in the form of a right *stricto sensu*, but more in the capacity of an indirect benefit accruing to a third party by virtue of a specific agreement to that end between other contracting parties.

Likewise, the other United Nations materials which the Soviets have been so fond of citing in the past as upholding their thesis, notably the 1952 Resolution adopted by the General Assembly on "The Right of Peoples and Nations to Self-Determination," are even more susceptible of this interpretation. They also address themselves exclusively to the states members of the Organization, exhorting them to give effect to the various recommendations in the dependent territories under their administration. In dealing with the right to self-determination, then, both the Charter and the sundry pre-1960 U.N. documents voted pursuant thereto may perhaps more accurately be described as functioning in a mode akin to that of *pacta in favorem tertii*. In this case, the evidence strongly favors the conclusion that the right/duty relationship applies *in toto* only as between the individual members of the United Nations and between each of them and the Organization as a distinct personality, while the colonies enjoy, for the purposes of this arrange-

---

[36] For some of the objections to the idea of self-determination as a right in positive international law, see Eagleton, *Self-Determination in the United Nations*, 47 AM. J. INT'L L. 88 (1953); N. BENTWICH & A. MARTIN, A COMMENTARY ON THE CHARTER OF THE UNITED NATIONS 7, 143 (1951); L. GOODRICH & E. HAMBRO, CHARTER OF THE UNITED NATIONS, COMMENTARY AND DOCUMENTS 235 (1946); H. KELSEN, THE LAW OF THE UNITED NATIONS, A CRITICAL ANALYSIS OF ITS FUNDAMENTAL PROBLEMS 50-51 (1950).

It should be noted that among Soviet scholars, too, the opinion has sometimes been expressed that self-determination was a political concept, but that the Charter elevated it into a legal norm. See, to that effect, Molodtsov, *Raspad sistemy kolonializma i ego vliyanie na mezhdunarodnoe pravo (The Disintegration of the Colonialist System and its Influence on International Law)*, [1956] SOVETSKOE GOSUDARSTVO I PRAVO, No. 5, at 73, 81.

ment, the status of objects, passive recipients of privileges which others voluntarily choose to extend them.

As formulated above, the Soviet right/duty concept in conjunction with the Charter's pronouncements on self-determination cannot be sustained for yet another reason. In a relationship of this genre, rights and duties must be reciprocal, that is, both parties incur liabilities and gain assets, with one side of the ledger ordinarily neatly balanced against the other. However, the way Moscow approaches the issue, the situation between an imperial power and a colony is an entirely unilateral one—the metropolitan country carries all the debits, the colony owns all the rights, or, conversely, the former has no rights, only obligations, the latter has no duties, only rights. As a juridical construction, the scheme will not stand up to criticism. Again, it reminds one in its essentials of the conditions which obtain where two parties enter into an arrangement *in favorem tertii*.

In such a contingency, the right to self-determination would not properly amount to a right, and the companion duty to grant independence could not constitute a proper duty either. The Soviets will not accept this conclusion, but until they can make their own arguments more convincing, this line of reasoning will continue to find acceptance elsewhere.

The remaining propositions of this portion of the Soviet anti-colonial thesis can be disposed of quite briefly. The notion that colonialism as such is contrary to the U.N. Charter is, needless to say, impossible to substantiate. Otherwise, one can hardly explain how powerful states with vast colonial holdings who were among the chief drafters of the document would have welcomed an idea of this sort and freely subscribed to it. Likewise, the thought that several states endowed with colonial possessions would, on their own, embrace an agreement which, to all intents and purposes, vilified them as criminals in the eyes of the international community sounds well-nigh incredible. No one simply looked at colonialism that way when the San Francisco Conference met. Were it otherwise, the Charter would have been worded altogether differently, given the power alignment in those days.

As for the proposition that in the cause of promoting self-determination resort to force is thoroughly legitimate, just as it would be in the exercise of the innate national right of individual and collective self-defense, to urge it is to perpetrate a *reductio ad absurdum*. For the Charter is explicit on this score and restricts resort to armed violence on the international level to self-defense against overt attack alone and, even so, always subject to the Organization's ultimate approval. To say that a select group of states, picked on the basis of their colonial past, holds the right at any time and by its own choice to rely on force against an imperial nation in order to "liberate" the latter's dependencies is to conspire against the very *raison d'être* of the United Nations and the sundry procedural safeguards devised to ensure its effectiveness as a bulwark of peace.

If the United Nations is to mean anything, it can tolerate no differential standards for judging cases of outbreaks of international violence; and violence by ex-colonies against imperial nations is qualitatively indistinguishable from any other type of violence and therefore prohibited. To have the newly emergent nations enjoy privileges on this account that are forbidden to others would be tantamount to announcing officially that, though all the members of the United Nations are equally bound by the Charter, some are a little less so than others. By that token, the chosen few would be allowed to invoke the special prerogative of employing armed force with regard to a certain category of nations, while all other members would be required strictly to adhere to the general rule prescribing peaceful methods for settling disputes. The damage such discriminatory practice could cause to the image and authority of the United Nations is incalculable, probably irreparable, for this would come close to destroying the Organization as a meaningful instrument for world peace.

Furthermore, once these gradations of preferential status are introduced, who is to say that similar privileged treatment would not later be extended to various other groups of states chosen on the strength of yet other criteria, but always to the detriment of some segment of the Organization's membership? Indeed, there need be no logical end to the distribution of these extraordinary dispensations; and a single breach in this crucial sector is likely to bring about the early collapse of the rest of the elaborate machinery of the United Nations designed to forestall precisely this contingency. In any form of human association, use of an avowedly double standard to pass on the behavior of the participants commonly leads to mayhem in the end. On the international scene, with relations as tense as they are today and the balance of power so delicately poised, it would result in nothing less than chaos compounded.

IV

THE "JUST WAR" THEORY

The final chapter of the Soviet brief in defense of wars of national liberation is based on the idea of "just war." Though frequently encountered in Soviet literature today, that concept emerged only relatively recently as a recognized ingredient of the Marxist ideology. In effect, both Marx and Engels paid very little attention to the matter of qualifying wars which occurred in their lifetimes as just or unjust (there was, of course, no question as yet of branding armed conflicts as legal or illegal). When they did feel called upon to comment on some outbreak of hostilities between states, which happened on several occasions, they chose instead to treat the issue in terms of their own dichotomy of "progressive" versus "reactionary" wars. Under "progressive," they put all military hostilities which served to further the advance of the materialist course of history, as blueprinted by themselves; and under "reactionary," they grouped all uses of international coercion which they considered wishful attempts to stop or turn back the clock of history and therefore hopelessly foredoomed to ultimate failure.

True, the expression "just cause," applied to such situations, is sometimes featured in their voluminous writings, but it adds no new dimensions to their analysis of the events and leads to no special conclusions. Rather, the idea of "justice" in this context appears throughout in a strictly subordinate role, as a quality incidental to the notion of "progress" and a derivative product of the latter: What is historically "progressive" is automatically also "just."

This mode of thinking is characteristic, too, of Lenin's pronouncements in which every political item, be it domestic or international, is assessed exclusively on the plane of whether it promotes or hinders the revolutionary program. As a practical politician, Lenin grasped better than Marx or Engels, the abstract theoreticians, the appeal of "justice" as a popular political slogan and so exploited it commensurately. But even then, it remained in his hands a weapon of very secondary importance. So far as he also was concerned, "justice" represented a mere handmaiden of "revolutionary progress" and never amounted to an autonomous doctrinal element.

Today, when it is fashionable in the U.S.S.R. to denigrate Stalin and attribute almost everything worthwhile to Lenin's genius, the claim is made that it is Lenin who, "taking into account the new historical situation and the new tasks of the working class in the struggle for socialism . . . developed the Marxist definition of the character of war of the pre-monopolistic period, advancing the general moral-political principle of justice and injustice." And, according to these same sources, "this principle applies to the evaluation of all wars, but has an especially great importance for the analysis of wars of the modern era."[37] Actually, this is quite a fanciful interpretation of the record, for it is under Stalin, and not Lenin, that the maxim of just wars fully came to the fore. Indeed, the very definition of just wars quoted at the outset derives from a publication the authorship of which was officially credited to Stalin and where is also offered a definition of unjust wars as "wars of conquest, waged to conquer and enslave foreign countries and foreign nations."[38]

With Stalin's ascendancy, drawing a distinction between just or unjust wars

[37] Khomenko, in MARKSIZM-LENINIZM O VOINE I ARMII (MARXISM-LENINISM ON WAR AND ARMIES) 80 (2d ed. 1961).

[38] HISTORY OF THE COMMUNIST PARTY OF THE SOVIET UNION (BOLSHEVIKS) 168.

For Western analysis and critique of the Communist theories of just and unjust wars and interventions, see T. A. TARACOUZIO, THE SOVIET UNION AND INTERNATIONAL LAW 311-15 (1935); LUIS GARCIA ARIAS, LA GUERRA MODERNA Y LA ORGANIZACION INTERNACIONAL 213-31 (1962); I. LAPENNA, CONCEPTIONS SOVIÉTIQUES DE DROIT INTERNATIONAL PUBLIC 236-42 (1954); J. Y. CALVEZ, DROIT INTERNATIONAL ET SOUVERAINETÉ EN U.R.S.S. 68-72 (1953); H. KELSEN, THE COMMUNIST THEORY OF LAW 149, 167 (1955).

For some recent Soviet studies on the question of just and unjust wars, see, in particular, Pukhovskii, *Voiny spravedlivye i nespravedlivye (Just and Unjust Wars)*, in MARKSIZM-LENINIZM O VOINE, ARMII I VOENNOI NAUKE, SBORNIK STATEI (MARXISM-LENINISM ON WAR, ARMIES, AND MILITARY SCIENCE; COLLECTION OF ARTICLES) 34-43 (1955); Kurbatov, *Marksizm-leninizm o voinakh spravedlivykh i nespravedlivykh (Marxism-Leninism on Just and Unjust Wars)*, 12 PROPAGANDA I AGITATSIYA 42-49 (1951); Chuvikov, *Uchenie Lenina-Stalina o voinakh spravedlivykh i nespravedlivykh (The Teachings of Lenin and Stalin on Just and Unjust Wars)*, 7-8 BOLSHEVIK 14-26 (1945).

became common Soviet practice. The operative criteria always remained purely subjective, predicated on Moscow's assessment of the events from an ideological point of view alone, in turn reflecting, of course, the U.S.S.R.'s current diplomatic interests as well. Though unilateral in application and highly personal in conception, these standards were, nonetheless, unhesitatingly applied by the Kremlin to render judgment on various conflicts between states which happened to disturb the international scene. What is more, the invocation of this "moral-political principle" implied definite juridical consequences.

As far back as 1939, for instance, Stalin himself had publicly declared that "we stand for the support of nations which are the victims of aggression and are fighting for the independence of their country."[39] The U.S.S.R. was, at the time, still a member of the League of Nations and officially a champion of its collective security system. In these circumstances, this would be an orthodox policy statement. Yet, it should be noted, Stalin made no reference whatever to the League, all but moribund by then in any case. Furthermore, in Soviet circles his *dictum* was thereafter treated as an enunciation of a general rule, not dependent on participation in any particular international organization. Thus, according to Soviet legal commentators, the formula simply affirmed that, *ex principio,* "there cannot be a similar relationship with the aggressor and the victim of aggression" and "this means that a state waging a *just* war must receive assistance and aid. . . ."[40]

Following the German invasion of Russia, the Second World War assumed, in Soviet parlance, the character of a supremely just war. In spite of this designation, however, Moscow did not, in the midst of the fighting, choose to indulge in any wholesale revision or repudiation of the established laws of war and, throughout, insistently demanded that the enemy likewise abide by the letter and spirit of the customary and conventional regulations on modern warfare. Significantly, the only marked departure from the old norms for which the Soviet régime admitted responsibility during the hostilities and which its jurisconsults openly tried to justify concerned rules setting conditions for the conduct of guerrilla warfare.[41] Even so, the pleadings here rested on technical grounds and pursued their objective ostensibly within the frame of reference of established international law.

As soon as war came to an end, however, the Kremlin's erstwhile caution in handling this sensitive issue suddenly evaporated. Instead, Soviet jurists now rhetorically asked ". . . can we confine a sacred people's war against an aggressor and enslaver, a heroic struggle of millions of people for their country's independence, for its national culture, for its right to exist, can we confine this war within

[39] J. V. STALIN, REPORT ON THE WORK OF THE CENTRAL COMMITTEE TO THE EIGHTEENTH CONGRESS OF THE COMMUNIST PARTY OF THE SOVIET UNION (BOLSHEVIKS) 15 (1939).

[40] E. A. KOROVIN (ED.), *op. cit. supra* note 3, at 557. (Emphasis added.)

[41] See, in particular, the thesis developed by E. A. KOROVIN, KRATKII KURS MEZHDUNARODNOGO PRAVA, CHAST II: PRAVO VOINY (BRIEF COURSE ON INTERNATIONAL LAW, PART II: THE LAW OF WAR) 34-36, 78-79 (1944).

the strict bounds of the Hague rules, which were calculated for wars of a different type and for a totally different international situation?"[42] They forthwith answered their own query in the negative. In the same vein, though some Soviet lawyers still tried to argue their case for the legality of guerrilla warfare in legal terms, they, too, soon fell back on the technique of appealing to the "justice" of their cause. By that token, "popular guerrilla warfare in the rear of an aggressor—a warfare which will be supported by all freedom-loving peoples" enjoyed "the protection of international law," but *vice versa,* if the inspirer and defender of aggressive war, that is, unjust war, tries to use guerrilla methods of warfare, then such 'guerrillas' cannot be under the protection of international law."[43]

Subsequently, the pendulum swung even further in this direction. Things finally reached a point where Soviet publicists denounced outright all attempts to deal with the subject on accepted legal terms and flatly condemned all earlier efforts by their own compatriots to furnish a jural rationale for the changes that the régime had effected in the course of the late war in the stipulations of the Hague accords regarding guerrilla warfare. All these endeavors were now brushed aside on the grounds that their badly misguided authors had erroneously "analyzed the problems of partisan war without bearing in mind the Leninist-Stalinist teachings concerning just and unjust wars. . . ." Henceforth, ran the injunction, "the task of the Soviet lawyers consists in giving a learned justification of the legality of partisan wars on territories occupied by the imperialist aggressors, keeping in mind the Leninist-Stalinist teachings on just and unjust wars."[44] This task would take as its keynote the central theme that "in a war of liberation every person who takes up arms to fight against an aggressor fulfills a high patriotic duty, and his actions may not be regarded as criminal."[45]

The net effect of such an outlook would again amount to conferring total immunity on the party said to be waging a just war, irrespective of its actual behavior

[42] Korovin, *The Second World War and International Law,* 40 AM. J. INT'L L. 753 (1946).

[43] Trainin, *Questions of Guerrilla Warfare in the Law of War,* 40 AM. J. INT'L L. 561-62 (1946); YURIDICHESKII SLOVAR, *op. cit. supra* note 15, at 440; P. I. KUDRYAVTSEV (ED.), *op. cit. supra* note 15, at 101.

[44] Mankovskii, in [1950] SOVETSKOE GOSUDARSTVO I PRAVO, No. 7, at 69-71; F. I. KOZHEVNIKOV, VELIKAYA OTECHESTVENNAYA VOINA SOVETSKOGO SOYUZA I NEKOTORYE VOPROSY MEZHDUNARODNOGO PRAVA (THE GREAT PATRIOTIC WAR OF THE SOVIET UNION AND SOME QUESTIONS OF INTERNATIONAL LAW) 95-99 (1954).

A curious discrepancy occurs in Soviet literature on the question of "partisan" war which deserves to be noted briefly. Soviet sources have always claimed that guerrilla warfare was legal under international law, but YURIDICHESKII SLOVAR, *op. cit. supra* note 15, at 440, features a statement to the effect that "by virtue of this stipulation [Art. 4, para. 2], the Geneva conventions of 1949 establish the legality of a partisan movement on occupied territory, which was not foreseen in the 1907 conventions." This *lapsus calami* is corrected in the second edition of the work, P. I. KUDRYAVTSEV (ED.), *op. cit. supra* note 15, at 102, where it is said instead that "by virtue of this stipulation, the Geneva conventions of 1949 confirm the legality of a partisan movement on occupied territory."

[45] L. OPPENHEIM, MEZHDUNARODNOE PRAVO (INTERNATIONAL LAW) (6th ed., 1949, by H. Lauterpacht; tr. by Ya. I. Retsker & A. A. Santalov; ed. by S. A. Golunskii, Vol. II, Part I), editorial note on p. 235. See, also Modzhoryan, *Partizanskie otryady i vooruzhennye vystupleniya mass v period vtoroi mirovoi voiny (Guerrilla Units and Armed Action of the Masses in the Period of the Second World War),* id. at 282-86.

on the battlefield and behind the front—to giving it *carte blanche* to act as it wishes, while sentencing its opponent to suffer every indignity without recourse. And, it should be stressed, the bulk of these extreme pronouncements were heard well after the signature of the Geneva conventions of 1949, which the Soviets so often cite. There, a partial attempt was made to resolve the legal status of the irregular troops by putting them on equal footing, for certain purposes, with the regular armed forces. Such a venture, in turn, can realistically be expected to achieve success only if the guerrilla units, too, observe the established laws of war. The logic of the situation, however, seems to have escaped the Soviets who, instead, altogether absolve one side from any obligation whatever to respect the regulations and concurrently insist that the other side must nevertheless fully conform to the rules.

To want to punish an aggressor may be a laudible sentiment and one that deserves sympathy, but to do so by completely ignoring the laws of war, even if the wrongdoer is already guilty of that offense, can only make matters worse. To adopt, *a priori,* such an attitude when there is an outside chance that the so-called aggressor might after all mind the usual amenities is heedlessly, and needlessly, to precipitate the conflict into a lawless butchery.

The fact that Soviet legal experts focused primarily on issues of guerrilla warfare is crucial for the present discussion, for Soviet commentators are always quick to point out that, "where the imperialists attempt by force of arms to suppress the national-liberation struggle, the peoples rise in revolt which grows into national-liberation wars that customarily take on the form of a partisan struggle." And guerilla wars are, by definition, people's wars *par excellence,* hence "these are sacred wars."[46] As such, goes the inference, they stand above the petty limitations of routine law.

It would serve no good purpose to dwell at greater length on the detailed vagaries of the Soviet campaign in praise of "just" wars. Anything so subjective and, one may add, so contingent on political whim, simply does not lend itself to meaningful analysis. Suffice it to note than the very concept itself runs diametrically counter to the spirit and the substance of the basic principles on which the post-war legal order was erected. In effect, one of the key concerns of the drafters of the Charter lay precisely in foreclosing the possibility of unilateral appeal by states to some ill-defined, abstract so-called "higher principles" to circumvent the text's express ban against recourse to violence in the international sphere. They deliberately avoided using the word "war" so as to preclude the usual abuse of that term, and even eschewed all reference to *bellum legitimum* or *illicitum,* to say nothing of *bellum justum* or *injustum.* In short, the chief object of the Charter was henceforth to bar resort to force—plain force—in interstate relations; and its language clearly reflects that preoccupation.

46 Khomenko, *supra* note 47, at 106.

Yet, in spite of its loudly professed respect for the Charter's principles, Moscow continues to cling to an anarchistic device which the rest of the world has repudiated as fundamentally incompatible with its hopes for peace and security as embodied in the United Nations Organization. Nor, it should be emphasized, does the slogan of "just" war represent a weapon in the Kremlin's armory which it will wield only when the United Nations has failed to speak its mind when confronted with an outbreak of armed hostilities and its members must fall back on general international law. For the Soviet government has made it abundantly evident that, in proper circumstances, it will not hesitate to invoke these vague "higher values" to thwart even a decision of the United Nations with which it happens to disagree.

The Korean incident offers an excellent case in point. When, on that occasion, Vishinsky exhausted his store of legal excuses for the presence of the Chinese "volunteers" on the battle-front, he finally came up with that time-honored plea of all lawyers and statesmen who find themselves pressed for good arguments, namely, an appeal to indeterminate moral justifications, and solemnly declared: "The statement of the Ministry of Foreign Affairs of the People's Republic of China of November 11, [1950] to the effect that the Chinese people's voluntary aid to Korea and their resistance to United States aggression had a moral foundation, was fully justified."[47]

For that matter, the scope of the privileged status that Moscow claims for "just" wars in this respect can perhaps be gauged even better if one remembers that while those fighting for the right cause need not, according to Soviet authors, feel hamstrung by any undue consideration for legal technicalities, the United Nations itself cannot aspire to a like privilege and suspend the operation of the conventional rules. An exception might be allowed if the Organization is engaged in repelling and punishing an aggressor, so designated by unanimous vote of the permanent members of the Security Council supported by the required majority. However, in the latter instance, such liberty would probably be permissible again only because there could be no doubt that the United Nations' stand was "just," the U.S.S.R. having concurred in the collective action.

Otherwise, the Soviet view is that the United Nations must abide by the standard regulations. Thus, to cite once more the Korean experience, all Soviet spokesmen during that crisis insisted that the Hague rules continued to obtain; that the members of the United Nations remained bound thereby *in toto;* and that, furthermore, the Security Council could not on its own free the member states of the duties incumbent upon them by reason of these conventions. As an Austrian author generally sympathetic to the Soviet point of view put it in an article that appeared in the chief Soviet legal periodical, "the customs and laws of war are not mentioned

[47]A. YA. VYSHINSKII, *Third Speech Before the General Committee, December 5, 1950,* VOPROSY MEZHDUNARODNOGO PRAVA I MEZHDUNARODNOI POLITIKI (QUESTIONS OF INTERNATIONAL LAW AND INTERNATIONAL POLITICS 275 (1951).

in the Charter, as it only regulates part of the international legal relations of states, members and non-members alike." Therefore, "the Charter assumed that commonly recognized law is still in force," and no U.N. organ can contravene it by deciding *ad hoc* to set aside temporarily these well established norms, the stipulations of the various Hague accords, *inter alia,* since these documents function "at present as a universal expression of the customary law of war obligatory for all states. . . ."[48] Besides, it was argued, even the Security Council is technically incapable of such action because "the decisions of the Security Council . . . do not have the force of juridical precedent and, consequently, cannot create general norms of international law"[49] nor, apparently, supersede existing general norms.

Though urged as universally valid principles, these propositions obviously reflected the fact that the U.S.S.R. had not given its sanction to the United Nations' initial decision to intervene in Korea and refused to acknowledge the legality of the subsequent measures adopted by the General Assembly on this question as a usurpation of the functions of the Security Council. Nevertheless, the example does demonstrate that for a war to be "just," the Soviet leadership must pronounce it so; and that without its consenting vote, no other power on earth can achieve that result, not even the United Nations.

V

"JUST WARS" AND PEACEFUL COEXISTENCE

One need not further belabor the point that Soviet espousal of the notion of "just" war cannot be reconciled with the aims of the United Nations Organization as stated in its Charter. What also deserves to be noted, however, is that the concept of "just" war cannot honestly be brought into harmony with the current Soviet campaign on behalf of "peaceful co-existence," either.[50] Indeed, even "peaceful co-existence," the virtues of which the Kremlin so assiduously sings today and which it endlessly extols as a key to a better world, does not stand exempt from the basic reservation that it must give precedence to "just" wars, a superior instrument for "progress" in the dialectical scheme of history, if the interests of the two should collide.

First, then, "peaceful co-existence" must defer to "proletarian internationalism," since, as one Soviet source has frankly admitted,

While the principle of peaceful co-existence is designed for the historical phase of simultaneous existence on the international arena of two opposing systems, the principle

---

[48] Brandweiner, *Amerikanskoe tolkovanie mezhdunarodnogo prava—vyrazhenie mezhdunarodnogo bezzakoniya (The American Interpretation of International Law—An Expression of International Lawlessness),* [1954] SOVETSKOE GOSUDARSTVO I PRAVO, No. 6, at 46-47.

[49] Levin, *Falsifikatsiya ponyatiya mezhdunarodnogo prava burzhuaznoi lzhenaukoi (Falsification of the Concept of International Law by Bourgeois Pseudo-Science),* [1952] SOVETSKOE GOSUDARSTVO I PRAVO, No. 4, at 57.

[50] For an excellent survey and analysis of recent Soviet views on so-called co-existence, see McWhinney, *"Peaceful Co-Existence" and Soviet-Western International Law,* 56 AM. J. INT'L L. 951-970 (1962).

of proletarian internationalism is designed for a more lasting epoch, for, as V. I. Lenin indicated, national and state differences between peoples and countries "will yet persist a very, very long time, even after the realization of the dictatorship of the proletariat on a world-wide scale. . . ."[51]

Next, "peaceful co-existence" must likewise make way for "solidarity with the oppressed peoples' struggle for national liberation." For all Soviet spokesmen, from Khrushchev on down, make no secret of where their sympathies lie, publicly declaring that ". . . we are against imperialistic, colonialistic and, in general, against all wars, except those wars which peoples wage in fighting for their own liberation. These are sacred popular wars against slavery, against colonial regimes."[52] By the same token, oppressed nations can, they are continuously assured, count on the ready backing of the Soviet Union and its allies in their struggle for independence. Yet the latter still always insist that the support they willingly render to such "anti-colonialist" causes in no way detracts from their fervent desire for international peace. On the contrary, they maintain,

The socialist countries and the Communists all over the world will continue to aid and support the peoples who are waging an armed struggle against colonialism. Far from contradicting the concept of peaceful coexistence, this is an affirmation of that concept, since the issue at stake is respect for one of the basic principles of peaceful coexistence— the right of all peoples to order their own life as they see fit, to be masters in their own house.[53]

In what shape these deft exercises in dialectical casuistry leave "peaceful co-existence" may well be imagined. As a Western student of Soviet affairs has rightly remarked, "If peaceful co-existence is to be a reality . . . the concept of 'just' intervention or war will have to be put aside."[54] Until that is done, "peaceful co-existence" will remain a myth. Granted, convinced Communists are certain that Marxist ideology furnishes them with a sure guide to the future and that in defending "just" wars they are simply facilitating the march of progress. By the same logic, however, those who do not share their beliefs may credit themselves with like ideals. The door will then again stand wide open for every government and every political movement to appeal to heaven, figuratively speaking, and, firmly bearing aloft a banner incribed with an appropriately inspirational message, be it "Gott mit Uns" or "Dialectical Historical Materialism is on Our Side," proceed to spread by the sword the advantages of its superior culture and fulfill its civilizing mission among its benighted neighbors.

[51] M. AIRAPETYAN & P. KABANOV, LENINSKIE PRINTSIPY VNESHNEI POLITIKI SOVETSKOGO GOSU-DARSTVA (LENINIST PRINCIPLES OF THE FOREIGN POLICY OF THE SOVIET STATE) 65 (1957), referring to 31 V. I. LENIN, SOCHINENIYA (WORKS) 72.
[52] N. S. KHRUSHCHEV, I KOMMUNIZM—MIR I SCHASTIE NARODOV (COMMUNISM—PEACE AND HAPPINESS OF PEOPLES) 379 (1962).
[53] Ponomaryov, Some Problems of the Revolutionary Movement, 12 WORLD MARXIST REVIEW 13 (1962).
[54] Hazard, Codifying Peaceful Co-Existence, 55 AM. J. INT'L L. 118 (1961).

If the proletariat reserves for itself the right to liberate its fellow-workers from the yoke of capitalism, and newly independent nations feel destined to bring freedom to the still extant colonies from their imperial masters, the bourgeoisie could also assert the right to rally to the rescue of its class brethren imperiled by Communist revolutions and wars of national liberation. Unless one is blindly committed to an ideological code, objective observers must concede that if one party may excuse its otherwise unjustifiable behavior by invoking some abstract and totally subjective "sense of justice," all may do so. And overnight, the world will be back where it was fifty years ago; and the United Nations will be as dead as the League was towards the end of its ill-starred career.

OUTLOOK

The above sums up the Soviet position on the question of national-liberation wars and their status under present international law. This much remains to be said: there is no doubt that, today, the Soviets are successfully riding the crest of a popular wave of anti-colonialism—so much so that many of the slogans mouthed by Moscow, no matter how extreme, have as of late attracted a ready audience and in some quarters have come to be accepted as gospel truth. The annals of the United Nations, the General Assembly in particular, since the flood-like influx of new African and Asian states to its membership, will testify to that. In this connection, the 1960 session, with its General Assembly Resolution entitled "Declaration on the granting of independence to colonial countries and peoples,"[55] marks a watershed.

True, that document, as finally adopted, was not the original Soviet draft, but a compromise text sponsored by a large group of Afro-Asian states. However, as Soviet sources are quick to point out, the latter "included nearly all the most important propositions advanced by the Soviet government."[56] As a result, the General Assembly officially went on record as a champion of many of the most radical principles of the anti-colonialist thesis long expounded by the Kremlin which, in the past, had brought down on the head of the Soviet régime a storm of criticism ranging from charges of sheer irresponsibility to accusations of flagrant disregard for international law and the letter of the Charter.

Yet, by overwhelming vote, the General Assembly has now vindicated Moscow's stand, in all its essentials. In sweeping language, it, in turn, declared that:

1. The subjection of peoples to alien subjugation, domination and exploitation constitutes a denial of fundamental rights, is contrary to the Charter of the United Nations, and is an impediment to the promotion of world peace and co-operation.

2. All peoples have the right to self-determination; by virtue of that right they freely determine their political status and freely pursue their economic, social and cultural development.

[55] Resolution 1514(XV), RESOLUTIONS ADOPTED BY THE GENERAL ASSEMBLY DURING ITS 15TH SESSION, Vol. I, Supplement No. 16 (A/4684), at 66 (1961).
[56] CHERNOGOLOVKIN, op. cit. supra note 30, at 25.

3. Inadequacy of political, economic, social or educational preparedness should never serve as a pretext for delaying independence.

4. All armed action or repressive measures of all kinds directed against independent peoples shall cease in order to enable them to exercise peacefully and freely their right to complete independence, and the integrity of their national territory shall be respected.

5. Immediate steps shall be taken, in Trust and Non-Self-Governing Territories or all other territories which have not yet attained independence, to transfer all powers to the peoples of those territories, without any conditions or reservations, in accordance with their freely expressed will and desire, without any distinction as to race, creed or colour, in order to enable them to enjoy complete independence and freedom.

6. Any attempt aimed at the partial or total disruption of the national unity and the territorial integrity of a country is incompatible with the purposes of the Charter of the United Nations.

7. All States shall observe faithfully and strictly the provisions of the Charter of the United Nations, the Universal Declaration of Human Rights and the present Declaration on the basis of equality, non-interference in the internal affairs of all states, and respect for the sovereign rights of all peoples and their territorial integrity.

Of course, technically, this General Assembly Resolution is no more than a recommendation and does not create a formal legal obligation.[57] As an authoritative and prestigious statement of world sentiment, however, its weight and impact are undeniable. There is thus much truth in the comment of a Polish jurist to the effect that, if "the collapse of the colonial system is, next to the emergence of the world system of socialist states, one of the most important social phenomena of our epoch," then the "15th session [of the U.N.] . . . represents, in this connection, a decisive turning-point" and its Declaration "is one of the most important documents in the history of the U.N.O."[58] Indeed, what the resolution has done was morally to condemn colonialism in every shape and form, and to denounce all its practitioners *ex principio*. Legally, it could accomplish no more, but it went just as far as it could.

On the other hand, what the practical consequences of the declaration will be, no one can tell, except that they are quite likely to be *nil*. Extreme policies which

[57] Soviet authors take the same view. See, for instance, Starushenko, *supra* note 22, at 70, where the author writes that the resolutions of the General Assembly are not directives, but that their moral weight is nonetheless very great.

On the other hand, Modzhoryan, *Raspad kolonialnoi sistemy imperializma i nekotorye voprosy mezhdunarodnogo prava* (*The Collapse of the Colonial System of Imperialism and Some Questions of International Law*), SOVETSKII EZHEGODNIK MEZHDUNARODNOGO PRAVA 1961, at 37-38 (1962), claims that: "As distinct from the other resolutions of the General Assembly, the resolution of December 14, 1960, has not only great moral authority, but also legal force. Resolutions of the UNO General Assembly, 'adopted in accordance with the provisions of the UNO Charter, play an important role in the process of formation of new principles and norms of international law,' but in the instant case the reverse phenomenon took place: the resolution of December 14, 1960, confirmed a principle already widely enforced in international practice. For recognition of the illegality of colonialism even before the adoption of the resolution had become a norm of behavior for the socialist states, as well as for the young national states from the very day of their inception." The quote within the quote is from TUNKIN, *op. cit. supra* note 3, at 13.

[58] Antonowicz, *La Déclaration de l'O.N.U. sur l'Octroi de l'Indépendance aux Pays et aux Peuples Coloniaux*, ANNUAIRE POLONAIS DES AFFAIRES INTERNATIONALES 1962, at 24-30 (1962).

overlook the hard facts of life and, as here, attempt to settle a difficult problem by advocating a unilateral and inequitable, therefore unrealistic, solution, usually fail where a more moderate approach might have succeeded. In any event, it is improbable that a measure which, *a priori,* places all the *onus* of guilt on one party to a contested issue and acquits the other of all responsibility, will play a very constructive role in human affairs.

Finally, it should perhaps be noted that the spirit of the 1960 General Assembly Declaration seems greatly inferior in its understanding of and respect for the goals of international law when compared to the doctrinal superstructure erected earlier by the "imperialist" powers to justify their expansionist policies which it condemns. The latter simply denied the applicability of international law to their dealings with colonial peoples. These lay outside the proper province of international law; and no pretense was made that its rules in any way extended to the business of building empires. International law was absolutely irrelevant in this context. Neither side could seek comfort in its provisions. Today's anti-colonialist forces are infinitely less honest in their attitude, for they attempt to accomplish their ends within the framework of international law by abusing it for their own purpose. They demand the full protection of international law for the side they favor, yet completely deny the same protection to the one they oppose. This is but a travesty of law; and it would be far better simply to leave law out of it altogether and settle the issue as once before without reference to legal principles instead of playing fast and loose with the law, openly preaching a double standard of public conduct and, in the process, generally discrediting both the law and the United Nations that is supposed to preserve it. In our troubled times, the foothold maintained by international law in the daily repertoire of state diplomatic practice is precarious enough without imposing this added strain on its already slender resources.

BASIC PRINCIPLES IN SOVIET SPACE LAW: PEACEFUL COEXISTENCE, PEACEFUL COOPERATION, AND DISARMAMENT

ROBERT D. CRANE*

During recent years the Soviets have increasingly used law as a subtle but effective instrument to control the minds of men and thereby to prepare the general political environment for the more effective execution of Soviet policy. International law has become for the Soviets a potential matrix and framework for the entire Soviet policy of world revolution. Space law has become a particularly important part of the developing science of Soviet international law, because it serves to prepare the way for Communist military use of space to deter effective Western military opposition to Communist expansion here on earth.

I

PEACEFUL COEXISTENCE

The strategic doctrine which the Communists have adopted to pursue their expansionist foreign policies is known in the new Communist jargon as "peaceful coexistence." It is important to understand the nature of this revolutionary doctrine, because it determines all the basic principles of Soviet space law. In the introduction to the second symposium of the Space Law Commission of the Soviet Academy of Sciences, edited by G. P. Zhukov, the Deputy Chairman of the Soviet Space Law Commission, Professor G. P. Zadorozhnyy, stated that "every activity in outer space whatsoever which is incompatible with the principle of peaceful coexistence is illegal."[1]

Some scholars in the West believe that Soviet support of peaceful coexistence reflects, as Professor Edward McWhinney puts it, a "common interest in minimum rules of world order," and "a sort of nuclear age 'due process' governing fundamental East-West relations."[2] Professor McWhinney, who is a Canadian member of the International Law Association and a member of its committee charged with the study of peaceful coexistence, believes that this is particularly true after the Cuban crisis. He has stated that there is, to be sure, a "hard-line, neo Stalinist core of Soviet juristic thinking which would use peaceful coexistence as no more than a convenient camouflage for achieving 'proletarian internationalism' in the special

* A.B. 1955, Northwestern University; LL.B. 1959, Harvard University. Research Principal of The Center for Strategic Studies, and Chairman of its Study Program on Arms Control, Georgetown University.

[1] Zadorozhnyy, *In Honor of the Seventieth Birthday of Yevgeniy Aleksandrovich Korovin* (in Russian), in G. P. ZHUKOV (ED.), KOSMOS I MEZHDUNARODNOYE SOTRUDNICHESTVO 8 (1963). All translations from the Russian, unless otherwise indicated, are by the author.

[2] McWhinney, *"Coexistence," the Cuban Crisis, and Cold War International Law*, International Journal, Win. 1962-63, p. 68.

sense of coordinated world revolution."[3] He contends that this conflicts with "the currently orthodox Soviet thinking on peaceful coexistence, associated with Premier Khrushchev . . . which bears some comparisons obviously to Leninist notions of 'Socialism in one country.' " Professor McWhinney adds:

Peaceful coexistence, as so developed by Soviet jurists and policy-makers, is, of course, a somewhat static, conservative, even reactionary doctrine. . . . For peaceful coexistence in this sense amounts virtually to a legitimation of the political and military status quo of the cold war era. In so far as it would accept the de facto situation of the bi-polar division of the world into the two great military blocs dominated respectively by the United States and the Soviet Union, it would necessarily concede general control and responsibility by each bloc leader over its own sphere of influence. It would further proclaim a principle of non-interference by either the United States or the Soviet Union in the other's bloc, however great the temptation to profit by the other side's difficulties at any time might be, and however great the moral anguish at not being able to intervene in specific cases.[4]

I quote this statement by Professor McWhinney because it is the clearest statement I have ever encountered of exactly what "peaceful coexistence" is *not*, and because it conflicts completely with the Soviet's own definition of peaceful coexistence.

A colleague of mine at the Center for Strategic Studies, Richard Allen, has presented in some detail the Communists' own views on peaceful coexistence in a chapter he has written for the book, *Detente: Cold War Strategies in Transition*.[5] It would be enlightening to ponder the Communists' own statements on the subject of peaceful coexistence which Professor Allen has made available to scholars in the field.

A recent Communist book by H. Dona on peaceful coexistence published last year explains that "some try to reduce the notion of peaceful coexistence to the renunciation of war. But peace and peaceful coexistence are not one and the same thing." The Soviet author Shishlin comments on the detente following the recent test-ban treaty as follows:

In view of the Communists, peaceful coexistence between the two systems is certainly not a passive process in which there is some sort of parallel development of capitalism and socialism, no freezing of social relationships, or strengthening of the status quo in the relationship between the forces of socialism and capitalism, but an active and intense struggle, in the course of which socialism irresistibly attacks, while capitalism suffers one defeat after another.[6]

The above quoted book by Dona states that "the struggle of the people against reactionary regimes cannot be dissolved by international agreement. For this struggle to cease, the causes eliciting it must be eliminated, *i.e.*, capitalism must be liquidated."

[3] *Id.* at 69-70.
[4] *Id.* at 71-72.
[5] Allen, *Peace or Peaceful Coexistence?*, in ELEANOR LANSING DULLES & ROBERT D. CRANE (EDS.), DETENTE: COLD WAR STRATEGIES IN TRANSITION 23-62 (1964).
[6] See the discussion in Allen, *supra* note 5, at 30.

In the deterministic framework of Communist thinking, which most non-Communists find impossible to take seriously or even to understand, capitalism actually causes the Communists to wage a struggle against it, and therefore capitalism must be destroyed to stop the struggle. As Premier Khrushchev put it in August 1963 following the signing of the nuclear test ban treaty:

If everyone acted and thought in the Communist way then there would be no antagonistic classes and communism would already be victorious everywhere. However, while there are still two systems, socialists and capitalists, each system has its own policy, its own course, and we cannot but take into account the fact that two systems exist. A fight is in progress between these two systems, a life and death combat. But we Communists want to win this struggle with the least losses [note that he does not exclude the necessity for losses] and there is no doubt whatsoever that we shall win.[7]

Perhaps the best definition of peaceful coexistence by a Western student of the subject was given by Richard Allen, as follows:

Peaceful coexistence is to the Communists a *unilateral* strategic doctrine, which is imposed upon the "inevitably doomed" adversary through the combined inherent and physical "superiority" of the Communist system, and to which the adversary may only "respond" because he is denied a creative and participating role in determining its essence and application.[8]

This creative role of "peaceful coexistence" must be emphasized because the essence of peaceful coexistence is its revolutionary and aggressive nature, its commitment to total victory by whatever means are best suited under the given circumstances. These means include the use of armed force and nuclear blackmail whenever the Communists believe that the risks of such use are outweighed by the gains which may be achieved. The Cuban crisis, and any crises we may have in the future, are not necessarily aberrations from peaceful coexistence, but result merely from a specific application of this doctrine, perhaps sometimes unsuccessfully, in a given time and place. The remarkable thing about peaceful coexistence is that it is growing in complexity and sophistication to encompass almost anything the Soviets may want to do in pursuit of their goal of total global victory.

The most interesting development for the American lawyer and political scientist is the Soviet attempt to clothe peaceful coexistence in legal terms. The dean of Soviet space lawyers, Professor Yevgeniy Korovin, stated last April that

One of the consequences of Socialism's transformation into the decisive factor of international relations is that peaceful coexistence has gradually become an accepted principle of international law. Initially it was the expression of a peaceful "breathing space," but being a specific form of class struggle between Socialism and capitalism on an international scale, peaceful coexistence was filled with new content as the relation of world forces changed.[9]

[7] Nikita S. Khrushchev, Speech at the Soviet-American Hungarian Meeting, July 19, 1963, in Current Soviet Documents, Aug. 19, 1963, pp. 9, 13.

[8] Allen, *supra* note 5, at 33.

[9] Korovin, *An Old and Futile Demand*, International Affairs (Moscow), No. 4, at 100 (1963).

In an earlier address to the Advisory Council of the University of Moscow Law School in 1961, which first set forth the essence of the new international law of "peaceful coexistence," Professor Korovin stated that the time had come for Soviet international lawyers to wage what he termed an "offensive attack," that they should "proceed from our own concepts, from the democratic principles of international law, and then, having proclaimed their binding character and universality, to show that any theories hostile to them constitute a violation of the generally recognized and therefore generally binding principles of law. . . ."[10]

The implication for Soviet space law was clearly stated in the new Soviet space law symposium, as quoted earlier, that "every activity in outer space whatsoever which is incompatible with the principle of peaceful coexistence is illegal." If the task of peaceful coexistence is to ensure that communism triumphs over capitalism as quickly and as effectively as possible, the resistance which the non-Communist world may put up is basically contradictory to "law" and hence is "illegal."

II

Peaceful Cooperation

The second basic principle in Soviet space law, according to the introduction to the new Soviet space law symposium is "peaceful cooperation."[11] This principle has evoked considerable discussion among Soviet international lawyers because the initial dispute back in 1956 among Soviet and American international lawyers over "peaceful coexistence" arose from the the Soviet opposition to Western lawyers who wanted to replace the term "peaceful coexistence" with the term "peaceful cooperation." The Westerners preferred the term "peaceful cooperation" in order to portray the Western concept of increasing reliance on mutuality of interest in foreign affairs and to portray the idea that international institutions for conflict resolution should replace unilateral conflict management as the ordering element of international relations.

This problem received a thorough airing last year at the Sixth Annual Meeting of the Soviet Association of International Law. Movchan led off the discussion by a speech on the legal principles of peaceful coexistence, in which he reminded his listeners that the 1961 Program of the Communist Party of the Soviet Union foresees a real possibility that new principles put forth by socialism will triumph over the principles of aggressive imperialist states. He suggested that the codification of international law should serve to make the content of the existing principles and norms conform to the developmental laws of contemporary society, by which he meant the shift of the correlation of forces in favor of Communism. Movchan evoked considerable criticism by stating that the principle of friendly relations among states—and by implication "peaceful cooperation"—is the same as peaceful co-

[10] Korovin, *The Declaration of the Conference of Representatives of Communist and Workers' Parties and the Tasks of the Science of International Law* (in Russian), [1961] Vestnik Moskovskogo Universiteta 71-72. See also the discussion in Crane, *Soviet Attitude Toward International Space Law*, 56 Am. J. Int'l L. 685, 713 (1962).

[11] Zadorozhnyy, *supra* note 1, at 8.

existence. The critics, of course, objected that such a confusion of terms would ignore the character of the relationship of class warfare between the socialist and capitalist states. After all, as Zakharova had pointed out:

Contemporary international law, which regulates the relations both of socialist and capitalist states, does not require the establishment among such states of relations of broad and full cooperation and fraternal mutual assistance, because by virtue of the very nature of capitalist states such relations are impossible.[12]

The solution to this problem was suggested at the Sixth Annual Meeting of the Soviet Association of International Law by V. M. Koretsky, who is presently the Soviet judge in the United Nations' principal legal organ, the International Court of Justice. Mr. Koretsky pointed out, as indeed Mr. Tunkin had done himself on November 21, 1961, in the Sixth Committee of the United Nations, that the essence of peaceful coexistence as a doctrine must be distinguished from the principles of peaceful coexistence put forward as principles of international law. Koretsky stated that peaceful coexistence in its essence and intent is an historical category of class warfare, but that the legal principles put forth under the rubric of peaceful coexistence can permit compromises with capitalism to achieve agreements under specific circumstances to strengthen the peace, because "it is necessary to consider not only one's *intentions* but one's possibilities" at the present moment.

In effect Koretsky was reminding the Soviet international lawyers that Marxism distinguishes between strategy and tactics. The support of "peaceful coexistence" as a Communist term and "peaceful cooperation" as a term to use in dealing with the capitalists is quite consistent with the Leninist policy of dealing simultaneously with the proletariat and with the bourgeoise as explained in his treatise entitled *The Two Tactics of Social Democracy*. This technique is discussed both in Stalin's work, *Problems of Leninism,* and in the standard work on *Fundamentals of Marxism-Leninism,* the most recent edition of which was published last year.

The concepts of interdependence and supranational institutions, such as the United Nations and the International Court of Justice, which many Westerners consider to be basic elements and instruments of international cooperation, were attacked in the recent Zhukov symposium on space law, which specifically rejected the concept of a single global communications satellite system. They were also attacked at a recent Conference of International Lawyers in Moscow devoted to the discussion of legal order in a disarmed world. This conference, which was sponsored by the Commission on Legal Problems of Disarmament of the Soviet Committee on the Defense of the Peace, was reported in the October 1963 issue of *Soviet State and Law.* At this conference, Levin stated that as long as states of two different systems existed, international organizations with wide supranational powers would be impossible, because such organizations, as has been proven in the West, interfere with the internal affairs of states.

[12] Zakharova, *Bilateral Treaties of Friendship, Cooperation and Mutual Aid Among Socialist States* (in Russian), [1962] SOVETSKOYE GOSUDARSTVO I PRAVA, No. 1, at 80, 83 (1962).

103

The clearest Soviet statement on this problem is contained in an article by Solodovnikov:

It is stated that the development of the weapons of mass annihilation and the simplification of their manufacture will impel the two systems to seek points of "convergence" and agree to international inspection which will gradually grow into a "world government" placed above the still raging cold war.

This, it appears, is the end aim of "convergence," this is the path to salvation suggested by the apologists of capitalism.

The concept of a future in which capitalism and Communism will "converge" on an "equal footing" is Utopian through and through. *The time will come, of course, when there will be a world government, but it will be the government of a world Socialist community* in which there will be no place either for "free enterprise" or for the monopolies. Neither research nor the subtle sophisms of the apologists of capitalism can save it from the death predestined for it by history. . . .

Life will always smash the advocates of ideological compromises and their bleak illusions and attempts to find a "third way" in the struggle of the two systems.

Our Socialist world is definitely helping capitalism in one thing: *to dig its grave the more quickly.* Such are the facts of the *"fruitful"* competition of the two systems.[13]

Premier Khrushchev made this quite plain early this year when he stated that the Chinese Communists and the Soviet Communists had their disagreements on the correct line to follow during the present period, but that they both agreed that their basic policy was to bury capitalism. The Chinese and Soviets differ, and have since 1957, on the risks of nuclear escalation from certain types of expansionist moves and on the advisability of waiting until the Soviets could gain greater strategic power to reduce these risks.[14] They both look at international cooperation, however, as a tactic which can be used advantageously whenever it is called for by their respective strategic evaluations of the world situation.

One of the tactical uses which the Soviets make of their second basic space legal principle is indicated by the following statement of the Soviet representative to the U.N. Space Committee, Ambassador Platon Dimitrivich Morozov:

In any case in which discussion of international cooperation in any field takes place, it immediately becomes necessary to regulate the cooperation of the parties. Therefore, how is it possible to speak of international cooperation in space research if the foundation is not laid, if those principles are not established which are basic to this cooperation.[15]

The Soviets make international cooperation contingent upon regulation, and regulation contingent upon U.S. acceptance of the space legal doctrines advanced by the Soviet Union. The space legal doctrines of the Soviet Union are manipulated to support the strategic position of the Soviet Union and to undermine the legality and political acceptability of the national and international security policies of the

---

[13] Solodovnikov, *Speaking Different Languages,* International Affairs (Moscow), No. 11, at 46, 48-49, 52 (1963).

[14] This difference in revolutionary strategy is discussed in the author's article, Crane, *The Sino-Soviet Dispute on War and the Cuban Crisis,* 8 ORBIS 537-49 (1964).

[15] Verbatim Record of the Tenth Meeting, Committee on the Peaceful Uses of Outer Space, Sept. 10, 1962, at 61 (A/AC.105/PV.10).

United States.[16]   The Soviets have tried to drive home the propaganda charge that any U.S. opposition to Soviet space legal doctrines is contrary to the requirements of "peaceful cooperation."   By this tactic they are trying to brand the United States as an enemy of peace, and in turn to justify their own hostile activities.   The duplicity of the Soviet use of the term "peaceful cooperation" is well illustrated by the fact that the above quoted statement by Morozov was made on September 10, 1962, at the very time that the Soviets were suddenly and secretly establishing a strategic missile base in the heart of the Western Hemisphere 100 miles from the state of Florida.[17]

III

DISARMAMENT

The third basic principle of Soviet space law is "general and complete disarmament."   This principle is discussed in the new Zhukov symposium.   In his chapter entitled "Space Law as a Result of Technological Progress," M. I. Lazarev, who has for years been a principal interpreter of the interrelationship between Soviet military strategy and space law, states that "the most important goal in the development of space law will be the prevention of imperialist expansion and militarism in space."   He attacks the counterforce doctrines of Secretary of Defense McNamara, which are designed to limit any nuclear war, if one should break out, to military targets, in order to provide the maximum incentive for both sides to stop the war before it could spread to cities.   Soviet strategists oppose this doctrine primarily because it undercuts the Soviet use of the psychological threat that nuclear holocaust will be the inevitable result of any firm United States action against Communist expansionist moves.   The relationship of space law to Secretary McNamara's strategy consists in the fact that the American strategy of counterforce was made possible to a large extent by the perfection of space observation satellites which indicate with a still considerable degree of reliability where the military targets, such as ICBMs, are in the Soviet Union.   Lazarev warns that any attempt to legalize space observation satellites, or space interception and inspection, would lead to the creation of a Damocles sword hanging over mankind.   He states that this would result because the U. S. satellites [which in our view are in the nature of arms control satellites designed to prevent war] are launched, as he puts it, "to facilitate the unleashing of aggressive, so-called preventive war . . . against the socialist countries."[18]

[16] This manipulation of Soviet space legal doctrine is developed in detail in the author's article, Crane, *Soviet Attitude Toward International Space Law, supra* note 10.

[17] Analysis of Soviet negotiating tactics in the United Nations indicates that the obstructionist function of the unrealistic Soviet political demands in the U.N. disarmament committee is served in the U.N. space committee by the unrealistic Soviet preconditions for peaceful cooperation. It appears that recently the Soviets have started to mix their tactics by injecting some of their disarmament demands, such as the liquidation of foreign military bases, into the discussions in the U.N. Committee on the Peaceful Uses of Outer Space. See note 22 *infra.*

[18] Lazarev, *Space Law as a Result of Technological Progress* (in Russian), ZHUKOV, *op. cit. supra* note 1, at 163.

Lazarev states that space law and international space cooperation must be based on, and therefore are contingent upon, the prohibition of American military uses of space by the demilitarization and neutralization of outer space within the overall framework of what he calls "disarmament law."

This "disarmament law" had its genesis at the same time that the Soviets proclaimed the policy of "peaceful coexistence" during the mid-fifties. The Soviets attempt to provide a legal framework for their campaign for "general and complete disarmament" by interpreting the Charter of the United Nations to require the acceptance of the Soviet program of general and complete disarmament in order to fulfill the original goal of the United Nations, namely the creation of a world-wide system of collective security.

The Soviet writers on the law of disarmament, among whom the foremost is probably Mr. Bogdanov, base their attempt to create a new international legal principle of general and complete disarmament (GCD) on articles eleven and twenty-six of the United Nations Charter and on the unanimously approved Resolution 1378 of the Fourteenth Session of the U.N. General Assembly in 1959. Some Soviet jurists, among them Romanov, believe that neither articles eleven nor twenty-six create a legal obligation for GCD but merely provide jurisdiction for the U.N. General Assembly and Security Council over GCD. Most Soviet lawyers, including Tunkin and Bogdanov, admit that Resolution 1378, because of the nature of U.N. resolutions, cannot create a legal obligation. Therefore, the Soviets have embarked on a general campaign by their own efforts to create for their law of GCD the status of an accepted legal obligation.

They do this by insisting that the highest goal of mankind is the Soviet program for GCD and that this GCD therefore must be the original goal of the United Nations, though it was first announced as a Soviet foreign policy goal by Premier Khrushchev in 1959. Just as in their attempts to create an obligatory troika in the United Nations and in the International Court of Justice (an attempt which is repeated in the recent Zhukov space law book), the Soviets are attempting by their campaign of GCD to harness the entire United Nations and thereby the nations of the world to their own Soviet disarmament program.

The military advantages which the Soviets hope to gain from acceptance of its program of GCD are well known to disarmament negotiators. These derive mainly from the Soviet insistence on U.S. disarmament without the reliable inspection necessary to assure Soviet reciprocation; and from the Soviet insistence that in order to achieve GCD the United States must first agree to Soviet proposals to realign the power structure of the world under the guise of "reducing international tensions."

The first goal, i.e., U.S. disarmament, the Soviets hope to achieve by a psychological campaign designed to convince the peoples and leaders of the world that the future of mankind depends on American acceptance of disarmament without realistic inspection. This type of disarmament could result in unilateral disarmament of U.S. deterrent forces both through the voluntary destruction by the United States of its existing weapons and—more importantly—by the failure of the United States to modernize its weapons arensal. In a world of disarmament without realistic inspection, such a failure to modernize would permit the Soviets to win the technological arms race by getting a generation ahead in advanced weapons systems, particularly those which in the future may be most effectively used in outer space. This in turn would permit the Soviets in effect to force unilateral disarmament on the United States.

The nature of this Soviet goal has been explained by the Soviets often during the last half century and there is no evidence that this goal has changed. As early as 1916, Lenin stated: "Only after the proletariat has disarmed the bourgeoisie will it be able, without betraying its world historical mission, to throw all armaments on the scraphead." In 1928 the resolution of the Sixth World Congress of the Communist International emphasized that "The aim of the Soviet proposals for general and complete disarmament is to propagate the fundamental Marxian postulates that disarmament and the abolition of war are possible only with the fall of capitalism."

On January 6, 1961, Premier Khrushchev made the point that "The struggle for disarmament . . . is an effective struggle against imperialism." This struggle is also "an active struggle against imperialism," but above all it is an active struggle "for restricting its military potentialities."

On January 2, 1964, *Pravda* published the reply of Premier Khrushchev to the question, "What do you think should be done to ensure that atomic energy and the achievements of technology are used for the good of mankind." Khrushchev said: "The best solution of this problem is to get rid of all the social and national causes of the outbreak of any kind of war, a thing which can *only* be accomplished with the victory of socialism all over the world." It is noteworthy that one cannot accuse the Soviets of insincerity, because for those who take the trouble to study in detail Soviet policy on peaceful coexistence and disarmament, the Communists make it abundantly clear what they have in mind.

The second goal of the Soviet program of GCD which they have attempted to elevate to the level of international law is the requirement that prior to GCD the West must end the cold war. This was first put forth during the post-test ban period on November 8, 1963, when the Soviet Union circulated a proposed amendment to a resolution which would urge the Geneva disarmament conference in January 1964 to concentrate on tension reduction as a preliminary to disarmament. The Soviets wanted the United States to renounce the use of force *of any kind* in opposing Communist revolutions; to abandon its foreign bases and military commitments; to acknowledge Communist conquests, particularly in Central and Eastern Europe as permanent; and for good measure, to *help* the Communist world through trade, aid, and friendly relations to overcome its economic weaknesses and increase its political acceptability. Do all those things, say the Communists, and the cold war will end tomorrow. End the cold war and we can make progress on the most pressing problem of our time, namely general and complete disarmament.

The present complete impasse in Geneva on the agenda, I believe, indicates what the United States thinks of this abuse of the desires of the world for peace and security. The new Soviet "disarmament law" is of vital importance as a basic principle of Soviet space law because the use of the Soviet GCD bargaining game has become the story of our failure to reach any really meaningful agreements in this area.

I shall not go into a discussion of the specific principles of Soviet space law. These include "liability for damages to the interests of other states," and "freedom of outer space." The latter was discussed particularly clearly by Cheprov in the recent Soviet space law symposium and by the Hungarian representative to the United Nations Space Committee on December 3, 1963.[19] Suffice it to say that agreement on these principles is explicitly conditioned on U.S. acceptance of the Soviet concept of peaceful coexistence and of the Soviet program of GCD.

This is particularly true for one of the most important of all Soviet general principles of space law: demilitarization and neutralization of outer space.

Whereas the Soviets prior to 1962 advocated the adoption of a legal principle calling for the use of space for peaceful uses only—and by this they meant non-military purposes—this policy changed in 1962 to legalize military uses, and now has gone so far that the Soviets are beginning to designate even the attempt to inspect one of their military space satellites as an act of preventive war.

This Soviet policy of legalizing the military uses of space has been stated in increasingly plain terms by the Communist representatives to the U.N. Space Committee. On April 22, 1963, the Czechoslovakian delegate opposed the inclusion in a draft of space legal principles of a "provision prohibiting the use of outer space for war purposes." He added: "Practical implementation of . . . [article 2(4) of the Charter and operative paragraph 1(a) of the General Assembly Resolution 1721(XVI) on the peaceful uses of space] could be ensured only by the negotiation and conclusion of an agreement on general and complete disarmament."[20] On May 3, 1963, the Soviet representative stated that the Soviet Union had adopted what he called a "realistic approach to the question and considered that the problem of the prohibition of the military use of outer space could be solved only in the context of disarmament."[21]

The Soviet representative stated his position quite clearly in the First Committee during the discussion on International Cooperation in the Peaceful Uses of Outer Space, on December 2, 1963, as follows:

The draft declaration does not and could not, of course, deal with the matter of military uses of outer space. As the members of the Committee all know, the Soviet Union has often stated that it is prepared, within the framework of a program of general and

[19] Verbatim Record, U.N. First Committee, Dec. 3, 1963, at 28 (A/C.1/PV.1343).
[20] Summary Record of the Twentieth Meeting, U.N. Committee on the Peaceful Uses of Outer Space, Legal Subcommittee, April 22, 1963, at 9 (A/AC.105/C.2/SR.20).
[21] Summary Record of the Twenty-eighth Meeting, U.N. Committee on the Peaceful Uses of Outer Space, Legal Subcommittee, May 3, 1963, at 14 (A/AC.105/C.2/SR.28).

complete disarmament under strict international control [which is the standard Soviet jargon], to destroy all types of weapons. That would also solve the problem of prohibiting the use of outer space for military purposes. However, we did not agree and still do not agree with attempts to divorce the matter of the military uses of outer space from other measures of disarmament which are intimately linked to it. As has been stated many times, the question of the prohibition of the use of outer space for military ends is organically linked with the question of the liquidation of foreign military bases on the territory of other countries. It is quite clear that the question of the prohibition of the military uses of outer space can be solved only in the context of disarmament, with parallel and simultaneous liquidation of foreign military bases on the territory of other countries.[22]

This statement acquires particular importance because it is the first time since the Cuban crisis that the Soviet representatives in the U.N. Space Committee have tied the demilitarization of outer space to the abolition of U.S. military bases.

On December 5, 1963, the Ukranian delegate went even further and stated that:

The representative of the United States declared that the above mentioned agreements on space "should help to create the confidence needed here on earth for greater progress in disarmament and cooperation in all areas." Without challenging this statement, we nevertheless would like to stress that the main question is that of general and complete disarmament and it is upon *the way* in which this problem is solved that, to a large extent, hinges the solution of other unsolved problems.[23]

In other places the Soviet representatives made possibly ominous remarks to the effect that the wording of the agreement over which the United States was rejoicing was broad enough to encompass all of the original points (except the prohibition of private enterprise in space) which the Soviets had used for two years since the inception of the U.N. Space Committee to block all progress in the development of space law.[24] The clearest statement was made a year earlier, on December 10, 1962, during the post-Cuban detente by the Soviet representative who stated that the militarization of space could be overcome only by the "liquidation of the cold war," of course on Communist terms.

During the fall 1963 session of the U.N. Space Committee, Academician Blagonrarov commented on September 10, 1963 that after the test ban treaty "the Soviet delegation considers it essential once more to stress the importance of a com-

---

[22] Verbatim Record, U.N. First Committee, Dec. 2, 1963, at 41-42 (A/C.1/PV.1343).

[23] Verbatim Record, U.N. First Committee, Dec. 5, 1963, at 43-45 (A/C.1/PV.1345). (Emphasis added.)

[24] Provisional Verbatim Record of the Twenty-fourth Meeting, U.N. Committee on the Peaceful Uses of Outer Space, Nov. 22, 1963, at 51 (A/AC.105/PV.24). The provisional record includes the statement: "The draft includes the most important basic legal principles which, one way or another, were touched upon in the course of the work of our Committee and of the Legal Subcommittee. That is why, as has been stated here, the draft . . . will, we hope, meet the interests of all the Member States of the United Nations." In the Additional Report of the Committee on the Peaceful Uses of Outer Space, Nov. 27, 1963 (A/5549/Add.1), this wording was changed to read: "The draft includes important basic legal principles. . . ." On Dec. 2, 1963, the Soviet delegate used the following wording: "In it we find reflected most important fundamental legal principles which are mentioned in various guises during the discussion on this matter. Verbatim Record, U.N. First Committee, Dec. 2, 1963, at 37 (A/C.1/PV.1342).

plete solution of this question that prevents the arbitrary holding of space research and experiments. . . ."[25] Three days later, on September 13, 1963, he made the statement that the test ban treaty had "removed the possibility of harmful experiments in outer space *for the time being*."[26]

The most startling of all statements on the military uses of outer space ever made by a responsible Soviet citizen is contained in the introductory chapter of the Zhukov symposium on space law. Zhukov indicated, as he first did in August 1962,[27] that space observation is aggressive, but bombs in orbit are not. He stated that self-defense under article fifty-one of the U.N. Charter does not permit the interception of bombs in orbit because the mere presence of bombs in orbit does not constitute the necessary armed attack. He then proceeded to develop a new and remarkable principle of Soviet space law, namely that if a state finds out that the satellite of another country contains a nuclear bomb, any attempt to disable it would constitute an act of "preventive war." The strategic significance of this term consists in the fact that for the Soviets, knowledge of an impending preventive war is a legitimate cause for a just pre-emptive attack on the United States. This statement is undoubtedly designed as an attempt at psychological warfare to instill in U.S. readers the proper fear of nuclear escalation resulting from any American attempts at countermeasures, for example, through the explosion of a nuclear bomb in the vicinity of the bomb in orbit.

One of the reasons given for this new Soviet space legal principle is the difficulty, within the current state of the art, reliably to inspect space satellites. Zhukov states:

Under conditions where it is practically impossible to determine the character of the activity of a space apparatus, the recognition of the right of a state to capture the apparatus for inspection would be tantamount to the assertion of complete arbitrariness and lack of law in this new sphere of human activity. How would one have any guarantee that space ships with a cosmonaut on board following exclusively peaceful purposes would not be destroyed by a state which considered that it endangered its security.[28]

This reasoning is most interesting in view of the recent Soviet indication that the Soviets must push space military research and development and that "it is necessary to have suitable means of providing for the timely detection of space apparatuses of the enemy and for their rapid destruction or neutralization."[29] In

[25] Verbatim Record of the Twenty-first Meeting, U.N. Committee on the Peaceful Uses of Outer Space, Sept. 10, 1963, at 41 (A/AC.105/PV.21).
[26] Verbatim Record of the Twenty-second Meeting, U.N. Committee on the Peaceful Uses of Outer Space, Sept. 13, 1963, at 45-50 (A/AC.105/PV.22). (Emphasis added.)
[27] See Crane, *The Beginnings of Marxist Space Jurisprudence*, 57 AM. J. INT'L L. 615, 622 (1963).
[28] Zhukov, *The Legal Regime of Outer Space in the Contemporary Period* (in Russian), ZHUKOV, *op. cit. supra* note 1, at 33.
[29] V. D. SOKOLOVSKIY (MARSHAL OF THE SOVIET UNION) (ED.), VOYENNAYA STRATEGIYA (MILITARY STRATEGY) 395 (2d ed. 1963). The means which the Soviets may have in mind are indicated by another reference in this book which emphasizes the importance of electro-magnetic warfare for the "destruction or jamming of the electronic fuses of bombs and missiles by electronic radiation, and the interception of radio signals and generation of interference in the electronic equipment for aerial reconnaissance, navigation, bombing, and in-flight missile guidance." SOVIET MILITARY STRATEGY 337-38

other words, the Soviets are preparing for the interception and destruction of U.S. satellites but assert that similar action by the United States against Soviet satellites would be an act of preventive war.

CONCLUSION

This inconsistency is understandable only if one understands that the Soviets use international law not as a means to resolve and remove conflict, but rather to manage and direct conflict in the interests of Communist global expansion. The Soviets have orchestrated the manipulation of both legal and military doctrines so that they serve really as two sides of the same coin. They are merely two different aspects of the single discipline of conflict management. The principles of Soviet space law, including the three most basic principles of peaceful coexistence, peaceful cooperation, and disarmament, are fully understandable only within this framework of analysis.

<hr>

(translated and with analytical introduction and annotations by Herbert S. Dinerstein, Leon Goure & Thos. W. Wolfe, 1963). The Soviets are referring to electronic countermeasures to disable the circuitry of ICBMs passing through space and to de-trigger their warheads. In the revised edition of this book, published in August 1963, the Soviets also for the first time called attention to U.S. research in the military use of anti-gravitation, anti-matter, plasma and lasers. See *id.* 394, 405 (2d ed. 1963).

THE SOVIET VIEWPOINT ON NUCLEAR WEAPONS IN INTERNATIONAL LAW

PETER B. MAGGS*

. . . [T]he initiative in all ventures directed at limiting the miseries of warfare proceeds from Russia. . . . the history of missions accomplished by Russia for the good of all peoples convinces us, on the one hand, that the clarification of the basic principles of international law is one of the goals of Russian national policy, and on the other hand, that ultimately the ideas proclaimed by Russia will win general recognition. . . .[1]

INTRODUCTION

The Soviet Union, like Tsarist Russia before it, has consistently been in the forefront of the advocates of prohibiting or limiting the use of innovations in weapons of war.[2] The advantages of this policy have been twofold. First, it has created an image of love of peace and progress that has helped to counteract the unfavorable impression created by the reality of autocratic internal policy and pragmatic foreign policy. Second, the banning of advances in weaponry has served to help the nation retain its relative power position despite its technological backwardness.[3] The advent of nuclear weapons, followed by the emergence of the Soviet Union as the second super-power has complicated the application of this traditional Russian policy.[4] The Soviet dialecticians must reconcile the contradictions between Soviet inferiority to United States military might and Soviet superiority to the rest of the world;[5] beween the Soviet peace campaign and the implications of the possession of a nuclear arsenal.[6]

* A.B. 1957, LL.B. 1961, Harvard University. Assistant Professor of Law and Associate of the Center for Russian Language and Area Studies, University of Illinois. Member of the District of Columbia bar. Research Associate in Law and Associate of the Russian Research Center, Harvard University, 1963-64; exchange student, Leningrad State University, 1961-62. Contributor to legal periodicals.

[1] F. F. MARTENS, VOSTOCHNAIA VOINA I BRIUSSEL'SKAIA KONFERENTSIIA 1874-1878 G. [THE EASTERN WAR AND THE BRUSSELS CONFERENCE OF 1874-1878] 99 (1879).

[2] For a history of Russian and Soviet efforts in this area, see O. V. BOGDANOV VSEOBSHCHEE I POLNOE RASORUZHENIE (MEZHDUNARODNO-PRAVOVYE VOPROSY) [GENERAL AND COMPLETE DISARMAMENT (PROBLEMS OF INTERNATIONAL LAW)] 146-65 (1964). Galenin, K istorii voprosa o zapreshchenii varvarskykh sposobov vedeniia voiny [Toward the History of the Problem of Prohibition of Barbaric Means of Waging War], SOVETSKOE GOSUDARSTVO I PRAVO [Soviet State and Law; hereinafter cited as SGP], 1953, No. 1, p. 74, contrasts the Russian approach with American reluctance to adhere to treaty limitations on means of waging war.

[3] A frank discussion of the motives of Nicholas II's arms control initiatives may be found in WITTE, I VOSPOMINANIIA; TSARSTVOVANIE NIKOLAIA II [MEMOIRS; REIGN OF NICHOLAS II] 143 (1922).

[4] Stalin saw the necessity of combining the traditional Russian policy with an active weapons development program. In 1946 he stated: "Of course the monopoly of the possession of the secret of the atomic bomb creates a threat, but there are at least two answers to it: (a) the monopoly of the possession of the atom bomb cannot last long; (b) the use of the atomic bomb will be prohibited." Pravda, Sept. 25, 1946, p. 1, col. 5.

[5] For statistics as to American superiority, see address by President Johnson at the United States Coast Guard Academy, N.Y. Times, June 4, 1964, p. 27, col. 2.

[6] For a detailed history of Soviet nuclear weapons development, see ARNOLD KRAMISH, ATOMIC ENERGY

I

The Military Use of Nuclear Weapons

Both Soviet weapons policy and Soviet theory of international law form an integrated whole; thus any breakdown for analytical purposes is of necessity artificial. However, a beginning must be made somewhere; an abstract statement that nuclear weapons are legal or illegal means nothing. The question must be put whether or not a given action at a given place and time with respect to these weapons is legal. This article will first discuss the Soviet approach to legal problems connected with the military use of nuclear weapons, and then discuss their testing, construction, possession, stationing, transit, and transfer.

Soviet statements on the military use of nuclear weapons present on the surface a startling dichotomy. Official Soviet spokesmen clearly imply that the Soviet Union is prepared to use nuclear weapons for a variety of military purposes if the need arises and do not intimate that they consider such use unlawful. The Soviet United Nations delegation and Soviet legal scholars, on the other hand, consistently speak and write of the illegality of the use of nuclear weapons.

Soviet civilian and military leaders have been quite explicit about the situations in which they would use their country's nuclear weapons. Both former Chairman Khrushchev and leading Soviet military figures have repeatedly stated that the U.S.S.R., if attacked with nuclear weapons, will reply in kind. In an article published in the Soviet government newspaper, *Izvestiia,* Marshal Sudets, commander-in-chief of Soviet air defense forces, claimed that the Soviet Union had nuclear-armed anti-missile missiles, with which it could destroy attacking missiles before they reached Soviet targets.[7] In a newspaper interview published in September 1961, Khrushchev stated that either side "would undoubtedly use nuclear weapons" if it felt it was losing in a conventional war unleashed by the "imperialists."[8]

The official manual of naval law published in 1956 by the Soviet Ministry of Defense gives tacit approval to the legality of the use of nuclear weapons against military targets. In its discussion of forbidden weapons, it not only refrains from stating that the use of nuclear weapons is illegal, but specifically points out that no international convention banning their use in time of war exists.[9] In contrast, aerial bombardment of cities with nuclear weapons is condemned specifically in a later section of the book.[10] The textbook of international law published in 1964 and officially approved for use in Soviet law schools also refrains from any direct statement that the military use of nuclear weapons is illegal.[11]

IN THE SOVIET UNION (1959). A chronology of Soviet nuclear test explosions is given in N.Y. Times, July 26, 1963, p. 8, col. 5.

[7] Izvestiia, Jan. 5, 1964, p. 2, col. 1.

[8] N.Y. Times, Sept. 8, 1961, p. 11, col. 2; Pravda, Sept. 10, 1961, p. 3, col. 2.

[9] Voenno-morskoi mezhdunarono-pravovoi spravochnik [Naval International Law Handbook] 291 (Bakhov ed. 1956).

[10] Id. at 326.

[11] Mezhdunarodnoe pravo [International Law] 647-48 (Kozhevnikov ed. 1964).

In apparent contrast is the position taken by the Soviet Union in the United Nations and by Soviet legal scholars in their unofficial writings. The Soviet Union voted for the General Assembly resolution of November 24, 1961, declaring that the military use of nuclear weapons is illegal.[12] Soviet legal scholars, instead of developing theoretical justifications for their country's avowed intent to use nuclear weapons in certain circumstances, have unanimously affirmed that the military use of nuclear weapons is illegal. These scholars, including such leading authorities as Bogdanov,[13] Durdenevskii,[14] Korovin,[15] Romashkin,[16] and Trainin,[17] are thus in accord with the vast majority of non-Soviet jurists who have written on this issue.[18] The arguments used by the Soviet jurists are essentially the same as those used by their non-Soviet colleagues.[19] O. V. Bogdanov, Senior Research Associate of the Institute of State and Law of the Academy of Sciences of the U.S.S.R. puts them as follows:[20] the use of nuclear weapons violates the "Martens clause" of the Preamble to the IVth Hague Convention of 1907;[21] Article 23(d) of the Annex to the Convention; Article 23(a) of the same Annex; the customary international law principle of the prohibition of the direction of military activities against the peaceable civilian populace; the Geneva Convention of 1949 on the Protection of Civilian Persons in Time of War;[22] the Hague Convention of 1954 on the Protection of Cultural Property in the Event of Armed Conflict;[23] and the Geneva Protocol Concerning Gas and Bacteriological Warfare of 1925.[24] Bogdanov, like other Soviet authors, views the use of "tactical" nuclear weapons as being just as illegal as the use of "strategic" nuclear weapons.[25]

[12] U.N. Doc. No. A/RES/1653 (XVI) (1961). The history of the Soviet effort to obtain such a declaration is chronicled in BOGDANOV, op. cit. supra note 2, at 191-203.

[13] BOGDANOV, op. cit. supra note 2, at 165-91.

[14] Durdenevskii & Shevchenko, Nesovmestimost' ispol'zovaniia atomnogo oruzhiia s normani mezhdunarodnogo prava [The Incompatibility of the Use of Atomic Armament With the Norms of International Law], SGP, 1956, No. 5, p. 38.

[15] Korovin, Atomnoe oruzhie i mezhdunarodnoe pravo [Atomic Armament and International Law], Mezhdunarodnaia zhizn' [International Affairs], 1955, No. 5, p. 48.

[16] P. S. ROMASHKIN, VOENNYE PRESTUPLENIIA IMPERIALISMA [THE WAR CRIMES OF IMPERIALISM] 129 (1953). This work, which was written before Stalin's death and published soon thereafter, was ordered withdrawn from Soviet bookstores sometime before the end of 1955. V. N. BRUK, ALFAVITNYI SPRAVOCHNIK USTAREVSHIKH IZDANII [ALPHABETICAL HANDBOOK OF OBSOLETE PUBLICATIONS] 242 (1960). The reason for its suppression may have been that its violent anti-Americanism was considered unsuitable in view of the "peaceful coexistence" campaign. See Borisov & Khaliuta, Book Review, Kommunist [Communist], 1954, No. 10, p. 119.

[17] Trainin & Morozov, Podgotovka i propaganda atomnoi voiny—tiagchaishee prestuplenie protiv chelovechestva [Preparation and Propaganda of Atomic War—The Most Serious Crime Against Humanity], Kommunist [Communist], 1955, No. 8, p. 95.

[18] Exhaustive bibliographic citations and summaries of the views of writers on the subject are given in EBERHARD MENZEL, LEGALITÄT ODER ILLEGALITÄT DER ANWENDUNG VON ATOMWAFFEN (1960).

[19] E.g., NAGENDRA SINGH, NUCLEAR WEAPONS AND INTERNATIONAL LAW (1959); Russian translation with introductory article by O. V. Bogdanov published under the title IADERNOE ORUZHIE I MEZHDUNARODNOE PRAVO (1962); but see GEORG SCHWARZENBERGER, THE LEGALITY OF NUCLEAR WEAPONS (1958).

[20] BOGDANOV, op. cit. supra note 2, at 165-91.

[21] 36 Stat. 2277; T.S. No. 539.

[22] [1955] 3 U.S.T. & O.I.A. 3516; T.I.A.S. No. 3365; 75 U.N.T.S. 240.

[23] 249 U.N.T.S. 240.

[24] 94 L.N.T.S. 65.

[25] BOGDANOV, op. cit. supra note 2, at 178-79.

Article I of the limited test ban treaty of 1963 pledges the parties "not to carry out any nuclear weapon test explosion, or any other explosion" in the prohibited environments.[26] In the hearings on the treaty held by the Senate Foreign Relations Committee, some Senators expressed the fear that this phrase would be interpreted to prohibit the use of nuclear weapons in time of war.[27] This argument has not been made in any of the Soviet writings on nuclear weapons that have come to the attention of this author. Indeed, Soviet authors would have little reason to make this argument, since in their view the military use of nuclear weapons was illegal even before the signing and ratification of the test ban treaty. It is somewhat surprising that none of the legal arguments presented to the Foreign Relations Committee (in open session, at least) mentioned the fact that all Soviet legal scholars and many non-communist legal scholars were of the opinion that the use of nuclear weapons in war was already forbidden by international law.

Both the Soviet-supported General Assembly resolution of November 24, 1961, and the writings of Soviet legal scholars fail to elaborate upon the implications of the proposition that the military use of nuclear weapons is illegal. No answer is given to such crucial questions as whether or not such weapons may be used in reprisal (a) against a nuclear attack or (b) against an attack with conventional weapons which constitutes aggression in violation of the United Nations Charter, questions which have been given considerable attention by non-Soviet writers.[28] A few words are devoted to this problem in a 1957 article in the authoritative political weekly, *New Times*, by N. Arkadyev, who is apparently not a lawyer. He argues against the legality of the use of nuclear weapons as a reprisal against aggression, pointing out that a claim of aggression may be used to cover an aggressive intent.[29]

On closer examination the split between the statements of Soviet government leaders and official legal sources on the one hand, and the position of the Soviet United Nations delegation and the legal scholars on the other hand, is more apparent than real. The vague principle of the illegality of nuclear weapons can coexist peaceably with the clear statements of the Soviet generals and politicians preserving their freedom of action in those situations where a credible threat of the use of nuclear weapons is needed. Soviet legal scholars, by refraining from discussing the use of nuclear weapons in retaliation or self-defense, are able to maintain an over-simplified position, which will not stand close examination, but has undoubted appeal to world public opinion. In addition, this approach allows any legal scholars who are opposed to their government's announced position of being the first to use

[26] Treaty Banning Nuclear Weapons Tests in the Atmosphere, in Outer Space and Under Water, Aug. 5, 1963, T.I.A.S. No. 5433.
[27] *Hearings on Executive M Before the Senate Committee on Foreign Relations*, 88th Cong., 1st Sess. 76-78, 175-79, 201-02 (1963).
[28] One legal scholar mentions the problem, but fails to elaborate on it. A. N. TRAININ, ZASHCHITA MIRA I BOR'BA S PRESTUPLENIIAMI PROTIV CHELOVECHESTVA [THE DEFENSE OF PEACE AND THE STRUGGLE WITH CRIMES AGAINST HUMANITY] 211 (1956). The views of non-Soviet writers are summarized in MENZEL, *op. cit. supra* note 18 at 56-68.
[29] Arkadyev, *Nuclear Weapons and International Law*, New Times, 1957, No. 4, p. 9.

nuclear weapons in certain circumstances,[30] but are afraid to speak out on the subject, to maintain their integrity by silence.

II

THE PEACEFUL USE OF NUCLEAR WEAPONS

In the early stages of their country's nuclear weapons program, Soviet spokesmen placed great emphasis upon the peaceful nature of the uses to which these weapons were to be put.[31] However, once the Soviet Union achieved substantial nuclear capabilities, this approach was dropped, and the military nature of the Soviet nuclear stockpile was frankly admitted.[32] More recently, Khrushchev denounced American projects for the peaceful use of nuclear explosions as a cover for weapons development.[33] Article II of the 1962 Anglo-American draft test ban treaty contained a provision allowing nuclear explosions for peaceful purposes.[34] Apparently at the insistence of Soviet negotiators, this provision was deleted from the treaty approved in 1962. Article I of this treaty prohibits explosions causing "radioactive debris to be present outside the territorial limits of the state under whose jurisdiction or control such explosion is conducted." The effect of this provision is to make impossible the implementation of most previous proposals for the peaceful uses of nuclear explosives. Soviet efforts also were apparently responsible for the insertion in the 1959 Antarctic Treaty of clauses prohibiting peaceful use and testing.[35]

III

THE TESTING OF NUCLEAR WEAPONS

Both official and unofficial Soviet spokesmen have condemned testing of nuclear weapons by the United States as illegal. A Soviet government statement published in June, 1962, condemned United States high altitude tests in strong terms:[36]

. . . the United States Government does not stop and has no intention of stopping at the grossest violations of the elementary norms of international law, which prescribe that states must take the interests of all other states into account in their actions in international affairs.

[30] See the statements cited above, notes 7 and 8.
[31] KRAMISH, op. cit. supra note 6, at 121-53.
[32] Id. at 129-32.
[33] N.Y. Times, Sept. 8, 1961, p. 11, col. 1; Pravda, Sept. 10, 1961, p. 3, col. 1.
[34] Anglo-American Proposal Submitted to the Eighteen Nation Disarmament Committee: Draft Treaty Banning Nuclear Weapons Tests in the Atmosphere, Outer Space, and Underwater, Aug. 27, 1962, printed in UNITED STATES ARMS CONTROL AND DISARMAMENT AGENCY, DOCUMENTS ON DISARMAMENT 1962, 804, at 805 (1963).
[35] S. V. Molodtsov, Dogovor ob Antarktike [The Antarctic Treaty], SGP, 1960, No. 5, p. 64 at p. 68; see generally Kucherov, Sowjetische Ansprüche in der Arktis und Antarktis, 6 OSTEUROPA-RECHT 123 (1960); compare United States Circular Note Regarding Antarctica, May 3, 1958, 2 U.S. DEP'T OF STATE, DOCUMENTS ON DISARMAMENT 1945-1959, at 1020 (1960), with the Antarctic Treaty, Dec. 1, 1959, arts. I and V, [1961] 1 U.S.T. & O.I.A. 794; T.I.A.S. No. 4780; 402 U.N.T.S. 71.
[36] Pravda, June 4, 1962, p. 1, col. 1.

Soviet legal theorists have gone a step further, and have proclaimed that all American, British and French atmospheric tests have been illegal.[37]

Criticism has centered upon the United States hydrogen bomb tests in the Pacific. The legal objections to these tests were not originated by Soviet jurists. Rather they were first advanced by the parties injured in the United States Pacific test of a thermonuclear device in 1954.[38] As a result of American miscalculations, a number of the inhabitants of the Trust Territory of the Marshall Islands and a number of Japanese fishermen were injured by fallout from this test. The resulting protests made by Japan to the United States and by the islanders to the United Nations Trusteeship Council were quickly supported by both Soviet official spokesmen and Soviet legal commentators. It is interesting to compare the Soviet writings on this subject with the debate on the same topic published in the *Yale Law Journal* in 1955.[39] Professor Margolis opened that debate with the arguments against the tests that were later adopted by the Soviet jurists: the proclamation of closed zones for testing infringes upon the freedom of the seas; the use of the Trust area as a test site violates the agreement under which the United States holds the Marshall islands in trust; the intentional pollution of the sea and air with radioactive fallout violates a developing rule of international law which forbids actions of this type which do harm to other states. Professor McDougal and Mr. Schlei, replying, went extensively into the history of the trusteeship agreement to deny that it limited United States freedom to test. Their main argument, however, is the most interesting, for a mirror image of this argument has been used by Soviet lawyers to support Soviet testing while condemning American testing. McDougal and Schlei argue that the rules of international law are flexible and must be determined in the light of the policy interests involved. They state:[40]

The claim of the United States is in substance a claim to prepare for self-defense. . . . a claim to take certain preparatory measures under conditions comparable to those traditionally held to justify measures in self-defense. It is a claim to take certain actions in contiguous zones and upon the high seas, with the minimum possible interference to others, under conditions of high necessity. . . . As expectations of imminent violence in the world arena have become ever more realistic and intense, many of the nations of the free world have organized themselves . . . into regional groupings for their more effective self-defense. The United States has undertaken its program of atomic and thermonuclear weapons development to ensure that these coalitions of free nations are not lacking in retaliatory power which may deter aggression or in weapons of self-defense if deterrence fails.

[37] *E.g.*, Usachev, *Moskovskii dogovor o chastichnom zapreshchenii ispytanii iadernogo oruzhiia i mezhdunarodnoe pravo* [*The Moscow Treaty on the Partial Prohibition of the Testing of Nuclear Weaponry and International Law*], SGP, 1964, No. 3, p. 72 at p. 73.

[38] For the history of this incident and its legal repercussions, see Margolis, *The Hydrogen Bomb Experiments and International Law*, 64 YALE L.J. 629 (1955); McDougal & Schlei, *The Hydrogen Bomb Tests in Perspective: Lawful Measures for Security*, 64 YALE L.J. 648 (1955).

[39] *Supra* note 38.

[40] McDougal & Schlei, *supra* note 38, at 686.

Three Soviet scholars, who have written in detail on the subject of the legality of nuclear testing, Judge Koretskii,[41] O. V. Bogdanov,[42] and I. G. Usachev,[43] have relied upon many of the arguments presented by Professor Margolis to demonstrate the illegality of American hydrogen bomb tests in the Pacific. However, when faced with the difficult question of how to justify continued Soviet testing in view of the harm done by radioactive fallout, the Soviet authors fall back upon arguments that are just the reverse of those used by McDougal and Schlei. I. G. Usachev, for instance, states:[44]

. . . and if the Soviet government, for the purposes of strengthening the defense of the U.S.S.R. and the other countries of the socialist system, carried out nuclear tests, this was done in answer to the actions of the Western powers, which forced it to do so.

Thus, before the limited test ban pact was signed, all Soviet and some American commentators took a view which tied the legality of testing to national policy interests, effectively limiting international law restraints upon their own government's actions, while leaving the way open for the imposition of such restraints upon others.

The signing of the limited test ban treaty in 1963 has lessened, though by no means eliminated, the importance of the question of the legality of atmospheric testing under general international law. Two nuclear powers, France and China, have not acceded to the treaty. The most thorough Soviet discussion of the legal implications of the test ban treaty concentrates on the problem of China.[45] The author of that discussion pointedly quotes Khrushchev's statement, "There has been a sort of world wide plebiscite of governments, political parties and leading statesmen on the question of who is for lessening international tension and who is against."[46] Clearly aimed at China is that author's quotation of the Declaration of the 1960 Conference of Communist and Workers' Parties with respect to the necessity of achieving a nuclear test ban.[47] He does not, however, go so far as to state that a Chinese nuclear test would be a violation of international law.

Soviet legal scholars have presented little worthy of note in their analysis of the legal implications of the test ban treaty itself. O. V. Bogdanov's study, discussed in the preceding paragraph, is largely descriptive. I. G. Usachev, in a short article, makes only two arguments of any interest. He suggests that a state which conducts

---

[41] Koretskii, K voprosu o protivopravnosti ispytanii termoiadernogo oruzhiia v otkrytom more [Toward the Question of the Illegality of Testing Thermonuclear Weapons on the High Seas], Izvestiia vyshikh uchebnykh zavedenii; Pravovedenie [News of Higher Educational Institutions; Jurisprudence], 1957, No. 1, p. 100.

[42] O. V. BOGDANOV, IADERNOE RAZORUZHENIE [ATOMIC DISARMAMENT] 133 (1961); Bogdanov, Pravovye voprosy prekrashcheniia iadernykh Ispytanii [Legal Questions ot the Cessation of Nuclear Testing], SGP, 1959, No. 7, p. 51.

[43] Usachev, supra note 37.

[44] Id. at 75.

[45] BOGDANOV, op. cit. supra note 2, at 212-16.

[46] Id. at 213.

[47] BOGDANOV, op. cit. supra note 2, at 215. For the text of the Declaration, see N.Y. Times, Dec. 7, 1960, pp. 14-17.

atmospheric testing in violation of the treaty should be liable for damages caused by fallout, pointing to the United States *ex gratia* payment to Japan for injuries caused by its 1954 test as a precedent.[48] Secondly, he ties in the clause in the preamble to the treaty which reads, "Proclaiming as their principal aim the speediest possible achievement of an agreement on general and complete disarmament under strict international control in accordance with the objectives of the United Nations," with the theory expounded by a number of Soviet international lawyers of the existence of a positive legal duty upon all states to agree to complete and general disarmament.[49]

IV

THE CONSTRUCTION AND POSSESSION OF NUCLEAR WEAPONS

It is clearly in the interest of the United States, the Soviet Union and the world as a whole to prevent the attainment of nuclear weapons capabilities by countries now lacking them. Obvious dangers, along with possible benefits, are presented by any scheme to give such weapons to international organizations. It is therefore not surprising that an important aim of Soviet foreign policy has been the prevention of the spread of nuclear weapons. Nor is it surprising that the Soviet Union has sought to capitalize upon public aversion to the spread of nuclear weapons by accusing the United States of planning to give control of such weapons to the Federal Republic of Germany. In view of these facts, the restraint of Soviet international lawyers in condemning the spread of nuclear weapons is remarkable; their failure to develop workable concrete proposals for preventing such spread is regrettable.

Soviet legal scholars have never suggested that absent treaty restraints mere possession or construction of nuclear weapons is illegal, though, as mentioned above, there has been considerable discussion of an alleged legal obligation upon all nations to agree to complete and general disarmament. Of the specific treaty restrictions, which apply only to the former Axis powers and their allies, Soviet statements and legal writings have emphasized only the ban on construction of nuclear weapons by West Germany[50] and the severe restrictions of the Austrian state treaty.[51]

Generalizing from the provisions of the latter treaty, which clearly binds Austria not to construct or possess nuclear weapons, Soviet scholars have enunciated the principle that possession of nuclear weapons by a permanently neutral state

---

[48] Usachev, *supra* note 37, at 76.

[49] *Id.* at 77-78. See generally BOGDANOV, *op. cit. supra* note 2, at 217-32. Romanov, *Vseobshchee i polnoe razoruzhenie i mezhdunarodnoe pravo* [*General and Complete Disarmament and International Law*], 1960 SOVETSKII EZHEGODNIK MEZHDUNARODNOGO PRAVA [THE SOVIET YEARBOOK OF INTERNATIONAL LAW; hereinafter cited as SOV. YB. INT'L L.] 80 (1961).

[50] Korovin, *Mezhdunarodnoe pravo i atomnoe vooruzhenie FRG* [*International Law and the Atomic Armament of the German Federal Republic*], Mirovaia ekonomika i mezhdunarodnye otnosheniia [World Economics and International Relations], 1958, no. 10, p. 76.

[51] May 15, 1955, art. 13 [1955] 2 U.S.T. & O.I.A. 2360; T.I.A.S. No. 3098; 217 U.N.T.S. 223.

is prohibited by international law. Professor Durdinevskii and G. A. Osnitskaia, writing in the leading Soviet legal journal in 1960, presented the argument that possession of nuclear weapons is incompatible with a status of permanent neutrality, as contradictory to the ideas of peace and cooperation that form the basis of that status.[52] Nor, they argued, are atomic weapons suitable for defensive purposes, considering the inevitable results of atomic war upon the small territory of the three permanent neutrals—Austria, Switzerland, and Cambodia.[53] Furthermore, they argued, these small countries could not obtain atomic weapons without foreign aid, and such aid would inevitably come with strings attached that would compromise their neutrality.[54] The theory was polished a little more in a shorter version of the same article which appeared the next year in the *Soviet Yearbok of International Law* under Durdenevskii's name alone.[55] This version emphasized peaceful coexistence and added a paragraph explaining why the Soviet Union needed nuclear weapons while neutral nations did not.[56]

The function of the Soviet legal scholar in this case appears to have been that of an advocate, developing the detailed legal argument for a previously announced government position. A TASS announcement published in August 1958 had strongly protested the Swiss decision to produce atomic weapons and had suggested that the decision was in conflict with the neutral status of Switzerland.[57] Then in 1959 and 1960, the legal scholars presented the detailed arguments discussed above.

Some statements by Khrushchev in 1958 formed the starting point for an article by the same G. A. Osnitskaia which suggested a much broader concept of atomic neutrality that would apply to neutralist nations and nations in atom-free zones.[58] However, Soviet scholars have not developed this idea of atomic neutrality under international law.

The Soviet Union has consistently opposed the possession of nuclear weapons by the United Nations both now and in a possible disarmed world of the future. In the initial debates on the establishment of a United Nations military force, the U.S.S.R. found itself in agreement with all of the major powers except the United States that such a force, if established at all, should be a weak one.[59] The Soviet delegate to the Security Council made the quasi-legal argument that any United

---

[52] Durdenevskii & Osnitskaia, *Neitralitet i atomnoe oruzhie* [*Neutrality and Atomic Armament*], SGP, 1960, No. 2, p. 101.

[53] *Id.* at 104.

[54] *Id.* at 104.

[55] Durdenevskii, *Neitralitet i atomnoe oruzhie* (*v svete printsipa mirnogo sosuschchestvovania*) [*Neutrality and Atomic Armament (In Light of the Principle of Peaceful Coexistence)*], 1960 Sov. YB. INT'L L. 105 (1961).

[56] *Id.* at 107.

[57] *Pravda*, Aug. 9, 1958, p. 2, col. 5.

[58] Galina, *Problema neitraliteta v sovremennom mezhdunarodnom prave* [*The Problem of Neutrality in Modern International Law*], 1958 Sov. YB. INT'L L. 200 (1959). According to Robert Crane, "Galina" is a pseudonym for "Osnitskaia." Crane, *Soviet Attitude Toward International Space Law*, 56 AM. J. INT'L L. 685, 689 n.12 (1962).

[59] BERNARD G. BECHHOEFER, POSTWAR NEGOTIATIONS FOR ARMS CONTROL 95-97 (1961).

Nations military force should be composed "on the basis of the principle of equal contributions."[60] Since at the time of this debate only the United States was in a position to contribute atomic weapons, equal contributions meant no contribution of such weapons.

The proposals that have been advanced in this country to allow possession of nuclear weapons by a United Nations peace-keeping agency in a disarmed world were attacked in a Soviet review of Grenville Clark and Louis Sohn's book, *World Peace Through World Law*.[61] The reviewer argued that the retention of such weapons contradicted the principle of complete and general disarmament.[62]

V

THE STATIONING AND TRANSIT OF NUCLEAR WEAPONS

The Soviet Union participated actively in the negotiation and adoption of the one clear ban upon the stationing and transit of nuclear weapons, that contained in the unanimous General Assembly resolution of October 17, 1963 against stationing nuclear weapons in outer space.[63] It also gave its support to the General Assembly resolution of November 24, 1961, which called upon member states to "refrain from using the territory, territorial waters or air space of Africa for testing, storing, or transporting nuclear weapons."[64] The Soviet Union has also supported many other proposals for denuclearized zones, but with the exception of the outer space resolution, none of these has been acceptable to the United States.

It seems appropriate to discuss here Soviet doctrine with respect to the legal force of General Assembly resolutions. Some Soviet writers state that such resolutions are merely recommendations; this was the view taken in an article published in the January 1964 issue of the Soviet journal *International Affairs* with specific reference to the 1961 United Nations resolution against the use of atomic weapons.[65] Professor G. I. Tunkin, legal advisor to the Soviet Foreign Ministry, goes somewhat further, stating that General Assembly resolutions adopted by a unanimous vote or with the concurrence of the major world power groups can operate as stages in the development of rules of international law.[66] Other writers, in particular Minasian, would give binding force to such resolutions if they were "democratic" and "directed in the interests of peace" and if they "corresponded to the general principles

---

[60] U.N. SECURITY COUNCIL OFF. REC. 2d year, 149th meeting 1177 (S/PV 149) (1947).

[61] Vasiliev, *Book Review*, SGP, 1961, No. 5, p. 159.

[62] See above, note 49.

[63] U.N. Doc. A/C.1/L.324 [A/RES/1884 (XVIII)], quoted in 49 DEP'T STATE BULL. 754 (1963). See generally Zhukov, *Iadernaia demilitarizatsiia kosmosa* [*Nuclear Disarmament of Outer Space*], SGP, 1964, No. 3, p. 79.

[64] U.N. Doc. A/RES/1653 (XVI) (1961).

[65] Lvov, *Disarmament Problems in the U.N.*, International Affairs (Moscow), 1964, No. 1, p. 18, at p. 21; *accord*, P. I. LUKIN, ISTOCHNIKI MEZHDUNARODNOGO PRAVA [SOURCES OF INTERNATIONAL LAW] 118-24 (1960).

[66] G. I. TUNKIN, VOPROSY TEORII MEZHDUNARODNOGO PRAVA [PROBLEMS OF THE THEORY OF INTERNATIONAL LAW] 134 (1962); *accord*, Kozhevnikov in MEZHDUNARODNOE PRAVO [INTERNATIONAL LAW] 43 (Kozhevnikov ed., 1964).

of international law."[67] The last-mentioned view, which in effect would allow Soviet spokesmen to pick and choose among General Assembly resolutions, is probably more in accord with the general trend of the Soviet science of international law.

A similar tendency to use selected arguments in favor of the Soviet position is found in studies of the legal status of foreign bases, a problem closely related to the stationing of nuclear weapons. A number of arguments are advanced to explain why American and British bases are illegal, while Soviet bases are legal. The basic point made by many writers is that NATO, CENTO, and SEATO are illegal because their purposes are aggressive.[68] Judge V. M. Koretskii gave the more detailed arguments that were to become standard in an article published in 1953:[69] the bases are a violation of the sovereignty of the states upon whose territory they are situated; they are meant for uses contrary to the principles of the United Nations Charter; the keeping of bases on United Nations Trust Territories violates trust obligations under Article 76 of the United Nations Charter; the maintenance of bases in West Germany and Japan violates the Cairo and Potsdam declarations; the keeping of bases in Taiwan violates a decision of the Cairo conference.

The Warsaw Pact and the stationing of Soviet troops and weapons in the countries of Eastern Europe are, on the other hand, declared by Soviet spokesmen and scholars to be entirely legal and proper. Unlike the non-Communist alliances, they argue, the Warsaw Pact Organization is a truly regional organization with only defensive goals. It is, they say, therefore quite different from NATO which stretches from the United States to Turkey, and whose treaty provides for military aid to non-signatories.[70]

The Soviet and the American treatment of the legal problems raised by the Soviet Union's stationing of nuclear missiles in Cuba in 1962 and the apparently successful American effort to have them removed are worthy of consideration as illustrations of some of the major similarities and differences in approach to questions of international law.

Both sides recognized the importance of appealing to world public opinion with simple slogans related to principles of international law, though of course the slogans chosen were different. Thus the United States labeled the missiles "offensive" weapons,[71] while the Soviet Union called them "defensive."[72] The

[67] N. M. MINASIAN, ISTOCHNIKI SOVREMENNOGO MEZHDUNARODNOGO PRAVA [SOURCES OF MODERN INTERNATIONAL LAW] 112-32 (1960).
[68] M. I. LAZAREV, IMPERIALISTICHESKIE VOENNYE BAZY NA CHUZHIKH TERRITORIAKH I MEZHDUNARODNOE PRAVO [IMPERIALIST MILITARY BASES ON FOREIGN TERRITORY AND INTERNATIONAL LAW] 117-20 (1963).
[69] Koretskii, Sozdanie amerikanskikh voennykh baz na chuzhikh territoriakh—narushenie norm mezhdunarodnogo prava [The Creation of American Bases on Foreign Territories is a Violation of the Norms of International Law], SGP, 1953, No. 6, p. 120.
[70] MEZHDUNARODNO-PRAVOVYE FORMY SOTRUDNICHESTVA SOTSIALISTICHESKIKH GOSUDARSTV [INTERNATIONAL LAW FORMS OF COOPERATION OF SOCIALIST STATES] 99-162 (Shushalov ed. 1962).
[71] Radio-Television Address by President Kennedy on the Cuban Crisis, October 22, 1962, 47 DEP'T STATE BULL. 715 (1962); Letter From the United States Representative (Stevenson) to the President of the Security Council (Zorin) on the Cuban Crisis, October 22, 1962, 47 DEP'T STATE BULL. 724

American naval action was called a "quarantine" by the President of the United States; a "blockade," "piracy" and "aggressive" by Soviet spokesmen.[73] Both sides also used more detailed legal arguments, the case for the United States being presented at length by the Office of the Legal Adviser.[74]

The greatest difference between the American and Soviet treatment of the legal problems came in the area of unofficial comment. In the United States, some unofficial commentators upheld the legality of the use of a threat of force to stop Soviet weapons shipments,[75] while others questioned the legality of the American measures.[76] There are no Soviet scholars in a position analogous to that of the law professors who contributed unofficial views in the United States, for all Soviet legal scholars work in institutions and publish in journals controlled by the Soviet party-government establishment. While Soviet authors have repeatedly made clear that their views do not represent those of the Soviet government or Communist Party, they do not in practice differ publicly with official foreign policy or condemn government actions as illegal under international law. The best analogy in United States experience to Soviet scholarly legal writings is found in articles published by United States government lawyers with a disclaimer clause to the effect that "the views expressed herein are those of the individual author and do not necessarily represent the position of his department or of the United States Government." Such authors, like Soviet scholars, are free to discuss questions of international law not settled by official government statement. However, they, like their Soviet counterparts, are subject to many limitations, and do not in practice accuse their government of violating international law. It is appropriate, therefore, to compare the articles on the Cuban crisis published under disclaimer clauses by United States Navy specialists in international law[77] with an article by a Soviet legal scholar dealing with the same subject.[78]

Both the American and Soviet articles start with the question of the justification of the United States action in the light of the principle of the freedom of the seas and the limitations placed upon the use of force by article 2 of the United Nations

(1962); United States Draft Resolution Submitted to the Security Council: Removal of Soviet Missiles From Cuba, October 22, 1962, 47 DEP'T STATE BULL. 724 (1962).

[72] Message From Premier Khrushchev to President Kennedy, October 27, 1962, 47 DEP'T STATE BULL. 741 (1962); Message From Premier Khrushchev to President Kennedy, October 28, 1962, 47 DEP'T STATE BULL. 745 (1962).

[73] Kennedy, supra note 71, at 716; Soviet Government Statement, N.Y. Times, Oct. 24, 1962, p. 20, col. 2.

[74] Chayes, The Legal Case for U.S. Action in Cuba, 47 DEP'T STATE BULL. 764 (1962); Chayes, Law and the Quarantine of Cuba, 41 FOREIGN AFFAIRS 554 (1963); Meeker, Defensive Quarantine and the Law, 57 AM. J. INT'L L. 515 (1963).

[75] E.g., Larson, Letter to the Editor, N.Y. Times, Nov. 12, 1962, p. 28, col. 5.

[76] E.g., Wright, The Cuban Quarantine, 57 AM. J. INT'L L. 546 (1963).

[77] Christol & Davis, Maritime Quarantine: The Naval Interdiction of Offensive Weapons and Associated Matériel to Cuba, 1962, 57 AM. J. INT'L L. 525 (1963); McDevitt, The U.N. Charter and the Cuban Quarantine, 17 JAG J. 71 (1963).

[78] Kolodkin, Morskaia boklada i sovremennoe mezhdunaródnoe pravo [Naval Blockade and Contemporary International Law], SGP, 1963, No. 4, p. 92. See also Korovin, International Law Through the Pentagon's Prism, International Affairs (Moscow), Dec. 1962, p. 3.

Charter. The American authors then go on to discuss in detail the possible justifications for the United States action: that the United States was acting in accordance with its right of self-defense under article 51 of the United Nations Charter or that there was a legitimate regional action under article 52. The Soviet writer condemns the American naval action as an illegal interference with the freedom of the seas and a violation of article 2 of the United Nations Charter, but completely ignores the questions presented by the legal arguments which have been put forth in favor of the United States. Here, as in the case of the question of the legality of the use of nuclear weapons in reprisal against aggression, Soviet international lawyers have refused to enter into a dialogue with their American colleagues, preferring bold arguments that might appeal to legally unsophisticated readers to close analysis of the problems involved.

The proposal to station nuclear weapons on merchant ships to form a multilateral nuclear force has also been attacked as illegal by a Soviet spokesman. Admiral of the Fleet S. Gorshkov, Commander-in-Chief of the Soviet Navy, argues in an article published in May 1963[79] that according to one of the Hague Conventions on the Laws of War,[80] the use of such rocket launchers disguised as merchant ships would be classified as "brigandage at sea, as piracy which undermines the principle of freedom of the high seas." He goes on to say, "International law allows the destruction of pirate ships and the capture of pirates regardless of their citizenship and the bringing of them to legal responsibility. The Soviet Navy will use its legal rights arising from the Hague Convention."

VI

THE TRANSFER OF NUCLEAR WEAPONS

Since most states are unable to develop their own nuclear weapons because of lack of raw materials, monetary resources, and technical experts, and in view of the limitations of the test ban treaty, restrictions on the transfer of nuclear weapons are crucial to the prevention of their spread. There is no evidence to indicate that the Soviet Union has ever transferred nuclear weapons to any other country. It is less clear whether or not it has ever agreed to make such a transfer. According to a statement of August 15, 1963 by the government of the Chinese People's Republic, a Sino-Soviet agreement on new defense technology of October 15, 1957 bound the Soviet Union to deliver "models of an atomic bomb and technical documents for its production" to China. However, according to the same Chinese statement, the Soviet Union broke this agreement on June 20, 1959.[81] There is no indication in

---

[79] Izvestiia, May 19, 1963, p. 3, col. 1, at col. 4; *Current Digest of the Soviet Press*, June 12, 1963, p. 26 (condensed translation).

[80] Admiral Gorshkov is apparently referring to the Convention for the Adaptation to Maritime Warfare of the Principles of the Geneva Convention of July 6, 1906, Oct. 18, 1907, 36 Stat. 2731, T.S. No. 543 and/or the Convention Concerning Bombardment by Naval Forces in Time of War, Oct. 18, 1907, 36 Stat. 2351, T.S. No. 542.

[81] Statement by the Spokesman of the Chinese Government, Aug. 15, 1963, Peking Review, Aug. 16, 1963, p. 7, at p. 14.

the Chinese statement as to whether or not any nuclear weapons or related technical information were transferred between the dates of the alleged making and breaking of the agreement. However, the Soviet reply to this Chinese statement implies that the U.S.S.R. has not given China any atomic bombs.[82]

The Soviet Union has been cautious in the transfer of control over fissionable material to other countries. Its grants have been of such limited size and nature that they could not form the basis of a significant program of nuclear weapons development in any of the recipient countries.[83]

Despite the obvious interest of the Soviet Union in preventing the spread of nuclear weapons, and the importance of the legal question presented by the Chinese allegation, Soviet legal writers have not developed any theoretical basis for the limitation of such transfers.

Conclusions

All major powers have long made use of the concepts of international law in their international public relations activities. Since Stalin's death the Soviet leadership has become increasingly aware of the importance of such concepts in the formation of world public opinion. Using legal arguments, it has gained considerable popular support for some of its policies: restraining the United States from using nuclear weapons in local wars, ending Pacific H-bomb tests, and restricting American foreign bases.

However, the U.S.S.R. suffers from a great handicap in the use of international law. This handicap rests in the tight restrictions upon the views which its international law specialists may express in public. As a result of these restrictions, statements by its legal scholars, however sincere and objective, are regarded with suspicion. Furthermore, the leadership runs the risk of conditioning its legal advisors to a way of thinking which will prevent them from giving candid evaluations of legal problems even in private.

Soviet international lawyers are by no means alone in viewing international law as an instrument of government policy to be used, distorted, or discarded as the situation may demand. So long as there is no tribunal with ultimate jurisdiction over questions of international law, we may expect governments, those in their service, and many outside their service to proclaim the invariable legality of their country's foreign policy actions. The Soviet Union thus has little to gain in the struggle to influence world public opinion by forcing its legal scholars to join the ranks of government advocates, for their arguments will be met with equally able counterarguments.

However, while recognizing the fact that the main task of Soviet international law scholars is to defend the foreign policy interests of the U.S.S.R., we should not forget

[82] Izvestiia, Aug. 22, 1963, p. 1, col. 2, at p. 2, col. 6; Current Digest of the Soviet Press, Sept. 18, 1963, p. 8, at p. 10.
[83] Ginsburgs, Soviet Atomic Energy Agreements, 15 International Organization 49 (1961).

that Soviet and American interests often coincide with one another and with the interests of mankind as a whole. No thinking person wants a major nuclear war, wants nuclear weapons to spread, or wants to suffer from the fallout of unlimited testing. There thus remain many areas in which cooperation with Soviet jurists may be possible and constructive in the interests of world peace and security.

THE ECONOMIC CONTENT OF SOVIET TRADE WITH THE WEST*

Leon M. Herman†

I

The U.S.S.R. As a Commercial Power

The observer who follows the activities of the Soviet Union as a commercial power is plagued by a special kind of occupational insecurity. He often has the uneasy feeling that he may be looking at the object of his investigation through the wrong end of the telescope. What worries him, of course, is the all too obvious fact that somehow his own observations do not quite seem to tally with the findings of the rest of the community of scholars who are studying the same terrestrial entity through their own specialized scientific instruments.

Thus, for example, the student of Soviet international trade finds that the U.S.S.R. fails to turn up in his observations anywhere in the front rank of commercial powers. Although the Soviet Union is today unmistakably the second largest economy in the world, as a trading nation it turns up somewhere between France and Canada, *i.e.*, at a considerable distance behind the world's three leading commercial powers.

Broadly measured, by the total value of their exports (in billions of dollars), the score for the five principal trading nations was as follows in 1963: for United States, 23.4; for West Germany, 14.6; for the United Kingdom, 11.4; for France, 8.1; for the U.S.S.R., 7.3.

Measured by a more specialized yardstick, namely by the prime industrial component of these exports, *i.e.*, the amount of machinery and equipment placed into world trade channels, the U.S.S.R. recedes still further away from the front rank of trading powers, falling behind both Italy and Japan. The Soviet Union, which is known to be the second largest producer of machinery in the world, exported in 1962 only slightly over one billion dollars' worth of machinery and transport equipment to all destinations, within as well as outside the Soviet Bloc. Six other industrial nations exported a larger amount of machinery and equipment.

Much to his surprise, too, the observer finds that the Soviet Union turns up, instead, as the second largest importer of machinery among the trading nations of the world. This makes it necessary, by the rules of the game, to classify the U.S.S.R.

* A paper delivered before the Conference on "The Soviet Impact on International Law," held at Duke University on February 28-29, 1964. The views expressed herein are those of the author and are not to be attributed to the Legislative Reference Service or to the Library of Congress.

† B.A. 1932, Long Island University; M.A. 1935, University of Chicago. Specialist in Soviet Affairs, Legislative Reference Service, Library of Congress; Adjunct Professor, The American University; Consultant to The Rand Corporation.

as a net importer of machinery, by a ratio of nearly two to one. ($2.5 billion imports as against $1.4 billion exports.)

Another basic characteristic, which has the effect of reducing the influence of the U.S.S.R. on the world market at large, is the fact that Soviet trade in general, as well as its trade in industrial products in particular, is largely confined to a fixed circle of trade partners, namely to the dozen or so states that profess the same political philosophy. As measured by their ruble value, seventy per cént of all Soviet foreign trade transactions are conducted within the confines of the Communist Bloc; this intra-bloc trade absorbs five of the total $7 billions worth of exports.

As a result, the Soviet Union comes into the world market at large annually to exchange about $2 billion worth of goods. With this limited volume of merchandise at its diposal, the U.S.S.R. falls into the category of such lesser lights among the major trading nations as Sweden and Switzerland; in fact somewhere between the former and the latter.

As far as the non-Communist nations are concerned, therefore, the contribution made by the Soviet Union to their foreign trade in the course of any recent year, measured in aggregate terms, amounts to less than two per cent.

We cannot, however, ignore the fundamental fact that the Soviet Union functions in the world market as the leading member of an integrated commerical bloc of nations who follow a common trade policy. Hence, the impact exerted upon the world of commerce is generally recognized to be a regional impact. The problem of trading with the U.S.S.R. does, in fact, tend to be viewed by every nation, or group of nations, as inseparable from the issue of trading with the Soviet-dominated region as a whole. Translated into dollar terms, therefore, we have to augment the $1.8 billion worth of Soviet export commodities by another $2.3 billion, representing the export total, and the purchasing power, of the countries of Eastern Europe.

Here, it may be noted with some interest, we have another telescopic effect—in reverse again. The volume of trade of the three main political components of the Communist Bloc seems to be inversely proportional to the size of their population: China has been importing only some 0.7 billion dollars' worth of merchandise from all non-bloc sources in recent years.

II

THE IMPACT OF SOVIET BLOC TRADE ON OPINION WITHIN THE WEST

The plain economic fact that the Soviet Bloc as a whole is only modestly, one might say cautiously, engaged in foreign trade, especially with respect to the outside world, has not, however, prevented this trade from looming up as a subject of considerable controversy within the West. It is not, of course, a new controversy. The two protagonists in the debate, namely the United States and Western Europe, parted ways on this issue sometime in 1954, the year in which the post-Stalin leadership in Russia returned in force, so to speak, to the markets of Europe. Since then, the two components of the Atlantic Community have followed a divergent course of policy toward the trade of the Soviet Union and its allies. Over the intervening years, this difference in outlook has merely picked up some added conviction, in the measure as the nations of West Europe have gained in economic strength and self-confidence.

It goes without saying that our respective attitudes, on the two sides of the Atlantic, have developed within dissimilar climates of public opinion and under the impact of a different record of experience so far as the markets of the Soviet Bloc are concerned. We can easily recognize, to begin with, that there is one fundamental factor at work among the democratic allies on both sides of the Atlantic Ocean. In all cases, of course, these are free societies in which the policies evolved by their governments tend to be the kind of policies that the public of each country will support. We must assume, therefore, that their trade policies are no exception.

A. The Prevailing U.S. Attitude Toward East-West Trade

Under the influence of our own public opinion, we in the United States have kept ourselves largely aloof of the trade overtures which the Soviet leadership has made towards the West since the end of the Stalin era. We have tended to be more concerned with the political hazards inherent in the expansion of trade across the Iron Curtain than with the potential economic advantages. We have felt no strong economic pressure to accommodate ourselves to the principle of "business as usual" in our trade policy toward a coalition of states that follow an avowedly hostile policy against ourselves and our allies.

Our own experience during the past ten years, moreover, has persuaded us that we have not suffered any serious economic damage by keeping our commodity trade with the Soviet Bloc under a tight check-rein of security controls. As far as our commercial interests are concerned, Eastern Europe is, after all, far away, geographically as well as economically. Its prime export commodities—chiefly raw materials, mineral fuels, and foodstuffs—are of little interest to our importers. Hence, the dollar value of our imports has tended to hover around a figure in the tens of millions of dollars, as against the hundreds of millions of dollars of imports arriving annually from Eastern into Western Europe. In 1962, for instance, the actual figures were: $79 million imported from East Europe into the United States; $2,527 million into Western Europe. From Russia, in particular, we imported $16 million worth of commodities in the same year, while each of the four leading West European trading nations imported between one and two hundred million dollars' worth of merchandise.

B. The General Response of Western Europe to Trading With the Soviet Bloc

The West Europeans, who are normally joined by Japan on this issue, are generally disposed in favor of more or less normal relations with the U.S.S.R. and its allies in the sphere of trade. They tend, therefore, to minimize the political hazards inherent in trading with the Communist countries on an extensive scale, provided that such trade is understood to exclude highly strategic commodities. The reasons for their more favorable disposition are purely economic, and rather easy to identify. By comparison with the United States, these countries, without exception, are far more dependent upon external trade. This may be illustrated by the fact that the United States imports annually a volume of goods that is equal to some three per cent of its gross national product. By contrast, in the case of the countries of West Europe who are in the forefront in world trade—the United Kingdom, France, West Germany, and Italy—the value of their annual imports makes up seventeen, eleven, fourteen, and twelve per cent, respectively, of their national product. For countries like Belgium and the Netherlands the proportions are still higher, namely thirty to thirty-five per cent.

It needs also to be borne in mind, too, that the nations of Western Europe are more aware, economically, then we are of the markets of the East. This is simply a matter of old-fashioned economic complementarity. On that basis, there has long been in existence a steady and active exchange of goods between the West and the East on the European continent. In this exchange, the Eastern half has always been able to earn substantial purchasing power in the West by means of its traditional export of raw materials, such as timber, sawn lumber, pulpwood, plywood, coal, coke, crude oil, fuel oil, metal ores, flax, cotton, foodstuffs and furs. In foodstuffs alone, for example, the West imported over $500 million worth of merchandise from the East in 1962; in crude materials, $550 million; in mineral fuels, $450 million. The Western half of this exchange also has a long tradition behind it. The appetite of the East European countries for finished products from the Western half of the continent, especially industrial machinery, has been very strong and active for a matter of decades.

To this should be added the highly relevant fact that the manufacturers of West Europe are generally more outward-looking in their sales promotion than are their counterparts in this country. Their typically small domestic economies tend to place a high premium on keeping in constant touch with any and all potential foreign outlets. Given the narrow capacity of their internal markets, they view this as a kind of insurance against the ever present danger of under-utilization of existing capacity. Because of this pressing need for substantial external sales, the national governments of these countries are also, for their part, extremely reluctant to interfere in the normal activities related to trade promotion, except, of course, under conditions of imminent danger of war; or, as at the present, with respect to a limited list of war-related export commodities.

Then, too, the West European nations are, as a general rule, deficient in low-cost domestic raw materials and foodstuffs. Accordingly, they must function economically as the workshop to the rest of the world. This is reflected, for example, in the high proportion of machinery and other finished products (seventy-eight per cent) in the composition of their exports. In the light of this particular pressure, they operate on the assumption that their best markets are to be found in the countries undergoing rapid industrial development. The countries of Eastern Europe, of course, represent this kind of market. As the trade record shows, some two-thirds of all of West Europe's exports to the Soviet Bloc ($1.3 out of $2.0 billion) fall within two broad groups of merchandise, namely machinery (including vehicles) and manufactured goods.

It has long been a matter of some surprise to the American observer of West European commercial practice that despite the fact that a high proportion of their exports to East Europe consist of advanced types of machinery, the Western manufacturers do not seem to be particularly concerned over the Soviet habit of importing advanced models of production equipment as prototypes, with the purpose of copying in mind. It seems that they have learned from decades of experience that by the time a new model of a machine is fully copied by the Russians and placed into serial production there, this model has already been superseded by one or more newer versions of the same product. As a result, the West Europeans indicate that they see in this practice, if anything, a rather effective, if unintended, way of building a systematic lag into sectors of the production system of the countries of East Europe.

At the same time, the West Europeans are too experienced and sophisticated a group of nations to allow their economies, or their trade, to become seriously dependent upon the markets of the Soviet Bloc. As a matter of fact, they have not, and this may be demonstrated quantitatively. Thus, for example, even in the case of the two nations that are most actively involved in trading across the Iron Curtain at present, West Germany and Italy, their exports to the entire Communist Bloc account for less than six per cent of all exported merchandise. For Western Europe, as a whole, the relevant percentage has remained at about 4.5 per cent for the past several years.

Still another significant fact that needs to be taken account of in this connection is the unique system of state trading employed by the countries of East Europe. This, too, serves as a source of effective pressure upon their trading partners in the Western half of the continent. Thus, while it is true that as a trading area the Communist Bloc is in itself not large enough to exercise any serious economic influence either upon the total external commerce or upon the general economic level of the Western countries, individual commercial transactions of the kind that are typically offered by the Communist-ruled states, especially by the U.S.S.R., are often large enough to produce a strong impact upon the business community of the individual Western nation. This becomes less surprising when we recall that one order of such magnitude may make the difference between a profitable and a middling year for an individual business firm in the West. Again, it is worth noting that a transaction of the same size would not necessarily cause the same splash in the capacious domestic market of the United States.

Taken together, those elements of commercial self-interest add up to a complex of pressures in favor of trading with the East which no national government within these societies has in the past been willing or able to resist.

III

The Economic Realities of East-West Trade

The present dialogue within the Atlantic community on the subject of East-West trade is certainly as timely as it is necessary. Thus far, however, our dialogue seems to be proceeding under a rather serious handicap, namely without the benefit of any clear and precise knowledge of the economic content of this trade. There seems to be very little awareness in our intra-Western discussions of precisely what kind of commodities are being exchanged between the Western and the Communist halves of the European continent. As a result, most of the terms in which the present Western dialogue across the Atlantic is conducted have become largely irrelevant to the current realities of East-West trade.

Thus, for example, there is not much point in continuing to argue about this trade as if it were largely an operation by means of which the Soviet Bloc allows the Iron Curtain to be parted from time to time in order to bring in some odds and ends of Western products or materials needed to help build up the military potential of the U.S.S.R. The plain fact is that East-West trade today is not this kind of an exercise at all. If anywhere, the Soviet Union is manifestly self-sufficient in the realm of military production. Moreover, if and when it does come up against a missing ingredient in this sphere of production, as we know from past experience, the Soviet military high command does not choose to rely on the overt commercial channel to make good the deficiency. There is very little leverage, therefore, that we can exert against the military component of the Soviet economy through the flow of commodity trade. The basic Soviet determination to generate a volume of military production that is heavily out of proportion to the available supply of resources and prevailing level of productivity of the Soviet economy is a fact of life over which we are not, we must admit, in any position to exert a direct influence. At the same time, as we will try to show at a later point, this determination in itself is important because it lies at the root of many of the current observable shortages within the Soviet economy.

It is equally unrealistic, we submit, to view with alarm the present exchange of commodities in East-West trade as an operation in which the countries of Western Europe are running the risk of developing a dangerous degree of economic dependence on the markets of the East. If this were true, it would indeed make Western Europe vulnerable to the arbitrary will of the Communist strategists who could, whenever it suited their purpose, sever the commercial lines of communication across the Iron Curtain. The current economic content of East-West trade, however, does not point to any observable degree of dependence on the part of the Western nations. To begin with, all the goods exported by Western Europe to the Soviet Bloc add up to some 4.5 per cent of their global exports; the proportion on the import side, as may be expected, is of the same order of magnitude. Furthermore, from the standpoint of the types of commodities involved, it is fair to say that there is not a single category of import goods now being received from East Europe for which there are not available ready and adequate replacements in the non-Communist world. Even in the much publicized case of petroleum products, the sobering fact to bear in mind is that Western Europe at present draws less than ten per cent of its total imports from the Soviet Bloc.

It is generally recognized, therefore, that as far as the Western European countries are concerned, the principal pull of the markets of the East comes from the export side of their trade interests. The countries of Soviet Europe interest them primarily as an outlet for the products of their highly developed, expanding, and surplus-producing industrial plants. They look upon Eastern Europe as an area that represents a rather permanent outlet for the great variety and volume of their manufactured products, especially for commodities in the vast category of industrial machinery. At present, for example, the exportation of machinery and transport equipment from the countries of Western Europe to those of Eastern Europe comes to an annual figure of $750 million. What is more, this figure has been growing steadily in recent years. At the same time, manufactured products other than machinery, valued at another $600 million, have also been shipped out annually by the producers of Western Europe to the markets of the Eastern half of the continent.

Yet, it is important to stress that as far as Western Europe is concerned, these sales do not bear the mark of a distinctive dependence upon the unique requirements of the Soviet Bloc. They do, to be sure, represent an extremely valuable additional outlet for current sales. This, in turn, has the effect of reducing the pressure of surpluses upon the economies and the price levels of the exporting countries. To this extent, of course, West European exports to Eastern Europe help to solve important short-term, quantitative problems. But there is no evidence that this market represents a specialized, qualitative outlet for Western manufacturers. Thus, for example, most observers would agree that an expansion in the capacity of any other market, either at home or anywhere abroad, would provide a fully acceptable substitute in the sense that it could easily take up the slack created by the loss of outlets in Eastern Europe.

For the countries of the East, on the other hand, the specific economic content of their trade with the West is of a much higher order of significance. In the first place, it absorbs a far more substantial proportion of their total trade. For the U.S.S.R., as well as for the Bloc as a whole, the nations of the industrial West account for eighteen per cent of all trade transactions. As a proportion of total trade, therefore, East-West trade is four times as large for the Eastern as it is for the Western group of trade partners.

Viewed in commodity terms, the East European countries display a far more impressive degree of specific localized dependence upon the industrial countries of the West. As exporters of raw materials (minerals, forests products, and farm commodities), they find their most natural and ready outlet among the nations that represent the largest concentration of processing industries in the world. At the same time, the goods they export are in no sense unique raw materials. Nor are the quantities involved significant. The West, for example, managed quite well without Soviet petroleum before 1955. Now, after a major Soviet export effort, the petroleum it markets in Western Europe add up to something like eight per cent of the region's imports from all sources. To the U.S.S.R., on the other hand, the market of Western Europe represents forty per cent of the entire volume of its petroleum exports.

Clearly, however, the heart of the matter, so far as the countries of the East are concerned, is to be found on the import side of their trade with the West. They obviously attach enormous value to the access it affords them to the abundant reservoir of industrial products represented by these diversified, demand-sensitive economies. This is for them a distinctive, precise, and responsive source of supply for which there is no substitute either within the Bloc or in any other segment of the world economy.

To begin with, Western Europe has proven itself to the hilt as an ever abundant source from which the East can, and does, help itself to compenate for the periodic shortfalls in production that are characteristic of its centrally and imprecisely planned economies. In recent years, however, the economic contribution made by the West, via the channels of trade, has revealed a new dimension. The U.S.S.R. in particular has begun regularly to turn to the industrial West for advanced models of production equipment in a variety of fields. This particular type of importation has been undertaken in a systematic effort to modernize selected branches of the domestic civilian economy. The fact that the West has served as an increasingly useful reservoir of industrial prototypes can be demonstrated quantitatively as follows: machinery and transport equipment now account for forty-seven per cent of all Soviet imports from the Industrial West, as compared with thirty-one per cent in 1958.

SOVIET IMPORTS OF MACHINERY FROM THE INDUSTRIAL WEST

Year	Millions of Dollars	Percent of total imports from these countries
1958	194.1	31.2
1959	293.9	38.8
1960	456.4	42.7
1961	469.8	43.2
1962	596.0	47.1

To the regular observer of the Soviet economic scene, the present large-scale Soviet intake of chemical equipment from the West with a view to modernize the domestic industry is not in any sense a novel departure; it is only the latest, most advertised manifestation of a settled Soviet policy of industrial modernization through the importation of prototypes. The fact is that within the past decade, as shown by the record, the U.S.S.R. has turned to the West for new ideas and techniques, via selected

U.S.S.R. IMPORTS OF MACHINERY AND TRANSPORTATION EQUIPMENT
FROM THE INDUSTRIAL WEST IN 1962

Item	Millions of Current U.S. Dollars 1962
Machinery and Transport Equipment, Total[a]	596.0
Metal cutting tools	15.8
Power generating and electrical equipment	28.2
Crushing and grinding equipment	12.4
Rolling mill and foundry equipment	2.9
Food and light industry equipment	89.9
Food industry	58.8
Chemical industry equipment	88.4
Pulp and paper industry equipment	141.2
Industrial fittings	12.4
Professional scientific and controlling instruments and apparatus	13.9
Railway vehicles	3.2
Motor vehicles and parts	2.5
Ships and marine equipment	144.1
Other	11.6
Unspecified	29.3

a. Because of rounding, components may not add to the totals shown.
Source: FOREIGN TRADE OF THE U.S.S.R. IN 1962 (in Russian) Moscow. 1963.

imports, in such diverse fields as electric locomotives, merchant ships, marine engines, tankers, fishing trawlers, truck tires, textile machinery, synthetic rubber, man-made fibers, oil-pipe machinery, cement mills, and paper production equipment.

Moreover, the whole course of the East-West commodity exchange over the past ten years has demonstrated beyond any doubt that the pattern of procurement followed by the U.S.S.R. has been something more than a mere adjustment to passing shortages that have tended temporarily to befall its rapidly expanding domestic economy. On the contrary, this procurement has displayed all the earmarks of a studied method on the part of Soviet planners to employ imported Western innovations as a compensation for the structural failure of the economic system of the U.S.S.R., along with the rest of the Soviet Bloc, to develop new technical ideas along the entire spectrum of industrial production.

While this is a calculated method for absorbing important innovations, it is nevertheless not an easy or a pleasant choice for the Soviet planners to make, nor for their political superiors to approve. They simply have no choice in the matter. There are no other means at hand by which to bridge the wide gaps that continue to persist in the U.S.S.R. with respect to such categories as newly-developed products, new processes, new materials, or research talent for the advancement of the productivity of civilian economy across the board. It is generally agreed among outside observers, moreover, that these gaps will continue to plague the Soviet leaders as long as they remain committed to the scheme of resources allocation which they follow at present, namely the kind that will generate a variety and modernity of military production that is palpably out of proportion to the magnitude and productivity of the domestic industrial plant.

The above brief review of the economic content of East-West trade would seem to warrant the conclusion that the U.S.S.R. derives from this exchange a variety of benefits that are both unique and seminal in terms of economic diversification. It enables the U.S.S.R. to maintain a pipeline between the West and the East by means of which new ideas, processes and market-tested results are fed into the Soviet industrial plant. There is no doubt that this represents an important long-range political advantage of a kind that Moscow is not likely to under-value.

Does it follow from the above that the nations of West Europe, for their part, have been drawn into a one-sided commodity exchange in which all perceivable long-term advantages are on the other side? Is this an exchange in which the West is dissipating its superior resources in innovation? The weight of the evidence, it seems to us, is against any such harsh judgment. The nations of Western Europe, it must be said at the outset, have, after all, consistently kept their commodity exchange with the East within reasonable quantitative bounds, somewhere near four per cent of their total world commerce. It needs also to be recalled that Western Europe has regularly withheld from the Bloc a list of goods jointly classified as of likely strategic importance to the military potential of the nations on the other side of the Iron Curtain. The list has not been as comprehensive as the United States would have liked. But it is a roster of critical goods based on the West's own assessment of the practical hazards inherent in this trade. What is more, the withholding of goods on this small strategic list is known to have been strictly enforced. To this should be added still another fact, namely that the Western countries have been able, in their exchange with the East, to pursue and strengthen their traditional role in the international division of labor, ever widening, in fact, the range of their specialization in the export of advanced production equipment.

Quite apart from the above, however, the West European trading nations have achieved an effect of exceptional political importance. By following their natural bent toward trading with all comers in time of peace, these nations have succeeded in building up among the economies of the East a significant and continuing dependence upon the tested industrial techniques and products of the West. By means of this remarkable utility, they may have built up some sort of modest economic deterrent against any reckless line of international action on the part of the production-minded politicians of the Soviet camp.

All in all, the experience of the past ten years should have demonstrated to the Soviet leadership the valid proposition that under present conditions of rapidly moving technological change, economic modernization can only be maintained within the setting of a cooperative enterprise. Any nation today that wants to continue to benefit from the explosion of new technical ideas cannot afford to live in isolation. The plain fact is that no nation can reasonably count on having encompassed within its own boundaries enough resources in risk capital, enough ingenuity, or enough "breaks" to develop all the improvements in productivity that could possibly enable it to share fully in the benefits flowing from the main stream of technical innovations. Today, it is quite clear, only the society that opens its doors full and wide to welcome all technological influences from abroad can truly keep up with the movement of social and economic progress. The Soviet leaders have obviously not yet arrived at the acceptance of the idea that progress is indivisible. Perhaps, however, they could be nudged in that direction.

APPENDIX TABLE 1

EXPORTS FROM THE WEST TO EASTERN EUROPE

(In million U.S. Dollars)

Products	From the United States				From Western Europe			
	1959	1960	1961	1962	1959	1960	1961	1962
TOTAL EXPORTS.....	89.1	193.3	133.0	124.8	1,366.6	1,727.0	1,910.0	2,087.8
Food and live animals....	35.5	103.9	36.7	50.8	111.3	116.5	127.2	178.9
Beverages and tobacco...	1.4	2.8	1.9	1.5	34.1	30.1	34.5	27.4
Crude materials inedible, except fuels..........	20.8	25.2	32.4	38.1	150.0	160.6	172.9	160.5
Mineral fuels, lubricants and related materials.............	—	.1	.3	.1	1.1	3.2	3.0	3.6
Animal and vegetable oils and fats..........	10.7	9.3	24.7	15.8	18.1	14.2	19.4	16.2
Chemicals..............	4.3	6.2	6.2	4.0	134.6	168.0	183.8	204.8
Manufactured goods classified chiefly by material..........	3.9	19.1	6.8	2.1	471.0	642.1	634.3	675.5
Machinery and transport equipment...........	10.3	23.4	20.5	7.6	397.5	534.5	671.3	756.3
Miscellaneous manufactured articles.......	.7	1.1	1.2	1.5	38.0	47.1	47.2	47.2
Commodities and transactions not classified according to kind......	1.1	1.7	1.9	3.5	10.6	10.2	15.8	17.5

Source: Analytical Abstracts, O.E.C.D., Paris, Jan.-Dec., 1962. Series B.

APPENDIX TABLE 2
IMPORTS FROM EASTERN EUROPE INTO THE WEST
(In million U.S. Dollars)

Products	Into the United States				Into Western Eurpoe			
	1959	1960	1961	1962	1959	1960	1961	1962
TOTAL IMPORTS............	78.9	80.2	80.3	78.4	1670.2	1952.0	2095.2	2253.4
Food and live animals..........	24.7	31.1	30.4	28.3	432.2	464.4	564.2	542.6
Beverages and tobacco..........	.2	.2	.2	.3	12.2	14.0	15.0	22.6
Crude materials inedible, except fuels.......................	16.9	14.0	16.1	18.7	360.7	499.3	518.4	548.1
Minerals fuels, lubricants and related materials..............	.3	.2	.2	.2	340.9	399.1	410.1	455.5
Vegetable oil and fats..........	—	—	—	—	7.3	16.1	16.1	20.5
Chemicals.....................	16.2	11.5	11.0	5.0	97.4	117.0	113.2	108.3
Manufactured goods classified chiefly by material...........	10.8	11.6	11.3	13.4	251.8	280.3	270.0	358.4
Machinery and transport equipment..................	4.2	4.1	3.0	3.6	90.7	97.9	112.3	112.4
Miscellaneous manufactured articles....................	4.8	6.7	7.3	8.5	48.2	58.0	70.1	78.4
Commodities and transactions not classified according to kind.......................	.4	.5	.5	.5	8.3	5.6	4.8	6.8

Source: Analytical Abstracts, O.E.C.D., Paris Jan.-Dec., 1962, Series B.

MACHINERY EXPORTS IN WORLD TRADE
(1962)

	Millions of dollars	Percent	To less developed countries [$ Millions]
Machinery Exports, Total..................	33,140	100.0	8,600
Free World Developed Countries..........	28,630	86.4	7,820
U.S.................................	8,350	25.2	—
F.R.G..............................	6,130	18.5	—
U.K...............................	4,650	14.0	—
France.............................	1,980	6.0	—
Italy...............................	1,409	4.3	—·
Japan..............................	1,230	3.7	—
Communist Countries.....................	4,230	12.8	590
USSR..............................	1,169	3.5	286

Source: United Nations Monthly Bulletin of Statistics, March 1964. Special Table C.III.E.

COMPARATIVE IMPACT OF TWO-WAY TRADE BETWEEN WEST AND EAST EUROPE
(1962)

	Millions of dollars	Percent
Exports of West Europe, Total.................................	56,794	100.0
To East Europe..	2,391	4.2
Imports of West Europe, Total................................	64,359	100.0
From East Europe...	2,527	4.0
Exports of East Europe, Total................................	15,965	100.0
To West Europe...	2,527	15.8
Imports of East Europe, Total................................	16,186	100.0
From West Europe...	2,391	14.8

Source: Annual data of U. S. Dept. of Commerce, United Nations Monthly Bulletin of Statistics March 1964, pp. 90-91.

COMMUNIST ECONOMIC OFFENSIVE
SOVIET FOREIGN AID—MEANS AND EFFECTS

BRANKO M. PEŠELJ*

I

HISTORICAL BACKGROUND

It is reported that Lenin once said: "The road to Paris and London leads through Bombay and Calcutta."[1] This statement clearly indicates the importance which Marxism-Leninism has attached from the very beginning to the political and socio-economic problems of the former colonial and less developed countries in the world.

In exposing the doctrine of the historical inevitability of socialism, Lenin believed that the underdeveloped and colonial countries of the world, in given conditions and with the support of Socialist states, will be able to bypass the capitalist stage of the historical economic development and launch directly upon the building of socialism.[2]

However, in the early stage of the Bolshevik regime, as a practical foreign policy towards the underdeveloped areas, Leninism envisaged that the colonial and semi-colonial states would attain their "ultimate and complete freedom" in two stages: (1) the national and political liberation of the country from its colonial status; and (2) the political and socioeconomic liberation of the country from its domestic exploiters.[3]

For the realization of the first stage, Lenin and later Stalin advocated collaboration of indigenous communist movements with nationalist and bourgeois elements—provided, however, that the forces and the organization of the local communists were kept as separate political entities and that they remained all times independent in their political decisions.[4] Once the first stage of the liberation is achieved, Leninism

---

* LL.B. 1931, J.S.D. 1932, University of Zagreb (Yugoslavia); Ph.D. 1950, Georgetown University; M.Comp.L. 1954, George Washington University. Adjunct Professor of Law, Georgetown University Law Center. Member of the bars of the District of Columbia and the Supreme Court of the United States. Author, INDUSTRIALIZATION OF PEASANT EUROPE (1954). Contributor to the *Encyclopedia Americana* and to legal and economic periodicals in the United States, Europe, and South America.

[1] A. Z. RUBINSTEIN (ED.), THE FOREIGN POLICY OF THE SOVIET UNION 341 (1960) [hereinafter cited as RUBINSTEIN].

[2] Herman, *The Political Goals of Soviet Foreign Aid,* in DIMENSIONS OF SOVIET ECONOMIC POWER 478 (1962) [hereinafter cited as Herman].

[3] These two stages are expounded in Lenin's theory of imperialism, Stalin's views on the solution of national and colonial questions, and the Program of the Communist International of 1928. Cf. RUBINSTEIN 341-72. This policy is applied also today, openly by the Chinese communists, especially in Africa, and more subtly by the Soviets in the formerly colonial areas of the world. Cf. Cooley, *China's Push in Africa,* 79 COMMONWEAL 424 (1964); also Paasche, *Sowjetische Konzeptionen fuer Unabhaengigge-wordene Entwicklungslaender [Soviet Views Concerning the Newly Created Underdeveloped Independent States],* 14 OSTEUROPA 409 (1964).

[4] Lenin's and Stalin's theses on the position and strategy of the communist forces in colonial states and underdeveloped areas are explained in several of their works, articles, and speeches. See XENIA JOUKOFF EUDIN & ROBERT C. NORTH, SOVIET RUSSIA AND THE EAST, 1920-1927, at 45-71 (1957).

139

teaches, the local Communist Party, supported by the international proletarian movement, must wage the battle for the attainment of the second stage, the establishment of the Socialist state.[5] Thus, in pursuing its eventual goal in colonial countries and underdeveloped areas, Leninism has always recognized the necessity of temporary compromises with the nationalist and bourgeois forces if, in final analysis, such compromise furthered the accomplishment of the ultimate aim, the World Socialist revolution.[6]

Although the ideas of Lenin and Stalin concerning Bolshevik policy and tactics towards colonial and semi-colonial states in the early period of the Soviet regime were primarily of a political nature, Lenin pointed out as early as 1920 that on the path to their ultimate political and economic freedom these countries "must maintain also a close economic alliance with the Soviet Republic."[7]

Naturally, in the early 1920s the Soviet Union was not strong enough to undertake any sizable economic steps which would support its political and ideological offensive beyond its borders.[8] The Soviets' primary concern was to consolidate their internal political stability and to build up their own independent economy. The latter was accomplished with the great help of the Western Powers, notably by the private economic concerns of the United States, during the period of the New Economic Policy.[9] At the same time the Soviet Union began to penetrate into the sphere of international economic relations by concluding its first trade agreement with the United Kingdom on March 16, 1921.[10]

Subsequently, in the period between the two world wars, the Soviets have signed a large number of international trade agreements, but only a few of these could be regarded as treaties offering foreign aid in form of credits or direct grants. The latter

[5] This doctrine, in its essence, has not been changed until today in spite of the more flexible tactics adopted by the Soviet government. See Editorial, *Marksistichko-leninskaia teoria revolucii i sovremenoe istoricheskoe razvitie* [*Marx-Lenin Theory of Revolution and the Contemporary Historical Development*], 5 VOPROSI FILOSOFII 3 (1958); also, JOHN M. MACINTOSH, STRATEGY AND TACTICS OF SOVIET FOREIGN POLICY 51-58 (1963).

[6] A typical example of the communist and other leftist collaboration with the bourgeois-nationalist elements in the two stages of national liberation and social revolution is offered in Algeria. In the first stage—the struggle for the national and political liberation of the country—the communists cooperated fully with the bourgeois-nationalist strata of the population and their leaders. In the second stage—the building up of a socialist Algeria—the moderate and nationalist elements have been completely eliminated and, where necessary, suppressd. The second example, more familiar to American observers, is Cuba. Cf. ROGER HILSMAN, THE SINO-SOVIET ECONOMIC OFFENSIVE THROUGH JUNE 30, 1962, at 6-7 (1962) [hereinafter cited as HILSMAN].

[7] RUBINSTEIN 359.

[8] At one moment during the Civil War, the Soviet economy was nearing total collapse. Only ten per cent of Russia's former coal supply, less than twenty-five per cent of iron foundries, and less than one half of the grain-producing areas were under the control of the Soviet government. Cf. MAURICE DOBB, SOVIET ECONOMIC DEVELOPMENT SINCE 1917, at 98 (1948).

[9] *Id.* at 125-207; also, WERNER KELLER, OST MINUS WEST = NULL, DER AUFBAU RUSSLANDS DURCH DEN WESTEN, 226-277 (1960).

[10] JAN F. TRISKA & ROBERT M. SLUSSER, THE THEORY, LAW AND POLICY OF SOVIET TREATIES 294-95 (1962). It is of interest to note that this treaty, though commercial in character, contained also purely political clauses, such as the prohibition of hostile activity and propaganda on the territory of the other party, non-interference in domestic matters, and so on.

was true especially in the Middle East to which the Soviet economic penetration was directed in the late twenties and early thirties. Thus, as a predecessor of the present Soviet foreign aid, the Soviet-Turkish Treaty of May 8, 1932 should be mentioned.[11] According to this treaty, the Soviet Union gave a credit to Turkey in the amount of eight million dollars for the purchase of industrial and agricultural machinery. In addition, the Soviet Union made a present to Turkey consisting of ten tractors, five tanks, two trucks, and one bus. The credit loan was made without interest and was repayable over a period of twenty years in Turkish produce. The eight million credit was later used by Turkey for the purchase of textile machinery from the Soviet Union.[12]

In World War II, the Soviet economy suffered severe blows, but its recovery was rather swift and efficient.[13] The emergence of a number of Socialist states in Eastern Europe and in Asia between 1945 and 1948 demanded from the Soviet régime for the first time a close economic cooperation with these countries in assisting their political and economic consolidation. Thus a series of agreements offering credits and technical assistance, or cancelling debts of individual Socialist countries, was concluded between the Soviet Union and the newly created socialist states in the period from 1945 to 1953, totalling transactions in the amount of approximately 2.5 billion dollars, which amount increased to 6.5 billion dollars by the end of 1962.[14]

In the same period, certain colonial countries in Asia, notably Burma, Ceylon, India, and Indonesia became independent states. However, their independence was not the result of political or revolutionary action of the local communist forces but the consequence of the changed political conditions in those parts of the world. As a rule, it was the outcome of peaceful compromises reached between the former colonial powers and the nationalist movements. For this reason, the early Soviet attitude towards the newly established régimes in South-East Asia was not favorable. Stalin, following rigidly the established Leninist doctrine of liberation of colonial states, considered these régimes as puppet governments controlled by their former colonial masters, and was therefore unwilling to support them politically or assist them economically.[15]

In 1949, when the United Nations debated the mode and the volume of the economic aid to be given to the underdeveloped areas of the world, the Soviet Union at first reacted favorably and advocated that such assistance be given through the United Nations.[16] Later, the Soviets changed their mind and refused to contribute anything for this purpose because Stalin was, in principle, still opposed to economic

[11] VIOLET CONOLLY, SOVIET ECONOMIC POLICY IN THE EAST 49 (1933).
[12] Id. at 49-50.
[13] DOBB, op. cit. supra note 8 at 290-312.
[14] Carnett & Crawford, The Scope and Distribution of Soviet Economic Aid, in DIMENSIONS OF SOVIET E NOMIC POWER, op. cit. supra note 2, at 474 [hereinafter cited as Carnett & Crawford]; see also JOSEPH S. BERLINER, SOVIET ECONOMIC AID 52-53 (1958) [hereinafter cited as BERLINER].
[15] RUBINSTEIN 389-94; see also BERLINER 13-14.
[16] BERLINER 15.

aid to any country which was not communist dominated, or in which, in his opinion, the conditions were not ripe for a communist take-over.[17]

One of the factors which contributed to the eventual change of the Soviet view was the communist seizure of power in China. The Chinese communists adopted from the very beginning of their rule a more flexible approach to the problems of foreign economic aid and cooperation with the neighboring Asiatic countries. Yet, the official Soviet attitude could not be changed until after Stalin's death.[18]

Stalin died in March 1953; and the disposition of his successors towards the policy and problems of foreign aid to non-socialist countries became immediately much more flexible and pragmatic. As early as August 1953, the first foreign aid agreement was concluded between the Soviet Union and Argentina, by which the former gave credit of 30 million dollars for the purchase of oil drilling equipment.[19] This agreement was followed by substantial credit allowances of Afghanistan in 1954, and then to India and Burma in 1955.[20] The formal turning point in the policy of the Soviet economic offensive was marked by the speech of Chairman Khrushchev, delivered at the 20th Congress of the Communist Party of the Soviet Union on February 14, 1956. Discussing the new aspect of the Soviet foreign economic policy towards the former colonial countries and underdeveloped areas of the world in general, Khrushchev said:

These countries, although they do not belong to the socialist world system, can draw on its achievements to build up an independent national economy and to raise living standards of their people. Today, they need not go begging for modern equipment to their former oppressors. They can get it in the socialist countries without assuming any political or military commitments.[21]

Khrushchev elaborated further the objectives of the Soviet economic offensive in his speech of January 27, 1959, in which he said:

Our country builds its relations with all states on principles of complete equality and collaboration without any conditions of military or political nature. Of course, we are not engaged in charity. Soviet Union gives aid on fair commercial principles. Socialist countries help the undeveloped nations to create their own industry, while the United States seeks to sell to them consumer goods which have no sale on other markets.[22]

II

MOTIVES AND OBJECTIVES

Soviet authors and statesmen describe their motives and objectives in providing economic aid to underdeveloped countries as most noble and unselfish. Socialist economic assistance, they assert, facilitates the advance of these nations on the road

---

[17] RUBINSTEIN 393-94.
[18] HILSMAN 2-4; BERLINER 14. For Stalin's ideas on the structure of the socialist economy and its goals, see JOSEPH STALIN, LES PROBLÈMES ÉCONOMIQUES DU SOCIALISME EN U.S.S.R. (Moscow, 1952).
[19] BERLINER 198.
[20] Id. at 198-99.
[21] RUBINSTEIN 395.
[22] Id. at 401-02

to progress. "We were taught this by the great Lenin," says Mikoyan, and adds, "This is an example of proletarian internationalism in action under modern conditions."[23]

The truth, we submit, is different, and the Soviet motives and objectives are not so benevolent as official Soviet statements suggest.[24]

It should be borne in mind, in the first place, that the foreign economic policy of every Socialist country controlled by the communists is an integral part of foreign relations in a broader sense.[25] It is therefore rigidly controlled by the respective communist governments, and adapted to the needs and objectives of communist world strategy. As Khrushchev said bluntly on one occasion: "We value trade least for economic reasons and most for political reasons."[26] Consequently, any foreign aid which the Soviet Union or other Socialist states are extending to former colonial and underdeveloped nations is devised to be one of the instruments through which the final goal of Marxism-Leninism—the world revolution—is to be achieved.[27]

The immediate objectives of the communist economic offensive are, of course, more limited. They are designed

(a) to neutralize the recipient country politically and economically;

(b) to achieve a gradual pro-Soviet or pro-Chinese inclination of the recipient;

(c) to increase the political and economic prestige of the socialist camp among the underdeveloped nations;

(d) to infiltrate the countries which receive foreign aid politically, economically and culturally;

(e) to bolster the global military posture of the communist orbit (in cases where military assistance is offered to individual underdeveloped states).[28]

In the countries which are already dominated by the communist régimes, which is the case in Albania, Yugoslavia or Cuba, the principal purpose of foreign aid is the political strengthening and economic consolidation of that régime.[29]

Political and economic neutralization of an underdeveloped country is of special importance where the recipient has had in the past a close and long relationship with

[23] Pravda, Moscow, Oct. 22, 1961, p. 1. At the 22nd Congress of the Communist Party of the Soviet Union (CPSU), in October 1961, Anastas Mikoyan pointed out that the world-wide economic offensive of the Soviet Union and other socialist states is an example of the just methods of maintaining economic ties on the basis of equality and of the noble intentions of facilitating the advance of these peoples on the road to progress. Pravda, Moscow, Oct. 22, 1961, p. 1; see also Fedorenko, *The Soviet Union and African Countries*, The Annals, July 1964, pp. 1-8.

[24] The true motives of the Soviets in offering economic and military aid to underdeveloped nations are questioned not only by the free world but also by Communist China. The latter has openly warned the former colonial countries and less developed nations that they will be eventually subject to Soviet domination if they accept aid from Moscow. N.Y. Times, June 22, 1954, p. 1, col. 6.

[25] BERLINER 8; Fieri, *Foreign Trade*, in INFORMATION U.S.S.R. 359 (1962). Harmstone, *Foreign Trade and Aid*, in ENCYCLOPEDIA OF RUSSIA AND THE SOVIET UNION 177-82 (1961).

[26] RUBINSTEIN 383.

[27] Herman 477-79; see also BERLINER 21-26.

[28] Carnett & Crawford 461-462; BERLINER 17-29.

[29] RUBINSTEIN 375 *ff*.

the West. This pattern is demonstrated by the Soviet economic offensive in India, Ceylon, and Burma, in the countries of the Middle East, and also in the African states that were formerly part of the British or French colonial empires.[30] Political neutralization—which is also promoted by Yugoslavia in her economic policy towards the so-called non-aligned nations[31]—is aimed at the destruction or weakening of the existing defense agreements or military alliances which these countries may have with the Western powers.

The political and economic prestige of the socialist camp is expected to be increased by stressing the friendly character of the economic help extended by the Soviet Union or other socialist donor—assertedly given as a part of the policy of peaceful coexistence, without any conditions of a political or military nature.[32] At the same time, accusations are levelled at the capitalist countries, in particular at the United States, which, the communists say, offer foreign help for their selfish purposes and whose aid is but another form of economic colonial exploitation.[33]

′ Political, cultural, and economic infiltration is achieved by sending to the recipient country, pursuant to the aid agreement or mutual cooperation agreement, a large number of technical experts, military advisers, and cultural workers. These individuals, in most cases, in addition to their professional skills and backgrounds, are also politically trained to extoll the successes of the Soviet Union and of other socialist countries, and are instructed to publicize the advantages of socialism.[34]

III

FORMS AND CONDITIONS

Soviet bloc foreign aid is given by bilateral international agreements between the donor and the recipient, and is expressed in four different forms:

(a) by the opening of credit or giving loan in a specified amount for a project or group of projects;

(b) by a straight grant for a designated purpose;

(c) by military assistance supplying the recipient with arms and ammunition;

(d) by a mutual cooperation agreement.[35]

The most common form of economic aid is extension of credit. This form of aid is preferred by the Soviet Union and other Socialist countries, except China, for two

---

[30] MACINTOSH, op. cit. supra note 5, at 135-40.

[31] Cf. PRESIDENT TITO'S MEETINGS WITH STATESMEN OF ASIAN AND AFRICAN COUNTRIES 30-44 (Belgrade, 1961); see also KENNETH R. WHITING, THE SOVIET UNION TODAY 334-40 (1962).

[32] Carnett & Crawford 465.

[33] Khrushchev, in his speech of Jan. 27, 1959, as reported in RUBINSTEIN 395.

[34] BERLINER 26-29; A. Rankovic, the Yugoslav Vice-President, commented on the position of these technical experts and cultural workers with the following words: "They are ambassadors of our development and of our concepts, and of our desire to help friends whose difficulties we can easily understand as our own difficulties were similar." THE ATTITUDE OF THE LEAGUE OF COMMUNISTS OF YUGOSLAVIA TO CURRENT INTERNATIONAL PROBLEMS 69 (Belgrade, 1963).

[35] HILSMAN 12-16; Carnett & Crawford 462-65; Sino-Soviet Bloc Economic Assistance to Less Developed Countries, State Department Memorandum, February 1963, pp. 3-6 (Unpublished) [hereinafter cited as Memorandum].

principal reasons. First, credit extension gives the impression of a fair commercial deal to which no political or military conditions are attached. Secondly, credit agreements, the execution of which is extended over a longer period of time, serve at the same time as a control of and as a brake on the recipient country.[36]

The credit is given, as a rule, for a specific project or a number of projects to be undertaken in the recipient country, and can be drawn upon during a number of years, depending upon the anticipated length of construction, usually up to seven years. The projects for which the credits are extended vary, but industrialization and mining account for almost seventy per cent of all the credit arrangements.[37] This trend is fully in line with Lenin's theory that the creation of an industrial proletariat is necessary for the strengthening of revolutionary forces in the country predestined to play the decisive role in the anticipated socialist revolution.[38] Credits are also given for amelioration works in agriculture. These constitute about twelve per cent of the total credits extended. The rest, about thirteen per cent, is given for transport facilities, road building, and other minor projects.[39]

Credits are never given to private entrepreneurs or corporations, but always to the public sector of national economy of the recipient state. Thus, the eventual nationalization of the economic system as a whole is being facilitated.[40]

Every credit agreement is usually divided into two parts: the general conditions under which the credit is extended (*i.e.*, its amount, interest, and repayment), and the mode of its utilization. The latter stipulates specific conditions, such as the contribution to be given by the recipient for the realization of the project, the terms of utilization of the credit (which are usually subject to the completion of the individual stages of the project), arrangements for the exchange of a number of individuals from the recipient country who will be trained for the work on the project, and so on.[41] The second part of the credit extension agreement covers also the number of the expert technicians to be supplied by the creditor, as well as their salaries and conditions of employment.

It is believed that by the end of 1962, about twenty-seven per cent of all economic credits extended by the socialist countries have actually been utilized. In military assistance, the utilization has been much larger and amounts to eighty-five per cent.[42]

The money value of new economic credits has been temporarily in decline from 1961 to 1963. In 1960, the extended economic credits reached their peak at 1.176 billion dollars. In 1962, they have declined for more than fifty per cent, to 519 million dollars. The utilization of the credits extended was largest in 1962, when it amounted to 395

[36] HILSMAN 12-13; Carnett & Crawford 462.
[37] Herman 481.
[38] BERLINER 25; EUDIN & NORTH, *op. cit. supra* note 4, at 68-70.
[39] HILSMAN 12; Herman 481.
[40] Herman 482.
[41] HILSMAN 11; Carnett & Crawford 464.
[42] HILSMAN 12; *Memorandum* 7. It appears that the utilization of the new and previously extended credits was the highest in 1963, though the exact figures have not been disclosed so far.

million dollars.[43] However, since the beginning of 1963, the foreign economic aid of the Soviet Union and all other communist controlled states has again been on the increase. One of the reasons for this trend is the rivalry for prestige and leadership between the Soviet Union and Communist China in Asia and in Africa. Within the last year, since the Fall of 1963, the Soviet Union alone has extended over 800 million dollars in new credits to various underdeveloped states.[44]

The extension of credit for a specific project is regularly contingent upon the contributions to be made by the recipient to the common venture. These contributions usually comprise the supply of the local building material and non-qualified labor.

The interest rate on credit, is usually 2-2.5 per cent,[45] though the Chinese have given large credits, as for instance to Burma in 1961 in the amount of 84 million dollars, without any interest.[46] Interest rates of the satellite countries are often higher, and amount to four or five per cent.[47] Yugoslavia's interest rate is usually three per cent.

Approximately seventy-five per cent of all the credits granted by the Soviet Bloc are to be repaid in twelve annual installments beginning with the year after the project is completed. In some instances, the period of repayment is much longer and may be extended over fifty years with deferred payments up to twenty-five years. A small portion of the credits granted by the Satellites (twelve per cent) is shorter in duration and repayable within a period of five to nine years after the completion of the project.[48]

Repayment is stipulated either in gold or in hard currency (United States dollars or British pounds sterling), or by the export of raw materials and goods from the recipient country to the creditor at the regular world prices prevailing at the time when the installments are due.[49] It is for this reason that Soviet economists sometimes tend to interpret regular commercial agreements which provide for the exchange of machinery and technical equipment with raw materials and foodstuffs also as foreign economic aid.[50]

Direct grants are given mainly by China, and have totalled approximately 120 million dollars. They were granted to Cambodia, Ceylon, Nepal, Egypt, Yemen, Guinea, and Zanzibar.[51] The Soviet Union occasionally also gives direct grants for

[43] Memorandum 1.
[44] The principal recipients were in Africa and in the Middle East, Egypt, Algeria, Kenya, Somalia, and Zanzibar, and in Asia, India, Afghanistan and Iran. Cf. N.Y. Times, June 21, 1964, p. 5, col. 1. China's new credits within the last year amounted to approximately 150 million dollars.
[45] HILSMAN 13; Carnett & Crawford 463.
[46] Very recently, Red China has extended interest free loans to Zanzibar (14 million dollars), to Somalia (20 million), and to Pakistan (60 million). Cf. The Washington Post, June 9, 1964, pp. A 11, B 27; N.Y. Times, Aug. 1, 1964, p. 1, col. 4.
[47] HILSMAN 13; Memorandum 6.
[48] HILSMAN 13-14; Carnett & Crawford 463.
[49] Memorandum 6.
[50] BERLINER 5.
[51] Memorandum 6; N.Y. Times, June 21, 1964, p. 13, col. 1.

specific purposes; for instance, 80 million dollars to Afghanistan in 1959, and also minor grants to other countries in Asia, notably to Nepal, Burma, and Indonesia.[52]

The total value of military assistance offered by the Soviet-Sino Bloc until the middle of 1962 was over 2.5 billion dollars.[53] Since then, this type of foreign aid has increased considerably, especially to Cuba and to some other countries in Asia and in Africa, such as Indonesia, Somalia, Ghana, Algeria, and Zanzibar.[54] In giving military assistance, the political and strategic motives of the donor have been of primary consideration, and no requirements have been made that the arms delivered must be used for defense purposes only.[55] The deliveries of the military material include all types of arms and ammunition, such as small arms, artillery, tanks, aircraft, submarines and other small boats, and in some instances even rockets.[56]

The main recipients of the Sino-Soviet Bloc military aid were, in Asia, Indonesia and Afghanistan; in the Middle East, Syria, Iraq and Egypt; and in Africa, Somalia, Guinea, Mali, Ghana, Algeria and Zanzibar. Yugoslavia has also offered military assistance to a number of underdeveloped countries, notably to Indonesia and Algeria.

A special form of foreign aid, which is usually but not necessarily contingent upon the utilization of a credit, is technical assistance. This type of aid is sometimes stipulated in the mutual cooperation agreements concluded between individual socialist states and underdeveloped countries.[57] Technical and cultural assistance is extended in two ways: either the donor assumes the obligation to provide a number of technical experts or cultural workers to supervise the anticipated project and to train and educate local personnel, or the recipient sends to the donor's country a number of individuals for training and education. Of course, both alternatives can be carried out simultaneously.

It is believed that approximately 13,500 economic and technical experts and cultural workers from various Socialist countries are currently working in 30 underdeveloped countries on four continents.[58] In addition, about 8,500 military technicians are employed as instructors in the countries which receive military aid from the Soviet Union and other Socialist states. The greatest number of "military instructors" are presently in Cuba (over 6,000); and the rest are employed in the Middle East (about 1,300), and 1,200 in Africa and Asia.[59]

[52] HILSMAN 24-28; Carnett & Crawford 467-69.
[53] HILSMAN 14-15.
[54] The Evening Star, Washington, D.C., Feb. 3, 1964, p. A 5; The Washington Daily News, Feb. 4. 1964, p. 7; The Washington Post, June 9, 1964, p. B 27; N.Y. Times, May 7, 1964, pp. 1 and 6.
[55] HILSMAN 15; BERLINER 48-50.
[56] N.Y. Times, Feb. 15, 1964, p. 2, col. 6.
[57] HILSMAN 15-16; Carnett & Crawford 464-65.
[58] Memorandum 3.
[59] Id. at 3. The total number of the so-called military technicians of the Sino-Soviet Bloc in various underdeveloped countries has never been officially revealed. Of course, the concept and definition of a "military technician or instructor" varies and often it is impossible to distinguish between the genuine military technicians and the combat ready military units.

IV

VOLUME AND BENEFICIARIES

The total economic foreign aid of all socialist states to underdeveloped nations, from 1954 until the middle of 1964, has been approximately 6.6 billion dollars. To this amount 2.5 billion dollars in military assistance should be added. Hence, the total amount of all foreign aid, economic and military, extended in that period, amounted to 9.1 billion dollars.[60] The distribution of economic aid by individual Socialist countries is as follows: the Soviet Union, 4.4 billion; European Satellites, 1.2 billion; China, 700 million; and Yugoslavia, 300 million.

In the period from 1954 to 1960, when the amount of foreign economic aid was on a permanent increase, the aid was given at an average rate of 700 million dollars yearly. Since 1960, the amount of the economic aid offered by the European Satellites has also been increasing; and in 1962 these countries contributed almost as much in new credits as the Soviet Union.[61] There is no distinguishable pattern of the division of geographical areas, or of types of projects, of credit extensions by the Soviet Union and the Satellites. However, the steadily increasing larger participation of the European Socialist countries, outside the Soviet Union, indicates their capability of independent economic action in the communist economic offensive.[62]

Areas, individual underdeveloped countries, and amounts of foreign aid extended by the Socialist states are shown in the following table:

TABLE 1[63]

SINO-SOVIET BLOC ECONOMIC CREDITS AND GRANTS EXTENDED TO LESS DEVELOPED COUNTRIES
January 1, 1954–July 31, 1964
(Million U.S. dollars)

Area and Country	Total Economic Credits and Grants
Asia	Total *2.722*
Afghanistan	574
Burma	97
Cambodia	65
Ceylon	69
India	1.182
Indonesia	638
Nepal	54
Pakistan	93
Middle East	*1.495*
Cyprus	1
Iran	46
Iraq	218
Syria	193
Turkey	17
Egypt	996
Yemen	24

[60] These figures are approximate only and have been determined according to the data published so far. The increased amounts of military assistance by the communist orbit since July 1962, which are known but were not published, are not included in these figures.

[61] *Memorandum* 3.

[62] *Ibid.*

[63] This table has been compiled on the basis of table 4 of the Memorandum, at p. 8, and has been

TABLE 1 Cont.

Area and Country	Total Economic Credits and Grants
Africa	*1.028*
Algeria..	236
Ethiopia.......................................	114
Ghana...	246
Guinea..	125
Mali..	98
Morocco.......................................	17
Somalia.......................................	98
Sudan...	23
Tunisia.......................................	46
Zanzibar......................................	25
Latin America	*849*
Argentina.....................................	104
Bolivia.......................................	2
Brazil..	74
Cuba..	669
Europe	*156*
Iceland.......................................	5
Yugoslavia....................................	151

Yugoslavia to underdeveloped countries (see Table 2).............................	*300*
Grand Total	6.600

There is no indication of geographical preference of individual Socialist countries in the extention of credits, except that China has demonstrated specific interest for South East Asia, Albania, and more recently also for Africa.[64] The credit agreements of the Soviet Union and the satellite states, as well as their military assistance, are spread over four continents, and it is clear that the industrially more advanced Satellites, *i.e.,* Eastern Germany, Czechoslovakia, and Poland, participate in economic aid with a larger share than the others.[65] Albania is the sole Socialist country which has received only foreign economic and military aid, while Yugoslavia, on the other hand, is the only Socialist state which receives foreign aid and also extends it on its own account to underdeveloped nations.

Scrutinizing the geographic areas to which economic aid is extended, and individual countries, we see that in Asia the most important recipient is India, with

supplemented by the recent available data published in the daily press until Aug. 1, 1964. All figures are approximate. The aid of China to Albania, in the amount of 124 million dollars, is not shown in this table.

[64] Since the rivalry for leadership between the Soviet Union and Red China has been intensified, the Chinese Communists have directed their efforts of political and economic penetration, in particular, to Africa. On this continent, they hope to achieve great successes by giving grants and offering interest-free loans to newly created states. There is no doubt that the Chinese are skillfully using their racial advantages, pointing out that the Western Powers, as well as the Soviet Union and the European Socialist states, are all dominated by the white man who, as an image, still represents to a great number of Africans the symbol of colonialism and political and economic oppression. Cf. Harry Schwartz, "Chou Bid in Africa," N.Y. Times, Feb. 7, 1964, p. 6, col. 1; also Washington Post, Jan. 11, 1964, p. 1 and A 9; also FitzGerald, *The Sino-Soviet Balance Sheet in the Underdeveloped Areas,* The Annals, Jan. 1964, pp. 40-49.

[65] Carnett & Crawford *op. cit.: Memorandum 8 ng*

The total amount of the Yugoslav credits to less developed countries is given variously as 300 or 330 million dollars.[81] These credits have been extended on a steadily increased yearly basis since 1957, and have attained seventy million dollars per annum in 1963.[82] The interest rate is usually three per cent, and the repayment period is set between twelve to twenty-five years. Considerable part of all the credits has been given for the purchase of the Yugoslav industrial equipment and other products. It is believed that approximately twenty-five per cent of all the credits have been utilized so far.

The table below shows that Yugoslavia has extended commercial credits to less developed countries around the world in the total amount of 357.6 million dollars. However, in this sum are also included the credits given to Brazil (65 million dollars) and to Argentina (45 million dollars), for ships to be built by the Yugoslav shipyards.[83]

TABLE 2[84]

YUGOSLAVIA'S ECONOMIC CREDITS TO LESS DEVELOPED COUNTRIES, 1957-1964

(Million U.S. dollars)

Area and Country	Total Economic Credits and Grants	
Asia		Total *89*
India......................................	40	
Indonesia.................................	10	
Cambodia.................................	6	
Ceylon....................................	15	
Pakistan..................................	10	
Afghanistan...............................	8	
Arab Countries and Middle East		*47*
Yemen....................................	2	
Egypt.....................................	10	
Sudan....................................	15	
Tunisia...................................	5	
Morocco..................................	5	
Algeria...................................	10	
Africa		*47*
Ethiopia..................................	10	
Ghana....................................	10	
Guinea...................................	7	
Mali......................................	10	
Tanganyka................................	10	
Latin America		*174.6*
Argentina.................................	45	
Brazil....................................	122	
Chile.....................................	0.6	
Bolivia...................................	5	
Uruguay..................................	2	
	Grand Total	*357.6*

[81] Granfil, *supra* note 78, at 17; THE ATTITUDE OF THE LEAGUE OF COMMUNISTS OF YUGOSLAVIA TO CURRENT INTERNATIONAL PROBLEMS, *op. cit. supra* note 34, at 41.

[82] GEORGE W. HOFFMANN & FRED WARNER NEAL, YUGOSLAVIA AND THE NEW COMMUNISM 356 (1962); Privredni Pregled, Belgrad, Sept. 13, 1959; THE ATTITUDE OF THE LEAGUE OF COMMUNISTS, *op. cit. supra* note 34, at 41.

[83] SÜDOSTEUROPA 65-67. It is questionable whether this type of credit could be called economic aid to underdevloped countries.

[84] This table is compiled on the basis of information given in SÜDOSTEUROPA 28-73; 6 JUGOSLOVENSKI

The participation of Yugoslavia in the communist economic offensive in the underdeveloped areas of the world is considerable. Computed on per capita basis, Yugoslavia's contributions are only twenty per cent lower than those of the Soviet Union, equal to the amount offered by other European socialist countries—some of which are much more industrialized than Yugoslavia—and fifteen times larger than the foreign aid given by Communist China.[85] It is understandable, therefore, that from the political point of view, this "independent foreign aid" offered by Yugoslavia has greatly enhanced her prestige among many underdeveloped nations which commence to believe that the so-called neutral and non-committed position in the world affairs is not so bad after all.

VI

EFFECTS AND CONSEQUENCES

Although the total figure of foreign aid of all Socialist countries combined, during the last decade, was less than ten per cent of the foreign aid extended by the United States alone during the same period,[86] the economic offensive of the communist world in less developed areas and its effects on the global international situation should not be underestimated.

The first thing to be recognized is the adaptability of the Soviet and other communist leaders to the present political and economic realities. Instead of the rigid dogmatism practiced by Stalin, new and more flexible methods for the promotion of communist goals have been adopted. The second stage in the development of the former colonial countries—the socialist revolution—is, in the opinion of the present communist leaders, to be achieved by a slow economic and political penetration rather than by the exclusive use of direct revolutionary means. This new international economic policy, practiced under the slogan of active and peaceful coexistence, by no means alters the ultimate goal of Marxism-Leninism which is the victory of socialism under proletarian dictatorship.[87] However, because of its subtlety and

---

PREGLED 11-12 (1963); MIODRAG SUKIJAKOVIĆ, PRAVNE KARAKTERISTIKE DVOSTRANIH TRGOVINSKIH UGOVORA FR JUGOSLAVIJE [LEGAL CHARACTERISTICS OF THE BILATERAL TRADE AGREEMENTS OF THE FPR YUGOSLAVIA] 122 ff. (Belgrad, 1959). It should be noted that not all of the agreements concerning foreign economic or military aid have been reported. Some of them have remained undisclosed for reasons of state security.

[85] The ratio of the population to the foreign economic assistance extended by the countries of the communist orbit to underdeveloped nations is as follows:

	Population in million	Foreign aid in million dollars
U.S.S.R.	220	4.400
European Satellites	95	1.200
Yugoslavia	18	300
People's China	700	825

[86] For the foreign economic and military assistance of the United States in the period 1953-1963, see Statistical Abstract of the United States, 1963, pp. 858 ff.

[87] Swearingen, Technique of Communist Aggression and the Moscow-Peking Axis, in NATIONALISM AND PROGRESS IN FREE ASIA 307/318 (1956); see also the program of the CPSU, accepted at 22d Congress

finesse it is often more dangerous for the free world than the overt revolutionary actions. Briefly, this new economic trend makes the fight against communist expansion much more difficult and sometimes less effective.

The question arises, how successful have been, so far, the new methods of the communist international offensive?

For searching for an answer to this question, the general disposition of the individual leaders in the former colonial countries should be considered to be of prime importance. In the underdeveloped countries where the political leadership is already inclined to regard Lenin's socialism with sympathy, as in Ghana, Guinea, Algeria, and Zanzibar, the communist economic offensive is undoubtedly very effective. It helps the leaders of these states to demonstrate to their peoples that the future of their nations lies in close cooperation with the Communist Bloc and in the eventual introduction of socialism under a single party system.

In the countries with genuine democratic traditions, such as India, Tunisia, Argentina, or Brazil, the economic aid of the Communist Bloc, though a challenge to the free world, is not a force which would, at this time, seriously endanger the ties which these countries have with the West, or imperial their democratic traditions. The Arab countries of the Middle East, notably Egypt, Syria, and Iraq, are in a special situation. There is little doubt that in spite of the substantial economic and military assistance which they have received from the communist camp, a deep mistrust exists between the leaders of international communism and the representatives of Arab nationalism which is the controlling ideology of that area.[88]

Generally speaking, the economic offensive of the Communist Bloc in the underdeveloped areas of the world, and especially among the newly created former colonial states, is favored by the following factors:

(a) Many peoples of the underdeveloped countries and former colonial possessions have never lived under a genuine democratic system and for this reason are unable to grasp the true meaning and the brutal reality of the proletarian dictatorship.[89]

(b) Some of the leaders in the underdeveloped states are impressed by the rapid industrialization of the Soviet Union and its achievements under socialist order. The fact that only sixty years ago the geographical area of the Soviet Union was one of the underdeveloped parts of the world, incites them to emulate the Soviet example by using socialist doctrine as a generating force also in their own countries.[90]

(c) Many leaders of these countries maintain a certain degree of grudge against their former colonial rulers and the Western world in general. In this respect, the Soviets, who claim that they have never been a colonial power,

---

in October 1961, N.Y. Times, Aug. 1, 1961, pp. C 14-15, cols. 8 and 1-4; see also Tito, *supra* note 76, at 17-19.

[88] See Khrushchev speech of January 27, 1959, in RUBINSTEIN 400-01.

[89] See WLADYSLAW W. KULSKI, PEACEFUL CO-EXISTENCE 240-51 (1959).

[90] HARRY SCHWARTZ, THE SOVIET UNION—COMMUNIST ECONOMIC POWER 60-62 (1963).

have certain advantages, not mentioning the Chinese who, in addition to their former semi-colonial status, exploit very adroitly their brotherhood in color and race.[91]

The foreign economic drive of the Communist Bloc represents a challenge to the free world and to its policy to secure freedom and peaceful progress in the underdeveloped areas. This challenge must be met with determination and appropriate counter moves. It cannot, of course, be expected that the American, or any other type of Western political and economic system, can be propagated and imposed through media of economic aid or military assistance. Nevertheless, it is mandatory that the policy of the free world in those areas be directed towards one basic goal. This goal is the preservation and implementation of fundamental human rights, among which is the right of every man to express freely his mind and conviction and to elect without restraint the political and economic system under which he wants to live.

[91] Cooley, *supra* note 3; Fitzgerald, *supra* note 64. For a good evaluation of the Sino-Soviet competition and rivalry in the underdeveloped nations, see Dienerstein, *Rivalry in Underdeveloped Areas*, 13 Problems of Communism 64-72 (1964).

FEDERAL REGULATION AND PROHIBITION OF TRADE WITH IRON CURTAIN COUNTRIES

STANLEY D. METZGER[*]

INTRODUCTION

American federal regulation and prohibition of trade with Iron Curtain countries can be discussed from many angles. There is the historical approach—how our present levels of trade restriction came about. There is the economic analysis—how efficacious these controls have been to accomplish whatever economic objectives they were or are thought to serve. There is the political assessment involving international politics—how the expansion, or maintenance, or contraction of trade regulation has served or serves our international political objectives of creating and maintaining the cohesion of the West against efforts in the East to frustrate a world striving to develop in diverse ways. There is the political assessment involving domestic politics—how the creation, expansion, maintenance, and contraction of trade regulation by the Administration in power is related to efforts by the political party out of power to make domestic political capital out of the level of trade regulation with Communist or Communist-dominated countries. And, finally, there is the military analysis—how does trade regulation in fact affect the military potential of putative enemies.

A truly adequate analysis of our regulation of trade with Iron Curtain countries would need to include and to combine all these approaches. Obviously this task is beyond the scope of this paper if something more than a series of declaratory propositions of doubtful utility were desired, wholly apart from problems of competence to perform it.

I propose instead to undertake a somewhat more manageable task, though one which may nonetheless be of some interest and importance. I should like to outline briefly the existing levels of our restrictions on trade with Iron Curtain countries; to indicate the extent to which they differ from those of our allies and friends in the West; to point out the extent to which our restrictions are imposed by Act of Congress or are merely authorized by Congress and thus can be changed by an administration without formal congressional participation; and finally, to indulge in some mild guesses as to future levels of our regulation of trade with Iron Curtain countries in view of the circumstances thus disclosed, and the fact that there has been on foot for some time progressive relaxation of trade restrictions which appears highly likely to continue.[1]

* A.B. 1936, LL.B. 1938, Cornell University. Professor of Law, Georgetown University Law Center. Author, INTERNATIONAL LAW, TRADE AND FINANCE (1962); TRADE AGREEMENTS AND THE KENNEDY ROUND (1964).

[1] There is a growing literature on trade restrictions, but it is spotty; to my knowledge there is no systematic critical analysis of our restrictions affecting trade with all countries. A recent good, short

I

Present Levels of Restrictions on Trade with Iron Curtain Countries

It is necessary to make distinctions, some quite sharp, within the general term, "Iron Curtain" countries, because United States trade regulation has done so. The Iron Curtain countries may be differentiated, for trade regulation purposes, into four groups: (1) Communist China, North Korea, and North Viet-Nam; (2) the U.S.S.R. and her European allies other than Poland; (3) Poland and Yugoslavia; and finally, (4) Cuba.

A. The Communist China Group

In the first group, (which also is foremost in terms of the degree of trade restriction), stands Communist China, North Korea, and North Viet-Nam. We have prohibited export and import trade with Communist China and North Korea, blocked their assets in the United States, prohibited persons subject to our jurisdiction to engage in financial transactions with their residents, forbidden U.S. flag vessels from plying to Communist Chinese ports, and forbidden others to use dollar currency or credits to finance trade with them since the Communist Chinese armed participation in the Korean conflict, beginning in December 1950.[2] Neither the embargo on all trade nor the freezing of assets and denial of financial transactions are required by the Export Control Act, on the one hand, or section 5(b) of the Trading with the Enemy Act, on the other; both statutes authorize the actions but neither requires them, and both give very wide discretion to grant licenses. As a matter of policy, however, we utilize the authority granted by these statutes almost to their limits and in fact have granted very few licenses.

Subsidiary trade discriminations, such as denial of most-favored-nation tariff treatment,[3] and prohibition of sale of surplus agricultural commodities to them for local currency,[4] both in the form of mandatory legislative prohibitions, followed in train,

description of American trade and financial restrictions, with emphasis upon the mechanics of export control, is found in American Law Institute-American Bar Association, Joint Comm. on Continuing Legal Education, A Lawyer's Guide to International Business Transactions 56-92 (Walter S. Surrey & Crawford Shaw ed. 1963) [hereinafter cited as Surrey & Shaw], together with a selected bibliography, id. at 98-100. A good comprehensive summary of restrictions on trade with the Soviet Union, as of 1959, is contained in Berman, The Legal Framework of Trade Between Planned and Market Economies: The Soviet-American Example, 24 Law & Contemp. Prob. 482, 504-528 (1959). The best descriptions of the levels of trade restrictions of the allies and friends of the United States can be found in the sixteen Battle Act Reports to the Congress, the reports of the Administrator of the Mutual Defense Assistance Control Act of 1951, 65 Stat. 664 (1951), 22 U.S.C. § 1611 (1958).

[2] The embargo on trade with North Korea was invoked in June 1950, 15 Fed. Reg. 4189 (1950). It was extended to Communist China in December 1950, 15 Fed. Reg. 8563 (1950). Financial restrictions, including blocking of assets, were applied to Communist China and North Korea by Treasury Regulations issued December 17, 1950, 31 C.F.R. §§ 500.201, 500.204 (1950).

[3] Sec. 5, Trade Agreements Extension Act of 1951, repealed, 76 Stat. 882; § 231, Trade Expansion Act of 1962, 76 Stat. 876, 19 U.S.C. § 1861 (Supp. IV 1962).

[4] Sec. 101 of Pub. L. No. 480, 68 Stat. 455 (1954), as amended, 77 Stat. 390 (1963), 7 U.S.C. § 1701 (Supp. 1964), authorized the President to negotiate and carry out agreements with "friendly

as well as strong steps in the direction of securing parallel action on the part of our allies.[5] In this latter effort we have had indifferent success, especially and progressively as time has lengthened since the Korean armistice of 1953.

At no time did other countries, even apart from the Soviet bloc, mount an embargo on China trade, with the exception of Nationalist China, and certain other countries of Southeast Asia, whose policy of embargo has been a matter more of form than of substance, given the range of their trade. There was, however, a "China differential" observed by the major world trading nations, in terms of greater restriction on trade with Communist China than with the Soviet European bloc, until 1957, when our allies decided to eliminate the differential.[6] And since the international list of goods which the western allies had agreed was to be denied to the Soviet European bloc had itself been curtailed in 1954,[7] and was further shortened in 1958,[8] this means that for the past seven years there has been a marked difference in the trading restrictions which the United States on the one hand, and the rest of the major trading nations of the Western world on the other, have maintained against Communist China, North Korea, and North Viet-Nam. We embargo; they trade in a wide range of both industrial and agricultural commodities.[9]

We can be quite certain that barring new international hostilities involving force, our allies will not change the policy which they have pursued since the mid-1950s. A fair sample of their views was recently expressed in an article in the *Washington Post* of December 29, 1963 under the headline, "Big Wheat Jubilee: Canada Just Keeps Selling Grain, Making Money," by Mr. G. V. Ferguson, editor of the *Montreal Star*. He said:[10]

> The [U.S.] embargo on shipments to Red China has no counterpart elsewhere, and nobody outside the United States believes that the embargo has any merit, except as a gesture which they believe as not necessary to a sound foreign policy.
>
> Certainly it can be taken for granted that Canada will sell its big wheat surplus to anyone offering reasonable deals and Trade Minister Mitchell Sharp's chief trouble is to find shippable wheat to meet the needs of long-standing customers in the face of a possible tendency to neglect the old unspectacular customers in favor of the big, new glamorous buyers behind the Iron and Bamboo curtains.

nations" to provide for the sale of surplus agricultural commodities for foreign currencies, and § 107 of that Act, 68 Stat. 457, 7 U.S.C. § 1707 (1958), defines "friendly nation" as "any country other than (1) the USSR, or (2) any nation or area dominated or controlled by the foreign government or foreign organization controlling world Communist movement."

[5] "The Strategic Trade Control System 1948-1956," pp. 33-35, 9th Report to Congress by Administrator of Mutual Defense Assistance Control Act of 1951 [hereinafter these reports will be cited as, e.g., "9th Battle Act Report"].

[6] 14th Battle Act Report, p. 5.

[7] 9th Battle Act Report, pp. 23-30.

[8] 14th Battle Act Report, pp. 1-4.

[9] 16th Battle Act Report, pp. 65-69. This report states that, in 1961, "Free World" countries exported $742.2 million worth of goods to Communist China, and imports from Communist China amounted to $637.5 million. Exports included food, chemicals, fibers, machinery, generators, transport equipment including ships, and so on, and imports ran the same gamut.

[10] The Washington Post, Dec. 29, 1963, p. E7.

Britain sold six Vickers Viscounts to Communist China in 1961, and its trade delegation to Peking has been making strenuous efforts to increase trade over a spectrum of non-strategic goods.[11] It has recently been reported that trade delegations from France, West Germany, Italy, Belgium, Sweden, the Netherlands and Japan have been in China to the same purpose.[12] Last year, Communist China's favorable trade balance with Hong Kong reached a "record of $230 million."[13]

B. The Soviet European Bloc

In the second group of Iron Curtain countries we find the Soviet Union, her Eastern European "satellites"—Hungary, Rumania, Bulgaria, East Germany, Czechoslovakia, and Albania and Outer Mongolia. We do not embargo exports and imports with those countries and areas. Rather we forbid those exports from the United States which we judge would make such "a significant contribution to the military or economic potential of" those countries that supplying them "would prove detrimental to the national security and welfare of the United States."[14] And we seek to have our allies cooperate by joining in the denial to those countries of "strategic" goods—we know that our allies will not cooperate in denying goods which merely contribute to the "economic potential" of the Soviet Union and its European allies.[15]

United States export controls have never been employed to deny shipment of all types of commodities to the Soviet Union and the other countries in this group. For example, ordinary foods and fibers have never been denied licenses for export as such.[16] On the other hand, not only have "strategic" goods—goods which contribute to the war potential of the Soviet bloc[17]—been denied exportation, but also such items as $100,000 dollars' worth of carburetors for cars and trucks in Rumania, and $43.7 million worth of automotive machine tools ($2.3 for Czechoslovakia, $41.4 for the U.S.S.R.), have been denied export licenses, because such exports "would have contributed significantly to the automotive capacity of the bloc."[18]

As indicated, this later type of export denial—goods which contribute to the "economic potential" of the "bloc"—has no counterpart in the export controls of our allies. And even as to strategic goods, their controls are not parallel with our own export control, since their view of what contributes substantially to the war potential of the Soviet Union is significantly more restrictive than ours.[19]

Any thought, however, that our export control statute is an inflexible instrument

[11] N.Y. Times, Jan. 13, 1964, pp. C37, 47, 55.
[13] The Washington Post, Dec. 22, 1963, p. A23.
[13] Supra note 11, at p. C47.
[14] Sec. 3, Export Control Act of 1949, as amended, 63 Stat. 7 (1949), as amended, 76 Stat. 167 (1962), 50 U.S.C. App. § 2023 (Supp. IV 1962).
[15] 16th Battle Act Report, pp. 4-6, 7-8.
[16] 9th Battle Act Report, pp. 11-14; 14th Battle Act Report, p. 49.
[17] 9th Battle Act Report, p. 12.
[18] 61st Quarterly Report (Third Quarter 1962) on Export Control by the Secretary of Commerce to the President and the Congress, p. x.
[19] 16th Battle Act Report, p. 7.

is wide of the mark. As construed by the Department of Commerce, which administers it, the statute indeed allows for very great flexibility in application. I refer here to the interesting exegesis of the amendments made in 1962 to the Export Control Act contained in the 61st Quarterly Report by the Secretary of Commerce (Third Quarter, 1962) on Export Control. For example, speaking of controls over goods contributing to the "economic potential" of the Soviet bloc, the Department of Commerce has indicated its approach to license applications in the following terms:[20]

When . . . it is found that an item will contribute significantly to the economic potential of the Soviet bloc, it may or may not be detrimental to the national security and welfare to approve it. There is, of course, a burden on any one who would argue that there is no such detriment. One situation where this burden can at times be met is where the same item, or a close equivalent, is readily available to the bloc from other free world sources. The Department has in particular cases concluded that, under such circumstances, and assuming that the United States is unable to persuade other free world countries to refuse to export the item in question to the Soviet bloc, it should properly conclude that export of the item from the United States would not be detrimental to the national security or welfare. In such cases the Department has decided that as long as the bloc can get the same or a similar item elsewhere, it is the fact of acquisition and use by the bloc that affects the security and welfare—not the source of the export. And, when it is considered that denial under such circumstances only operates to the detriment of U.S. business firms and workers, the Department believes it is not unwise in concluding on balance that there is, in such cases, more detriment to the national security and welfare in denial than there is in approval. There is, of course, a "grey" area between the military and economic, where one may find an item that appears to contribute to both potentials, but contributes significantly more to the one than the other. Such items must, of course, be dealt with on a case-by-case basis, in the light of such factors as the relative degree of contribution to the military or economic potentials, and the relative degree of effectiveness of U.S. control.

Even as to an article which may contribute significantly to the military potential of the Soviet bloc, there must be, first, a decision by the Commerce Department that in fact it does so contribute, which in a very large area involves judgments fully capable of changing from time to time depending on changing military assessments of the article; and second, a decision that exportation would prove detrimental to the national security and welfare of the United States. The Department has been careful to give itself some room even as to this second question, since it says that "it would most likely deny" exportation of items which in its judgment did contribute to military potential because "it is very difficult to see how" approval would "not prove detrimental" to U.S. security and welfare.[21]

In addition, the Commerce Department has construed a recent amendment to the Export Control Act as authorization to it to "vary the scope and severity of export control to particular countries, from time to time, as national security and foreign policy interests require; e.g., during a period of heightened tension." As we shall

[20] *Supra* note 18, at 6.
[21] *Ibid.*

see in regard to Poland, the Department has already varied the scope and severity downward in the reverse case—one of lessened tension.

Finally, the Commerce Department has read together two of the 1962 amendments in such a manner as to give it the very largest area of discretion in its choices of when to and when not to license. The first amendment was the third unnumbered paragraph in section 2 of the Act,[22] reading: "The Congress further declares that it is the policy of the United States to use its economic resources and advantages in trade with Communist dominated nations to further the national security and foreign policy objectives of the United States." The second amendment was that to section 3(a), third sentence,[23] which provides that "rules and regulations" shall provide for denial of export licenses "to any nation or combination of nations threatening the national security of the United States if the President shall determine that such export makes a significant contribution to the military or economic potential of such nation or nations which would prove detrimental to the national security and welfare of the United States." What the Commerce Department did was to read these together as follows: ". . . the Department regards the policy statement of this [the first] amendment as related to the policy expressed in the amendment to section 3(a) of the act [the third sentence], a finding of a trade advantage under the amendment to section 2 being one means, for example, of counterbalancing what might otherwise be a claim of 'detriment' under section 3(a)."[24] If I understand this rightly, the Department is saying that the act allows it, in its discretion, to find that the advantage to American exports and balance of payments from the sale of carburetors counterbalances any detriment to the security of the United States flowing from an increase in the "automotive potential" of the Soviet Union, and hence to license the export. Nor is this reading limited to exports which makes a significant contribution to "economic potential."

As with Communist China, the Soviet Union and her European satellites are by law denied most-favored-nation tariff treatment—their goods pay the 1930 Tariff Act rates, not the rates as reduced by trade agreements entered into since the 1934 Trade Agreement Act—and agricultural commodities cannot be sold to this group of Iron Curtain countries for local currency under the Agricultural Trade and Development Act—the P.L. 480 program.

Does this mean that our agricultural commodities cannot be sold to the Soviet Union at subsidized export prices—that is to say, at world prices, which are lower than our deliberately supported higher domestic prices? The Attorney General ruled in October 1963, in connection with the then contemplated wheat transactions with the Soviet European bloc, that we could sell at the world price.[25] The re-

[22] *Id.* at 47.
[23] *Id.* at 48.
[24] *Id.* at 5.
[25] U.S. Attorney General's Opinion on Wheat Sales, Dep't of State Press Release 520, Oct. 10, 1963, 49 DEP'T STATE BULL. 661 (1963); 2 INTERNATIONAL LEGAL MATERIALS [hereinafter cited as I.L.M.] 1194, 1198 (1963).

striction in P.L. 480 is limited to a prohibition of sale for local currencies, *e.g.*, for rubles, and does not apply to sales at world prices for dollars.

Are there financial or credit restrictions which hamper trade with the Soviet Union and her European satellites? We have not invoked section 5(b) of the Trading with the Enemy Act respecting the Soviet Union and her European bloc (with the exception of an *ad hoc* blocking of one steel mill bought by Czechoslovakia)[26] as we have with Communist China. This means that there is no blocking of Soviet assets in the United States, nor is there a general restriction upon the use of dollars or other currencies by persons subject to American jurisdiction or others for the financing of trade between the United States and the Soviet Union and her European satellites. There is, to be sure, a financial transactions control, ancillary to our own export control and to the multilateral strategic control system, which operates to prohibit the use of dollars in financing trade from third countries to the Soviet bloc of certain strategic items, but that is a quite limited control.

What about financing of trade through credits, of which we have been hearing quite a bit this past year? Are there legal restrictions on the granting of governmental credits to finance trade with the Soviet Union, or merely restrictions based upon policy considerations? Are there legal restrictions on private credit financing of trade with the U.S.S.R.? Are there legal distinctions between so-called short-term and long-term credits for this purpose?

The Attorney General's opinion of October 1963 answered a number of these questions. In the first place, the Johnson Act,[27] which forbids certain financial transactions involving foreign governments in default in the payment of their obligations to the United States (*i.e.*, the Soviet Union), is not applicable to the Government of the United States or to "public corporations created by or pursuant to special authority of Congress, or corporations in which the United States has or exercises a controlling interest through stock ownership or otherwise." This exception includes, for example, the Commodity Credit Corporation. Furthermore, it is not applicable to the Export-Import Bank, in view of the express exclusion from Johnson Act restrictions contained in the Export-Import Bank Act of 1945;[28] hence the Bank may participate in export sales financing "by issuing a guarantee of payment of the purchase price or otherwise." Nor does the Johnson Act apply to "private insurance companies, acting through the Foreign Credit Insurance Association, which might participate with the Bank in the issuance of such guarantees."[29]

---

[26] A LAWYER'S GUIDE TO INTERNATIONAL BUSINESS TRANSACTIONS, *op. cit. supra* note 1, at 86. After Czechoslovakia had jailed William Oatis, an AP correspondent, on spying charges, the United States forbade the export from the United States of a steel mill which had been purchased by Czechoslovakia for more than $16 million, and paid for, and then *ad hoc* blocked the property in order to prevent Czechoslovakia from selling it and realizing the funds to use in other ways. No other Czech property was blocked, however, nor were transactions with Czechoslovakia, other than in this steel mill property, prohibited.

[27] 62 Stat. 744 (1948), 18 U.S.C. § 955 (1958).

[28] 59 Stat. 529 (1945), as amended, 12 U.S.C. § 635h (1958).

[29] 2 I.L.M. 1195.

Secondly, sales by private American firms on a deferred payment basis are not "loans" to defaulting countries within the meaning of the Johnson Act; rather, they are "credits," which are not within the Johnson Act prohibitions. Further, discounting of commercial paper is not a "sale" of "obligations" under the Act, because the Act "relates only to sales of bonds and securities and 'other obligations' of like nature."[30] While the opinion dealt with proposed sales "on normal commercial terms," i.e., deferred payments up to eighteen months or so, this rationale by the Attorney General would appear to support the conclusion that private sales involving deferred payments over a longer term would also not run afoul of the Johnson Act, although there is no great practical likelihood of purely private trading transactions involving lengthy repayment periods, such as over five years.

The only other statute which might interdict credit financing of exports to the Soviet bloc is the Battle Act. This is the act named after a former Alabama congressman which supplements our Export Control Act by adding a mechanism for inducing other countries to embargo the shipment to the Soviet bloc of "arms, ammunition, and implements of war, atomic energy materials, petroleum, transportation materials of strategic value, and items of primary strategic significance used in [their] production."[31] The Battle Act provides for the termination of all military, economic, or financial assistance to any nation if it "knowingly permits the shipment to any nation or combination of nations threatening the security of the United States, including the Union of Soviet Socialist Republics and all countries under its domination," of any of the embargoed materials.

The Attorney General stated that this Act "did not purport to regulate private United States shipments to Soviet bloc countries, which were already subject to regulation under the Export Control Act." It "relates, rather, to trade with the Soviet bloc by countries receiving aid or assistance from the United States."[32] This analysis, of course, also supports the conclusion that the Battle Act does not purport to regulate public or governmental United States shipments to the Soviet bloc.

"Moreover," said the Attorney General, probably for the benefit of those who might not be entirely convinced by this analysis,[33] "the transactions to which this

[30] Id. at 1196. It is interesting to note that Professor Berman stated in 1959 that, "The term 'loan' in the Johnson Act has been construed . . . to apply to credits beyond six months," explaining that "This is the opinion of the Attorney General's office, as given informally in response to inquiries by American businessmen." Berman, supra note 1, at 516.

[31] Sec. 101 Mutual Defense Assistance Control Act of 1951, 65 Stat. 644 (1951), as amended, 22 U.S.C. § 1611 et seq. (1958).

[32] 2 I.L.M. 1199.

[33] Ibid. For many years the agencies of the U.S. Government had acted as if the Battle Act was applicable to one Iron Curtain country which shipped arms, ammunition, implements of war or atomic energy materials to another, just as it was deemed applicable to, e.g., Denmark, were she to ship such goods to an Iron Curtain country. The language of the act itself makes no distinction—it refers to "any nation." The issue therefore was not whether the Battle Act applied to the United States, in the sense that the United States was to be put in the place of Denmark or Czechoslovakia, but rather whether what the United States contemplated continuing to provide to Denmark or Czechoslovakia—assuming that either shipped such proscribed goods to an Iron Curtain country—constituted "economic assistance." If what the United States provided, either in money or goods, was such "assistance," it must be cut

opinion relates [wheat sales on deferred payment basis] would be purely commerical in nature from the standpoint of the purchasing countries, and would therefore not involve 'economic or financial assistance' within the meaning of the Battle
Act." It is difficult to perceive that longer term credits, rather than shorter term
credits, accompanying the sale of commodities for export would work a change
in the "commerical nature" of the transaction, from the standpoint of the purchasing country. It would in both cases be purchasing commodities for dollars, in
one case paying in a year and a half, in the other in five, six, seven, or ten years with
greater rates of interest in most instances, and, in all such cases, paying more dollars.
The Attorney General's opinion therefore appears to be saying that, however one
views the purposes of the Battle Act, it does not prohibit the exportation of goods
from the United States to the Soviet bloc on credit terms, long or short term, so long
as the purpose of the transition is to exchange goods for desired and desirable
American dollars.

If then, our legislation does not require us to refrain from extending credit
financing in the exportation of goods to the Soviet bloc whether the exports are
made through governmental instrumentalities or through private shipments, it is
clear that whether we do or do not extend credits is a discretionary act of policy of
our government. And, it might be added, none of the legislation we have been
discussing distinguishes the Communist China group of Iron Curtain countries from
the European Soviet Bloc.

What is our policy today on credits for financing trade? Since the Administration in the fall of 1963 announced willingness to extend governmental credits on
"normal commercial terms," i.e., 18-month deferred payments, to the Soviet European
bloc, and staved off strenuous efforts in the Congress to deny it the means to extend
such credits,[34] it must be taken that it is clear for the present, as it has not been
hitherto, that our policy embraces short-term credit financing of American exports
to the Soviet European bloc. On longer term credit financing—beyond five years—
it has also been made clear that our present policy is to refuse to offer such terms,
and, beyond that, to seek to persuade our allies to refrain from offering such longer-
term credit financing for their own exports.[35]

Here again, however, we appear to be running into difficulties which are unlikely to be surmounted short of a new outbreak of serious fighting. While the
Federal Republic of Germany appears to be prepared to join us in non-extension of

off; if it was not, it could continue to be provided. It seems therefore that the Attorney General was
greatly overstating the matter when he said that the Battle Act did not relate to United States economic
relations with Soviet bloc countries. Assuredly it does not, if such relations do not include "economic
assistance" to the foreign nation which is shipping proscribed goods to an Iron Curtain country.

[34] The President's communication of Oct. 10, 1963, H.R. Doc. No. 163, 88th Cong., 1st Sess. (1963),
related in detail why he considered it to be in the national interest to sell surplus agricultural commodities to the Soviet European bloc. Efforts thereafter to prohibit the use of apropriated funds for
such purposes, by the adoption of the Mundt Amendment to the Foreign Assistance Act of 1963, failed
oy narrow margins. See 109 CONG. REC. 19322 (1963).

[35] The Washington Post, Jan. 19, 1964, pp. A1, 13.

longer than five-year credit financing, it is clear that Britain will not, and therefore that France most likely will not.[36] And if the recent past is any guide to the near future, this means that in all likelihood the smaller European trading nations—the Dutch, Belgians, Swedes, Italians—will not join us, because to do so might disadvantage their competitive exports. This likely development, in turn, might well lead to a prudent judgment that West Germany will not long remain a spectator of an over five-year credit financing parade, when one gets underway.[37]

C. Poland and Yugoslavia

When we turn to the third "group" of Iron Curtain countries: Poland and Yugoslavia, we find further variations in the regulation of trade. In fact, Yugoslavia is not considered to be a "bloc" country and needs discussion principally because successive Administrations' treatment of Yugoslavia has over the years encountered difficulty in the Congress.

In 1957, after the Gomulka regime succeeded in asserting a marked degree of independence from Soviet domination and control over its internal affairs, we lowered the level of our control of exports to Poland.[38] In addition, beginning in 1956 the Administration found that Poland was no longer dominated or controlled by the Soviet Union within the meaning of P.L. 480 and thus was enabled to make

[36] *Ibid.* The Washington Post, Jan. 9, 1964. The British are negotiating a long-term credit with the U.S.S.R. for the sale of a chemical plant worth about $30 million, according to Flora Lewis, reporting from London to the *Washington Post.* She reports that the dispute with Washington over this question "is not just a dispute over tactics, but reflects basic and far-reaching differences of attitude on the key question of how to press the effort to taper off the Cold War." The British are in disagreement with the Central Intelligence Agency's recently publicized analysis that Russia is faced with a choice "between guns and butter unless the West provides up to $500 million a year in long-term credits." Moreover, "they do think a ban on long-term credits for America's reasons would be taken by the Russians as a form of economic warfare and put them more angrily on guard."

"The British not only disagree that a lean Russia would be less bellicose and more interested in negotiating with the West, they consider that there is a serious risk that if economic troubles get out of hand Moscow will revert to Stalinist-type belligerence. Hostile foreign relations have usually accompanied the need for strong domestic suppression of discontent.

"Therefore, the British hold that a fat Russia is in the interests of the West. They do not claim that a prosperous Russia is bound to be more docile. They consider it a possibility, and they are frankly interested in the huge trading opportunities that a prosperous, industrialized Soviet Union could offer."

It is obvious that there are no hornbook answers to this kind of question. It is equally obvious, however, that the British argument is, at the least, sufficiently strong to withstand efforts to change British policy. In this connection it is of interest to note that the latest (16th) Battle Act Report states that while economic sanctions served as a "marginal restraint" on Soviet aggressive capabilities during the tension of the Stalin and early post-Stalin years, "the inevitable process of industrial and economic growth during these 12 years has meant that the Soviets have developed their own productive capability in many of the areas where a restraining impact was necessary and possible 10 years ago" (at p. 8). [Since the above was written, the British concluded the sale, involving a 15-year government guaranteed credit.]

[37] Flora Lewis has reported, in connection with the German position:
". . . the British ask a little tartly, has the United States not noticed that West Germany has two outstanding long-term credit agreements with the Russians? One is for ships for 6 years, the other for a polyethylene plant for 8 years. Both are backed by provincial government guarantees, approved by the federal government, which is the German explanation of why they do not count as a breach by Bonn itself of America's recommended 5-year limit." The Washington Post, Jan. 19, 1964, p. A 13.

[38] 41st Quarterly Report on Export Control, p. 3.

a series of agreements for sales of surplus agricultural commodities to Poland for local currency.[39] The Administration was required to defeat efforts in the Congress to reverse its finding and hence to stop the sales, but it did so handily.[39a] Thereafter, in 1960, the Administration, making the same finding—that Poland was not so dominated or controlled—for the purposes of the Trade Agreements Act, accorded most-favored-nation tariff treatment to Poland at the same time as it secured Polish agreement to make a deferred-payment lump sum compensation agreement on account of Polish nationalizations of American-owned property in Poland.[40]

In 1962 the Congress, over strenuous Administration objections including the personal participation of the American Ambassador to Yugoslavia, provided in the Trade Expansion Act[41] for denial of most-favored-tariff treatment to Poland and to Yugoslavia (which had never before been denied most-favored-nation treatment) "as soon as practicable." In 1963, however, further strenuous Administration efforts to delete this prohibition, through an amendment in the foreign aid legislation,[42] succeeded, with the result that both Poland and Yugoslavia continue to receive most-favored-nation tariff treatment.

As has been indicated, the other legislative enactments authorizing restrictions on trade with Poland, with or without credit financing, permit a very high degree of discretion in the determination whether and to what extent trade should be restricted. In fact, there is no asset-blocking or financial transaction control,[43] and short-term credits are permitted. Moreover, our no over five-year credit financing policy is not applicable to trade credits to Poland.

So far as Yugoslavia is concerned, it is treated for export control purposes as a Western European country.

The reason for this, as well as for the absence of other trade or credit restrictions,[43a] and for the substantial American aid program to Yugoslavia, is of course

[39] The first of the series was signed and entered into force on June 7, 1957, T.I.A.S. No. 3839.

[39a] The Administration fared less well in the second session of the Eighty-eighth Congress, in 1964, an election year. Sec. 11 of Public Law No. 88-638, the act extending Public Law No. 480 authority, forbids sales of surplus agricultural commodities for local currency to Poland and Yugoslavia, though permitting dollar sales on five year credit terms. Needless to say, the Administration opposed this provision, and may be expected to press for its elimination in the next Congress.

[40] Agreement Relating to Settlement of Claims of Nationals of the United States Against Poland and Exchange of Notes, July 16, 1960, T.I.A.S. No. 4545, 11 U.S.T. & O.I.A. 1953.

[41] Sec. 231. While the Act itself did not specifically mention Poland and Yugoslavia, the House Committee Report made very clear the congressional intention that they be denied most-favored-nation benefits. H.R. REP. No. 1818, 87th Cong., 2d Sess., 4, 40-41 (1962).

[42] Sec. 402 of the Foreign Assistance Act of 1963 (P.L. 88-205) amended § 231 of the Trade Expansion Act of 1962 (P.L. 86-735) by adding a new subsection thereto reading as follows: "The President may extend the benefits of trade agreement concessions made by the United States to products, whether imported directly or indirectly, of a country or area within the purview of subsection (a) which, at the time of enactment of this subsection, was receiving trade concessions, when he determines that such treatment would be important to the national interest and would promote the independence of such country or area from domination or control by international communism, and reports this determination and the reasons therefor to the Congress."

[43] Other than the control over third country financing with dollars of trade in certain limited strategic goods.

[43a] See note 39a supra.

the fact that Tito broke with the Soviet Union in 1948 and is not in military alliance with the Soviet Union through the Warsaw Pact, and that the United States is satisfied that Yugoslavia has not since 1948 again become, in sum, a member of the bloc. The Administration's maintenance of this assessment, with its consequential results, has not been free from efforts in the Congress to upset them, but these efforts have been successfully repulsed.[44]

Almost needless to say, our allies and friends have been trading with Poland and Yugoslavia in a wide range of goods, involving substantial credits, for many years.

D. Cuba

American regulation of trade with Cuba began in 1960. Restrictive licensing began in the summer of that year and, effective October 19, 1960, exports of everything except certain foods and medical supplies were required by Commerce Department regulations, issued pursuant to the Export Control Act, to have validated export licenses, and the Department announced that no such validated licenses would be issued.

Although there was almost continuous consideration given to imposing controls over imports from Cuba, no controls were imposed until February 6, 1962, when the Cuban Import Regulations,[45] issued pursuant to the authority granted in section 620(a) of the Foreign Assistance Act of 1961,[46] were issued. These regulations prohibited the importation into the United States of all goods of Cuban origin and all goods imported from or through Cuba, except pursuant to licenses, which as a matter of policy have not been issued. As originally issued, the regulations did not apply to imports of goods manufactured in third countries containing Cuban components, but on March 23, 1962 they were amended to bar entry of such goods as well. The amended regulations were issued under the authority of section 5(b) of the Trading with the Enemy Act[47] as well as the aforementioned section of the Foreign Assistance Act of 1961, in view of the narrower scope of authority contained in the latter act. The reason for these import restrictions was stated to be that "the embargo will deprive the Government of Cuba of the dollar exchange it has been deriving from sales of its products in the United States," which, in turn "will reduce the capacity of the Castro regime, intimately linked with the Sino-Soviet bloc, to engage in acts of aggression, subversion, or other acts endangering the security of the United States and other nations of the hemisphere."[48]

[44] See 109 CONG. REC. 20111-12 (1963).

[45] 31 C.F.R. §§ 515.101-515.801 (1962). A good summary of trade restrictions with Cuba is contained in SURREY & SHAW, op. cit. supra note 1, at 91-92, from which this and the next following paragraph are drawn.

[46] Sec. 620(a) of the Act, 75 Stat. 444 (1961), as amended, 22 U.S.C. § 2370 (Supp. IV, 1962) provided: "No assistance shall be furnished under this Act to the present government of Cuba. As an additional means of implementing and carrying into effect the policy of the preceding sentence, the President is authorized to establish and maintain a total embargo upon all trade between the United States and Cuba."

[47] 40 Stat. 411 (1917), as amended, 50 U.S.C.A. App. § 5(b) (1962).

[48] Supra note 1, at 3.

167

The Cuban Import Regulations apply only to importations into the United States and to financial transactions incident thereto. Unlike the financial controls applied to Communist China, they do not apply to other financial transactions with Cuba, nor to American citizens or American subsidiaries located abroad unless the transaction involves an importation into the United States.

Other trade controls applied to Cuba include denial of most-favored-nation tariff treatment, as well as the preferential rates under the 1902 Convention and the exclusive agreement supplementary to G.A.T.T.,[49] pursuant to the requirement of section 401 of the Tariff Classification Act of 1962,[50] until the President determines that Cuba is no longer controlled by the foreign government or foreign organization controlling the World Communist movement. Obviously no credits or other facilities affecting trade are available to Cuba in view of our almost total embargo.

Our allies and friends in the West do not embargo exports to or imports from Cuba. In early January 1964 this divergence in policy was made apparent when the United States objected to a British sale under government-guaranteed credit of some $10 million worth of buses to Cuba, and the British Government and press rejected our efforts to stop the transaction. The British press was rather sardonic and mocking in the process.[51] Other Western European countries such as France and Spain, as well as non-Soviet bloc countries elsewhere, also trade with Cuba in a range of products, which is currently being expanded both as to type of goods and quantities.

II

Future Levels of Restrictions on Trade with Iron Curtain Countries

Any attempt to guess, however carefully and mildly, concerning future developments in American restrictions and prohibitions of trade with Iron Curtain countries must be based upon certain assumptions. If those assumptions are upset by events, so are the guesses; in fact, the guesses may be inaccurate in any event. With that exculpatory clause out of the way, one may hazard the future from the recent past on the single assumption that the various Iron Curtain countries and the various countries in the West will not engage in serious new fighting involving each other, directly or by proxy.

[49] See § 350(b) of Tariff Act of 1930, as amended, 19 U.S.C. § 1350(b) (1960); for the 1902 Convention, 33 Stat. 2136, T.S. 427, I Malloy 353; for the 1947 Exclusive agreement, 61 Stat. 3699, T.I.A.S. No. 1703, 119 U.N.T.S. 163.

[50] In addition, certain shipping controls have been applied to vessels which ply to Cuban ports. No shipments of cargoes financed by the Departments of State, Defense, Agriculture, the General Services Administration or the Agency for International Development may be made on a foreign flag vessel if such vessel has called at a Cuban port on or after Jan. 1, 1963 unless the person controlling the vessel assures that henceforth (from Dec. 16, 1963) or as early as possible following expiry of charters entered into prior to that date, it will not so ply. "Cuban Shipping Policy," Dec. 16, 1963. Moreover, § 301(e) of the Foreign Assistance Act of 1963, 77 Stat. 379 (1963), 22 U.S.C.A. § 2151 (Supp. 1964), cuts off aid to any country which fails to take "appropriate steps" to prevent its vessels from carrying goods to or from Cuba.

[51] The Washington Star, Jan. 9, 1964; The Washington Post, Jan. 13, 1964; N.Y. Times, Jan. 11, 1964.

A. Communist China

Since our allies and friends have been engaging in trade with Communist China in a wide range of goods for some time and show no signs of changing that policy—in fact, are intensifying efforts to expand their trade with China—it seems only a matter of timing dictated primarily by our domestic political considerations on the one hand, and intra-bloc relations on the other, before the United States will be prepared to relax its total embargo. This relaxation, when it occurs, will in all likelihood begin with licenses for the sale, for dollars, of wheat, and other grains which we have in substantial surplus, at world prices and for cash or on short credit "on normal commercial terms." Whether in fact we will be able to cut into the Canadian wheat market in Communist China is a question of some seriousness.

As evidence that this qualifies as a careful and rather mild guess, there is offered the third of ten different ways outlined by President Johnson in his State of the Union Message of January 8, 1964[52] to achieve "a world without war, a world made safe for diversity, in which all men, goods and ideas can freely move across every border and boundary." President Johnson's third way is: "Third, we must make increased use of our food as an instrument of peace, making it available—by sale, trade, loan or donation—to hungry people in all nations which tell us of their needs and accept proper conditions of distribution." These words—hungry people in all nations—must have been very deliberately chosen. Nor would it appear that there would be special conditions of distribution if there were dollar sales of wheat and other grains; at least I am not aware that there have ever been special distribution conditions imposed on dollar cash sales, as of course there have been on disaster relief grants or local currency sales.

Such a relaxation would not of course affect the existing status of non-recognition of the Communist Chinese régime, any more than did our commercial dealings with the Soviet Union before 1933. And it is probable that the licenses would issue to American private traders, enabling them to engage in such trade with Communist China, as in the recent wheat sale to Russia, so as to avoid directly dealing through the Commodity Credit Corporation.

Thereafter, over a longer time period, we would likely move toward trade in other "peaceful goods," since both the material and non-material reasons for not doing so tend to grow continually thinner as time goes on and our Western allies continuously step up their trading pace.

So far as most-favored-nation treatment and P.L. 480 sales for local currency are concerned, the prognosis is for no change for a very long time to come. In the absence of a substantial change in the character of the present Chinese régime, which hardly appears foreseeable, alteration of the status quo in these respects would require congressional action. And if there is any certainty remaining in domestic politics, it is that any Administration knows how difficult it is to ask Congress to

---

[52] II.R. Doc. 140. 251, 88th Cong., 2d Sess. 1964; The Washington Star, Jan. 8, 1964, p. A-8.

amend existing law if the effect of the amendment can be characterized as "helping the Communists," and avoids requesting such action if it is humanly possible to do so. The reasons for this are fairly obvious. The total foreign trade of the United States, imports plus exports, amounts to about $35 billion a year, out of a gross national product of over $600 billion a year. Using pre-trade restrictions and pre-war figures, in an effort to get to a "representative" year, those from 1938, we find that our foreign trade, imports plus exports including re-exports, with the whole Sino-Soviet bloc amounted to the grand total of $309,877,000—a little over $300 million.[53] This amounts to less than one per cent of our total foreign trade, and an infinitesimal fraction of our gross national product. Is it any wonder that a Congressman hesitates to take the political risks involved in primary and general election campaign attacks on him for being soft on Communism, when there is so little domestic political capital in it for him on the other side? In 1962 even so entrenched a Congressman, and one so seemingly impervious to such attacks, as the late Chairman of the House Un-American Activities Committee Francis E. Walter found himself charged with pro-Communism because he led the congressional battle to provide continuing aid to Yugoslavia. It may also be recalled that there are many aspirants to political office who have made careers on such issues.

Since it is not hard to avoid going to Congress in the case of Communist China, I would therefore expect that it will be avoided.

B. The Soviet European Bloc

Here again, the prognosis is for steady but unspectacular relaxation of trade controls, not primarily in those goods which we consider to be strategic while our allies do not, but rather in the range of commodities which we do not restrict for that reason, but because they contribute to the "economic potential" of the bloc. There is, of course, no prospect for relaxation on arms, ammunition, implements of war, or atomic energy materials.

As we have seen, our allies apply no trade restrictions on goods which they consider non-strategic and have no intention of doing so. The Commerce Department's careful explanation of its reading of the 1962 Amendments to the Export Control Act as permitting export licenses for goods which the bloc can secure anyway in adequate quantities from our allies, must presage willingness to grant licenses when restriction "only operates to the detriment of U.S. business firms and workers."

In fact, in the summer of 1963, the able Director of the Mutual Defense Control Staff of the Department of State, Robert B. Wright, underlined this relaxation in policy: ·

In cases where we cannot persuade other potential supplying countries to exercise an embargo policy and where the United States cannot be certain of withholding something

[53] 14th Battle Act Report, p. 48.

from the Soviet bloc under unilateral controls that cannot be alternatively supplied by other countries, there seems a prima facie case for allowing United States traders to compete with other potential Western suppliers to the Soviet bloc.[54]

As these relaxations occur, and even before (as in the case of food and fibre exports), credits facilities in connection with such exports may gradually extend even beyond eighteen months—up to five years.

None of these changes would involve formal congressional participation.

As for not granting credits beyond a five year term, while our present efforts to secure parallel action from our allies are not meeting with success, and the augury for the future is the same, it is nevertheless unlikely that we would do an about-face any time soon. Quick political about-faces are ungraceful, and not enough turns on this one anyway. Thus, there will likely develop a "Soviet credit differential" over the next year or two, which will persist for some time.

So far as most-favored-nation tariff treatment and P.L. 480 sales of surplus agricultural commodities for local currency are concerned, the prospects again are for no change in the near future, since both would require congressional action which any Administration will prefer to avoid.

I would offer only one possible caveat on this prognosis, applicable only to most-favored-nation treatment. Suppose the United States ever resumes once again Lend-Lease settlement negotiations with the Soviet Union, the last explanation of positions having occurred in January 1960, and these negotiations could result in a substantial cash payment by the Soviet Union over a period of years, paralleling the British and French Lend-Lease settlements. The atmosphere would then have been created for a strenuous Administration effort to secure from Congress a resumption of most-favored-nation treatment of Russia. For then the Soviet Union could point out that it needed to export more to us to earn the dollars to pay the installments called for by the settlement. In fact, I have been wondering for some time now why we have not suggested a resumption of Lend-Lease negotiations. We and the Soviet Union have been making a variety of suggestions to each other which might lower the temperature of the Cold War, and have accomplished successfully several of them. Can't we now make one which would help to liquidate World War II and also assist in re-establishing trade relationships beneficial to the American consumer?

C. Poland and Yugoslavia

Nothing much need be added to what has been said about these countries. It can be expected that relaxation of trade restrictions with Poland, which are not serious, will continue. Yugoslavia likewise, on the assumption that her basic political stance continues, can expect to continue to trade normally.

It is very possible that some of the other so-called satellite countries may in the

[54] "The State Department Role in East-West Trade Controls," address before Ninth Annual Corporate Law Institute, University of Wisconsin, Madison, Wis., July 18, 1963, p. 7.

future be given treatment more comparable to Poland than to the U.S.S.R. in the interest of encouraging more diversity and semi-independence within the Soviet European bloc. Developments in Rumania[54a] and Hungary particularly point in this direction, but there are also indications of increasing interest in improved relations with the United States in all the European bloc countries except Albania and East Germany.

D. Cuba

James J. Walker, "Hizzoner" the Mayor of New York, once replied to a reporter who asked what he thought about the suppression of James Joyce's *Ulysses*: "I never knew a girl who was ruined by a book." While few of us possess or profess the expertise about overthrow of governments which "Hizzoner" was reputed to have concerning his avocations, it nevertheless seems safe to say that none of us have ever known of or heard about a government that was ruined by a partial embargo such as now exists respecting Cuba.

With Cuba trading with the Soviet bloc and Communist China, and increasingly with Britain, France, Spain and many others, it is obvious that the U.S. embargo is not going to bring Castro down, or even interfere materially with his acquisition of money with which to attempt to subvert Latin American governments. If he falls, or desists in these efforts, or both, it is more likely to be because of his domestic economic policies, which appear to have been inept these past five years, if Theodore Draper's article in *Commentary*[55] is any guide.

Nonetheless, it is most unlikely that because our embargo has had and will continue to have an extremely limited effect upon Castro's retention of power or trouble-making activities[56] it will be changed any time soon. For our position of antipathy to Castro is staked out too firmly for the limited effects of our embargo to exercise real influence upon its continuation. As I have been indicating in various ways throughout this paper, domestic American politics has always had great motive power in causing the imposition as well as the retention of trade restrictions, and this has been true in Cuba's case as much as in that of Communist China. The cry, "don't just stand there, do something,"[57] when it becomes strident, results

---

[54a] Subsequent to the writing of this article, the United States and Rumania discussed "economic and trade matters" during May 18-June 1, 1964. The joint communique of June 1 (Dep't of State Press Release No. 263, June 1, 1964), states that "The United States Government agreed to establish a General license procedure under which most commodities may be exported to Rumania without the necessity for individual export license. In addition, the United States agreed to grant licenses for a number of particular industrial facilities in which the Rumanian delegation expressed special interest."

[55] 37 COMMENTARY 25 (1964).

[56] 16th Battle Act Report, p. 6, indicates that the large drop in Cuba's foreign trade was in part made up by U.S.S.R. trade and aid agreements. Recent activity, such as the bus deal with the United Kingdom, and the truck deal with France, indicates that Cuban foreign trade is now on the upswing.

[57] The Washington Post editorialized on Jan. 13, 1964, p. A 14, as follows:
"The dispute over trade with Cuba is another sign that the old simple world has vanished. Who would have thought that Generalissimo Franco, who asserts that he saved Spain from communism, would turn out to be a trading bedfellow with the Communist regime in Cuba? Spain is importing sugar from Cuba, and is giving serious consideration to an order for 100 ships for Mr. Castro's fleet.

in trade restrictions being imposed by Administrations, all of which are well aware that this "something" is usually very, very little, and in their being retained long after even these marginal effects have practically evaporated.

Thus, the present differences in trade restrictions with Cuba, as between the United States and our allies, seem destined to continue for the foreseeable future. This difference in trade restriction in turn reflects differing political assessments concerning Cuba, which again reflects the degree of concern felt by the various allies regarding the actions of Cuba's government.

CONCLUSION

If one may be permitted to generalize upon the foregoing, the following propositions would appear to be justified:

1. At present, American restrictions on trade and credits in and of trade with the U.S.S.R. and the European Communist bloc, with Communist China and her sphere of countries, and with Cuba are more severe than the restrictions of our friends and allies.

2. The restrictions of many of our friends and allies upon trade and credits with all of these Iron Curtain countries are being progressively relaxed, and trade between them is growing, with all parties taking strong initiative in that direction.

3. With the exception of most-favored-nation tariff treatment, P.L. 480 sales of surplus agricultural commodities for local currencies, and shipping restrictions on Cuba, the differences in the levels of trade restriction between the United States and its friends and allies are the result of policy determinations, not mandatory as a matter of law.

4. The imposition and the maintenance of these more severe restrictions by the United States has been very largely the result of domestic pressures upon successive Administrations which, without regard to the particular political party in power at the time, have attempted with much success to retain as much legal flexibility as possible in order to be able to relax restrictions as circumstances permit from time

---

And the Spaniards are downright annoyed that the United States has formally complained about this alliance between Europe's loudest anti-Communist and Cuba.

"In Great Britian, a similar dispute is arising over a 10-million-dollar order for buses that Cuba urgently needs. The British, too, are irked with U.S. criticism. 'The United States has a surplus of wheat,' one Briton was quoted as saying, 'We have a surplus of buses.'

"These differing views over trade wtih Cuba are natural, since the embargo is justified primarily in terms of hemisphere and national interest. Cuba's neighbors have deep grievances against the Castro regime. But countries that are not parties to the dispute find it hard to understand why they should be bound by the embargo—particularly when the issues do not seem to them quite so black and white as they tend to appear here.

"In fact, the embargo has been chiefly a negative policy, dictated in part by a desire to 'do' something about Cuba. Though the embargo has hurt Castro, it has also provided him with a propaganda excuse for all the troubles that beset his country. Rather than weaken Cuba's dependence on the Soviet Union, the embargo has strengthened the very connection that this country finds most objectionable.

"In the absence of a better policy, and in the circumstances of an election year, the Cuban embargo may still make negative sense—it is a less reckless way of expressing hostility to Castro than organizing an invasion. But Americans should not be surprised when other countries have their own views on the wisdom of the policy."

to time. All of these Administrations have been acutely aware of the limited effects which trade restrictions have had and have upon putative enemies.

5. All Administrations have also been acutely aware of the complications in our relations with our friends and allies—of the divisive effect caused by differences in our respective levels of trade restrictions with Iron Curtain countries.

6. In consequence of these circumstances, it may be expected for the near future that, apart from Cuba, within the tolerances deemed to be afforded by domestic politics, there will be progressive relaxation of our trade restrictions with Iron Curtain countries. But because our domestic tolerances will continue to be deemed to impede such relaxation, there will continue to be a differential between our trade restrictions and those of our allies, as both continue to reduce trade restrictions, and hence this source of friction in our relations will continue to exist. The United States may be expected in the future, however, to play these differences down rather than up, which has not always been the case in the past, including the recent past.

341.0947
B111

91332